OLFACTORY RHETORIC

NEW DIRECTIONS IN RHETORIC AND MATERIALITY
Allison L. Rowland, Christa Teston, and Shui-yin Sharon Yam, Series Editors

OLFACTORY RHETORIC

SNIFFING OUT ENVIRONMENTAL PROBLEMS

Lisa L. Phillips

THE OHIO STATE UNIVERSITY PRESS
COLUMBUS

Copyright © 2025 by The Ohio State University.
All rights reserved.

Library of Congress Cataloging-in-Publication Data
Names: Phillips, Lisa L. (Professor of English) author
Title: Olfactory rhetoric : sniffing out environmental problems / Lisa L. Phillips.
Other titles: New directions in rhetoric and materiality
Description: Columbus : The Ohio State University Press, [2025] | Series: New directions in rhetoric and materiality | Includes bibliographical references and index. | Summary: "Examines three contemporary environmental crises affecting historically marginalized communities—the Sriracha sauce factory controversy, the Salton Sea events, and the Blue Ridge Landfill emissions problem—to elevate olfactory rhetoric and forward an intersectional ecofeminist sensory-rhetorical approach to advocating for environmental justice"—Provided by publisher.
Identifiers: LCCN 2025017467 | ISBN 9780814215937 hardback | ISBN 0814215939 hardback | ISBN 9780814284247 ebook | ISBN 0814284248 ebook
Subjects: LCSH: Smell—Environmental aspects—Case studies | Smell—Physiological aspects—Case studies | Environmental toxicology—Case studies | Environmental justice
Classification: LCC QP458 .P47 2025 | DDC 612.8/6—dc23/eng/20250611
LC record available at https://lccn.loc.gov/2025017467

Other identifiers: ISBN 9780814259535 (paperback) | ISBN 0814259537 (paperback)

Cover design by Melissa Dias-Mandoly
Text design by Juliet Williams
Type set in Adobe Minion Pro

CONTENTS

List of Illustrations		vi
Preface	Environmental Injustice Stinks	vii
List of Abbreviations		xiii
INTRODUCTION	Rhetoric Comes to Its Senses	1
CHAPTER 1	Proposing a Sensory Rhetorical Approach to Environmental Problems	33
CHAPTER 2	Is It Pepper Spray or Sriracha Sauce?	70
CHAPTER 3	Something Smells Fishy at the Salton Sea	91
CHAPTER 4	Nasal Rangers at the Blue Ridge Landfill	125
CHAPTER 5	Launching a Call to Sense	157
Acknowledgments		179
Works Cited		181
Index		207

ILLUSTRATIONS

FIGURE 1	Cuyahoga River fire, 1952—Jefferson Street and West Third	7
FIGURE 2	Map of Irwindale, California, featuring Huy Fong Foods and the surrounding area	73
FIGURE 3	Map of Salton Sea region in Southern California	92
FIGURE 4	Patchy land ownership map featuring Torres Martinez land on the Salton Sea's north side	104
FIGURE 5	Map of the Blue Ridge Landfill location and adjacent communities	126
FIGURE 6	Nasal Ranger Field Olfactometer	148

PREFACE

Environmental Injustice Stinks

The air reeks of brimstone accumulating in Earth's lungscape, threatening damnation across species regardless of proximity to the source. Ammonia-laced air assaults my nostrils and burns my eyes. My throat constricts and I struggle to breathe. Waves of nausea and retching crash through me. Rage shakes me, floods my body with adrenaline, increases my blood pressure and cortisol, alters my immune system, suppresses my digestive system, and communicates with parts of my embodied brain and nervous system that affect mood, fear, and drive. Encounters with smell transform us physically and our senses edify us (Tsing et al. 58).

One neighbor says it smells like ammonia mixed with rotten flesh and embalming fluid—her father is a mortician. Another, a Vietnam veteran, says a medium day smells like Agent Orange and a bad day like the "Hanoi Hilton" where he suffered yet survived. To me, the odor morphs from sickly-sweet putrescence to a visceral rotten-egg smell. The residue lodges in my nose, embodied mind, hair, and clothing for hours afterward. Everything once supposed good then tastes and smells foul. A massive 17,000-plus hog breeding facility built less than a mile from my rural Illinois home blows this disgusting wind. The Vietnam veteran passed out due to fumes and effects that accumulated and hung in the valley by his home on a hot summer evening. Logging complaints with the Illinois Environmental Protection Agency (EPA) bears no fruit of relief because olfaction is supposedly unimportant to our health.

Too few humans ingest the nauseating health affects for the agency to care, never mind the nonhumans, and composite arts of "nosewitnessing" resist storied quantification. The "law of the senses" is also subjective (Valverde). That is, if one could measure a stench's impact by weight, volume, and chemical structure, then the quantifiable story becomes credible in court and in the mediated public sphere. If someone exposed my neighbors, family, and me to graphic pornography or thunderous noise, force-fed us, or punched us in the gut without our consent, then the perpetrators would face fines, jail, or other recompense. Olfactory assault violates our bodies too, spawning pain, trauma, and memories.

The prow of our facial profile rides crests of air, turns the rudder of attention in an instant, and anchors memory to moment. Unlike perfunctory breathing, taking a deep whiff and deliberating on the results turns our focus outward toward the larger world, though the initial act is private. Redolent air swirls with rhetorical activity, but you need to pay attention to notice. You cannot help but notice when a rank odor punches you in the face and you find no escape or relief. The visceral a/effect is immediate and arresting. The conventional idea that our sense of smell matters not must be overcome, for the examined life is the one worth living. Not just any kind of attention will do, either. It necessarily involves "quality of attention," attuned to the "need to cultivate care" (Hawhee, *Sense* 2): care for our shared environment and one another.

Environmentalists are made, not born—shaped over a lifetime or in an instant. For some, the material environment shapes the orientation. For others, witnessing environmental abuse that renders it lifeless provides the motive. For me, it is a combination of the two, as the opening gambit suggests.

My childhood involved unfettered outdoor activities in all sorts of weather. A spartan parental approach conferred upon me tousled hair, freckles, and calloused soles, as it imparted a guileless sense of the flora, fauna, and climate of my surround. Because I spent so much time outside, I feel shifts in environmental conditions.[1] For example, in the late 1970s to mid-1980s, when I was living on a family farm adjacent to the Cypress Creek National Wildlife Refuge in Southern Illinois, I used to ice-skate on a pond that froze consistently from late December to early February. The pond seldom freezes anymore, and when it does, the thin ice cannot support ice-skating. In the past,

---

1. *Environment* has several meanings. It can refer to a specific habitat in the natural world (e.g., a forest or field), a built environment (e.g., a classroom or workplace), or the holistic concept of nature. In Western contexts, the environment is separate from people and seen as a resource. In Indigenous contexts, the environment is part of us and vice versa. Indigenous approaches to the environment as webs of relation are more aligned with my thinking.

the "plant hardiness zone" spanned the 5b to 6a range, which meant extreme winter temperatures could drop to −15°F to −5°F (−26°C to −20°C). For now, the hardiness zone is 7a, which is in the 0°F to 5°F range (−17°C to −15°C). No wonder the pond seldom freezes. When sensing environmental change, our bodies are thermometers and barometers of presence and absence. My lived experience provides a different sort of data regarding global heating and environmental damage than the quantitative temperature zones the United States Department of Agriculture (USDA) provides or air quality assessments the Illinois EPA acts upon or neglects, respectively.

My parents worked the farm throughout the '70s, '80s, and '90s, though they branched out into custom-designed furniture in the late 1980s and did selective harvest of trees on timbered acreage. My parents continued to cultivate land classified as arable—land used for higher-yield crops. My dad used a variety of herbicides and pesticides (e.g., Roundup, Atrazine, and Paraquat, and the insecticide Malathion) and applied them using an open spray rig with little or no protective equipment.[2] The furniture business was also saturated with chemicals like paint, paint thinner, polyurethane varnish, and so forth. The chemicals I note in both the agricultural and furniture-making processes smell noxious and linger in the air. The odors warned of the chemicals' dangers.

When he was about sixty, my father said he could no longer smell anything. I dismissed it at the time because I did not give our sense of smell (olfaction) much thought. Losing one's sense of smell is a harbinger of Parkinson's disease, something he fell ill with likely due in part to Paraquat exposure (Cha; Copping; Reaves; Zou et al.). My mother developed Alzheimer's disease, which is similar to Parkinson's disease in its links to chemical exposures and the impairment of olfaction in the disease's early stage (Kovács et al.; Zou et al.). Ironically, to help Alzheimer's patients trigger long-term memory associations, one therapy is to use strong scents the patients may recall from distant memories to alleviate anxiety (Zou et al. 871). My parents' protracted diseases likely resulted from or were exacerbated by exposure to environmental toxins.

Globally, thirteen million deaths per year stem from unhealthy environments, which is about one in four deaths pre-COVID-19, according to the World Health Organization. An unhealthy environment refers to things like

---

2. Atrazine is linked to human and nonhuman congenital disorders and "neuroendocrine effects" and is banned in many countries (Reaves 12). Paraquat is linked to Parkinson's disease and other health problems and is banned in more than 100 countries (Cha; Tanner et al. "Disease" and "Rotenone"). Both are legal in the US, though Paraquat use is restricted to commercial entities. Malathion is a known carcinogen and neurotoxin and is banned throughout the world, though not banned in the US (Brocardo). Roundup is a glyphosate and known carcinogen used across the US (Copping).

polluted air and water, exposure to chemicals, global heating, ultraviolet radiation, catastrophic weather, and more. The poor, the elderly, and the very young suffer more from environmental hazards, and exposure rates are highest in the Global South (e.g., Africa, Asia, Latin and South America, Oceania, and poverty pockets in wealthier nations) (Di Chiro). Historically excluded, minoritized, and marginalized communities endure the most environmental damage in the United States and systemic biases steeped in extant power structures inform the inequitable results (Haas and Frost 171).

How are we to contend with the global scale and scope of unhealthy environments? How do people and nonhumans attend to local unhealthy environments? What and how does an unhealthy environment communicate to us, and how does this translate to action devised to combat the issue? The answers include evaluating olfaction's suasive nature and olfactory rhetoric tied to deteriorating environments as it emerges within the mediated public sphere. As an adjective, *mediated* refers to different forms of communication and multimodal and textual artifacts emerging from them that connect audiences through traditional means (e.g., newspapers, televised news broadcasts, public meetings, policy documents) and online modes (e.g., social media posts and videos) (J. Davis 66).

Olfactory Rhetoric: Sniffing Out Environmental Problems focuses on bodies that know when something is off in the environment as it interrogates failures in public policy that circulate in mediated publics. I draw from Jenny Rice's "publics approach" to places, people, nonhumans, development, and materiality to inform how we "can make the strongest interventions into imperiled places" (14). Addressing imperiled places and publics, this book lays out an intersectional ecofeminist sensory rhetorical (RISE)[3] approach to sensation and embodiment as rhetorically, textually, materially, relationally, and culturally informed processes, highlighting the role that olfactory persuasion plays in assessing environmental conditions and communication tied to them. Incorporating the sensate into how we evaluate environmental injustices requires rhetoricians to attend to how environments are sensed and interpreted by publics, including nonhuman and "more-than-human" considerations (Abram). This is rhetoric "not as a collective noun, but connective verb, with remainder" (Druschke). It also follows Thomas Farrell's account of rhetoric as "the art, the fine and useful art, of making things matter" and matter to others (470). Sensory rhetorics are gaining traction among rhetoric scholars who hope to address a world in distress and shape future publics

---

3. Rearranging the letters, I use RISE as the acronym rather than IESR, as RISE is easier to say and conceptually aligned with my intent and purpose.

(Ceraso and Stone; Hawhee, *Sense* and "Rhetoric's"). As Matthew Houdek and Ersula J. Ore note, "There's something in the air," and what is adrift breathes with possibility in both literal and figurative senses (85). The figurative signals "a foreboding yet cautiously hopeful sign of different [ontic-epistemic] worlds on the horizon," or "otherwise" worlds in which all may breathe freely (85–86). Currently, many do not in a literal sense.

The book's three case studies highlight specific environmental problems tied to a/effects on human olfaction and environmental health more broadly. All three have in common "high air-toxic cluster tracts" and "intersectional environmental inequality" (Liévanos 58, 51). High air-toxic cluster tracts classify places with higher rates of harmful chemicals, industrial emissions, odors, dust, pollen, and more circulating in the air, which correlates with higher rates of lifetime cancer risk and other health concerns for humans and nonhumans (53–56). Air-toxic cluster areas predominate in majority-minoritized communities (59–60, 63, 65); hence, high air-toxic regions feature intersectional environmental inequities and illustrate the impact of environmental racism.[4]

The 2015 "Rhetoric and Sensation" seminar leaders Debra Hawhee and Vanessa Beasley promised to "re-examine rhetorical theory in relation to sensation" and delivered a "preliminary" definition of the topic "as feelings emanating from perceptual contact." At length, Rhetoric Society of America seminarians discussed the "sensorium" as a concept that both "evokes sensation and sensory ecologies [that mediate] technologies and bodies." The sensorium refers to sensory and perceptual faculties taken together that constitute an individual's sensory experiences and composite sensations of a group or groups of humans, nonhumans, or more-than-humans. Nonhumans are living entities we share the Earth with, like plants, microbes, fungi, and other animals. More-than-human refers to nonliving and animated entities with whom we share the Earth (including rivers, lakes, mountains, and minerals) and tangible materials humans create, like digital sniffing technologies that sense the environment. The sensorium amounts to a layered and polyvalent assemblage of sensations and their a/effects enmeshed within our environment and us.

Sniffing out environmental problems involves risk assessment when environmental changes threaten public health. Exposure to environmental hazards and poor health outcomes like those my parents experienced are examples of the problem. However, broader environmental justice concerns are relational,

---

4. Environmental racism refers to overlapping axes of oppression that result in higher exposures to environmental hazards for people of color. The overlapping axes of oppression include lax rules, inequitable policies, lenient or unenforced regulations, and negligent government and corporate decisions that put communities of color in closer proximity to toxins ("Environmental"; Enríquez-Loya and Léon).

and rhetoricians ought to account for intersecting axes of oppression since environmental risks are unevenly distributed across the globe. Environmental justice scholar and activist Robert Bullard points out how "dominant risk paradigms" like those the US EPA and other global and local governmental agencies use routinely fail to account for "subpopulations" and "communities of color" in "various phases of assessing risk, including scoping, data gathering, discovery of alternatives, analysis, mitigation, and monitoring" (*Quest* 21). A RISE approach informs ways to evaluate how people circumvent, redress, and acknowledge environmental injustices and interrogate "traditional quantitative-risk models" commonly deployed in Western contexts (Bullard and Wright 3). Ultimately, virulent qualities of sensory experiences, particularly notable in unpleasant olfactory encounters with environmental hazards, move as a Moebius strip from embodied experiences to the mediated public sphere and circulate across sensory-rhetorical ecologies. Such encounters and circulations are the purview of this book.

ABBREVIATIONS

ArcGIS	Aeronautical Reconnaissance Coverage Geographic Information System
BIPOC	Black, Indigenous, and People of Color
CERCLA	Comprehensive Environmental Response, Compensation, and Liability Act (otherwise known as Superfund)
EPA	Environmental Protection Agency
ESRI	Environmental Systems Research Institute
FIDO	Frequency, Intensity, Duration, and Offensiveness (odor characterization charts)
NASA	National Aeronautics and Space Administration
RISE	Intersectional Ecofeminist Sensory Rhetoric
SCENT	Sensing and Searching, Context, Emplacement and Embodiment, Narratives, Tactics and Transformation
SWAPE	Soil, Water, Air Protection Enterprise
TCEQ	Texas Commission on Environmental Quality
TMDCI	Torres Martinez Desert Cahuilla Indians

INTRODUCTION

Rhetoric Comes to Its Senses

> The relation between composite sensations and future actions, the straining to discern that which is not, or not yet, certain, and acting accordingly, constitutes the world of rhetoric.
> —Debra Hawhee, *Rhetoric in Tooth and Claw*

Wrongly judged an impoverished sense, olfaction is the "Cinderella" of our sensorium (Barwich ix). Olfaction's vain stepsiblings sight and hearing generally hog rhetoricians' scholarly scenes, yet olfactory persuasion presents rich new directions for rhetoric and materiality. Our sense of smell helps us navigate, unlocks memories, unleashes feelings, and informs us about environmental conditions that require forms of nosewitnessing.

Mediated sensation—technological and fleshy—is the object of this book. Olfaction's suasive nature and olfactory rhetoric are its subjects. Inciting a riot of "breathable futures" is the aim (Houdek and Ore). Invoking sensation respects embodied experiences of people, nonhumans, and "elemental entities" in our shared molecular melee (Hawhee, *Sense* 37). Composite sensations—clusters of sensuous activity—unfold in the sensorium and mediated public sphere when environmental problems attract attention and spark future-oriented efforts through deliberative, epideictic, and forensic rhetorics. Deliberative rhetoric grapples with present and future actions and potential outcomes. Epideictic rhetoric assigns praise and/or blame to actors or agents in a network, and it is "a form of social action" meant to instruct publics about future a/effects and past practices (Rice 102–3). Forensic rhetoric pertains to legal cases, policy debates, grievance hearings, and more directed toward justice, though "justice" bears the unmistakable stamp of socioeconomic and political power. All three are informed by and through sensation. Like Jenny

Rice, I link epideictic rhetoric and public memory to current and future deeds among emplaced, embodied publics (17, 103). Like me, Rice is "interested in how to intervene in the negative aspects of development," which include harmful environmental results from industrial processes, fast capitalism, racism, colonialism, and a host of associated concerns including unprecedented fossil fuel–driven global heating (5). However, rather than argue for "*more investment*" in "ongoing scene[s] of debate" imagined to foster "sustainable futures," Rice suggests we disrupt "citizen nonparticipation" and circumvent old discursive debates (6). We can out-logic or out-argue one another, yet the world still burns replete with fumes of our own design.

This book shows how people, nonhumans, and more-than-humans are sensitive to environmental issues beyond words, illustrating how people can sense "themselves as public subjects who can and [do] intervene in . . . crises we currently face" (Rice 7). Facing Eastern ontologies and Luce Irigaray's "respiratory lens," or to avoid the ocularcentric context, a respiratory sensitivity seems fitting to the task of resuscitating Earth's clogged airways and other bloody tributaries in need of CPR. In ashen corners where a section of the planetary lungscape collapsed, or an artery clogged, as representative of this book's case study chapters, we need socially just ways to treat and evaluate the effects of decades of tar and other toxins on Earth's life support system. We also need ways to unpack the mediating role of sensory persuasion as it bumps up against the "Technopolis," a space of unrelenting "progress" in which the senses diminish in influence though not in import (Winner ix, 5).

To begin, presuppose two ideas. First, assume nondiscursive sensation and our senses are rhetorical and at work in public memory of environmental hazards. Nondiscursive sensation, or what Debra Hawhee might name the "other than rational," plays a role in deliberative, epideictic, and forensic acts because it persuades people to do or say something about an environmental issue (*Rhetoric* 7). Public memory as it relates to nondiscursive sensation relies on the "activity of collectivity . . . in addition to individuated, cognitive work" (Blair et al. 5). Second, consider odors rhetorical. People design and create smellscapes and scents for a variety of persuasive purposes, including to attract, sell, soothe, teach, motivate, delight, warn, threaten, disgust, and disguise (DiCaglio; Henshaw et al.; Weidner). Though truncated, the list shows openings for rhetorical awareness that I address in detail in the "Why Olfaction Matters" section. Nonhuman animals and plants also create and exude odors to persuade. Encountering a skunk's hindquarters when raised and aimed is one example that may tap some readers' olfactory imaginations. In the plant realm, the corpse flower (*Amorphophallus titanum*) fills the air with a putrid smell to attract carnivorous insects, and the dark burgundy color of the flower looks tasty to pollinators. Using thermoregulation, the world's largest flower can even warm itself up to 98°F (36.7°C) to further tickle a bug's fancy and spread its smell through self-generated rarefied air (Pollak qtd. in Bradford and Dobrijevic; Barthlott et al. 23). Such marvelous cookery, no?

Olfactory Rhetoric evaluates the effects of olfactory persuasion, as it deserves focused attention. Biological olfaction orients and persuades humans and nonhuman entities to attend to changes in environmental conditions and humans to praise, blame, deliberate, and act in response to those changes. Olfaction leads to action. Ask anyone at a scent marketing and branding firm (Medway and Warnaby; Minsky et al.; Thompson). The embodied, mediated translation process from olfactible experience to olfactory rhetoric is recursive. Regardless of category, our senses "guide thoughts and feelings as much as they guide the expression of those thoughts and feelings"; "stirred air stirs meaning," and odorous air stirs meaning, indeed (Hawhee, "Rhetoric's" 6–7). Sensation alone is meaningful because we act on it.[1] However, tools that measure things like air pollution, soil contamination, noise level, and so forth receive more respect than our natural senses or serve to legitimize sensory experiences. In legal contexts where dominant risk assessment paradigms involving air-as-chemical entity, test tubes, labs, science, and rationality are privileged, tools provide quantifiable evidence, yet people usually note the impact of environmental hazards and risks on and through bodily sensations that are "physical . . . tangible and felt" and informed by prior experiences and perceptions (DeVasto et al. 139; Hawhee, *Sense* 2). Scientific, vernacular, and mediated types of evidence differ in sociotechnical assemblages, but the stories they tell together expand how we sense and talk about environmental damage. Places like Louisiana's "Cancer Alley" and other environmental injustice zones where respiratory sensitivity calls for CPR face foul bouquets that forecast ongoing deadly effects.

Cultural training of attention shapes what sense perceptions humans attend to and neglect when evaluating a range of social and environmental issues. Olfaction, as one facet in a multifaceted sensorium, is currently downplayed in a Western hierarchical structure that privileges vision and hearing and mutes other sense perceptions (Classen, *Color*; Classen et al.; Corbin; Houdek and Ore; Jenner; A. Parrish). Olfaction's influence within this structure is malleable. Sensory studies scholar Constance Classen writes, "No sense has suffered such a reversal of cultural fortune as smell," as olfactive sensibilities were of great import in the past (*Worlds* 15; Corbin 5–7). The choice to

---

1. Barry Brummett argues the opposite in a 1976 article, writing, "Sensation alone is *meaningless*," noting that "experience is sensation plus meaning" (29). Brummett's constraint neglects how sensations make people respond nevertheless.

privilege ocularcentric and auditory paradigms is bound up with intersecting axes of oppression that render disabled, gendered, classed, queer, racialized, minoritized, and nonhuman bodies paradoxically as objects of and for a Western hegemonic gaze and as invisible or ideally silent, depending on the power dynamic involved. To illustrate, women are told they talk too much, queer couples are cautioned against public displays of affection, legally blind people may be advised to wear sunglasses to cover their eyes from another's uncomfortable stare, and so forth. Dominant power structures like white supremacy that reinforce the status quo by suffocating BIPOC people, silencing women-identifying people, oppressing LGBTQIA-plus people, shaming disabled bodies, and more inform the illustrations. As feminist biologists Carla Hustak and Natasha Myers put it, reading "athwart dominant logics . . . requires reading with our senses attuned to stories told in otherwise muted registers" (77). Olfaction itself is a muted register in our contemporary sensorium, and it has stories to tell us about environmental injustice. The Cinderella sense is in wont of a fairy godmother and a glass slipper moment. The slippered moment disrupts rhetorical anosmia enacted by those in positions of power who willfully ignore stinking environmental hazards and shut down victims.

In this chapter, I first highlight the role of sensation as a nondiscursive and/or extradiscursive element that shapes mediated publics.[2] Then, I explain what an intersectional ecofeminist sensory rhetorical (RISE) approach does as an overarching theme and address interdisciplinary audiences who might find RISE useful when evaluating intersectional environmental concerns,[3] as the concerns pertain to an array of sensual experiences including and beyond olfaction. Next, I introduce the book's ethical commitments, express my positionality as a matter of reciprocity and transparency, converse with literature that informs the book, and outline the book's primary arguments. This chapter also explicates what our breathy sense of smell does and why it matters for meaning-making and actions related to environmental issues. After defining and describing olfactory persuasion, I make plain olfactory rhetoric's import to socioenvironmental justice initiatives. I conclude the chapter with an overview of subsequent chapters.

---

2. I use the terms *extradiscursive* and *nondiscursive* interchangeably. However, *nondiscursive* pertains more to persuasive impacts of stimulus on the bodymind. *Extradiscursive* is more expansive because it includes sensational and rhetorical a/effects of stimulus resulting in perception and mediated texts that may emerge from and influence such experiences.

3. As explained in the preface, I've rearranged the letters and use RISE as the acronym, rather than IESR, as it is easier to say and more conceptually aligned with my intent and purpose.

Extradiscursive Sensations That Circulate in Mediated Publics

Analyzing composite olfactory sensations that circulate within the sensorium and across mediated publics exposes how discourse about environmental risk includes "extradiscursive actors and conditions," components that extend beyond human speech, writing, and multimodal composing (Scott, *Risky* 6). Extradiscursive elements merge within embodied material effects and affect how one makes sense of, discusses, and addresses environmental problems and the associated risks as well as evaluate what reverberates in a "rhetorical ecology" (Edbauer). Extradiscursive conditions and actors include things like more-than-human technologies, systemic power relations, nonhumans, and scent events. Scent events involve relational interspecies enmeshments and are framed by indeterminacy, contingency, and time, wherein time is not neutral. Extradiscursive conditions that create olfactory rhetoric emerge from embodied experiences with scent events and interactions that take place in a smellscape. For example, if one drives past a pet food factory or a massive animal confinement facility like a feedlot, the extradiscursive conditions may result in closing the windows or turning on the air-conditioning as one drives by to block the noxious odors and then opening the windows once past the facility to remove those noxious odors from the vehicle's interior. Upon arriving home or at the workplace, one may describe the stench to housemates or colleagues, using olfactory rhetoric to persuade them of the intensity of the experience. If one lives next door to one of those facilities, one may deploy olfactory rhetoric consistently to persuade local, state, and federal regulatory agencies to mitigate the harmful community health effects.

Understanding a complex environmental problem by starting with what the nose knows requires some invention and imagination. It also requires an expanded sense of rhetoric, a vital direction in materiality and posthuman inquiry other rhetoric scholars have begun and one I embrace in this book. As Alex Parrish substantiates in *Adaptive Rhetoric*, "If it is difficult to imagine . . . olfactory persuasiveness, that is only because we are unused to analyzing [the affiliated] behaviors as argument" (36). Such matters deserve critical reflection, for, as writer Amitav Ghosh notes, contending with "climate crisis" and environmental hazards requires us to attend to both "crisis of culture" and that "of the imagination" (9). *Olfactory Rhetoric* attends to cultural aspects of the olfactory imaginary and composite olfactive sensations rooted in material environmental conditions that emerge in the mediated public sphere, as it highlights changes in behavioral patterns and promotes more effective environmental responsibility across a spectrum of structural, intersecting inequities. I analyze olfactory persuasiveness as argument within the larger sensorium and face concerns important for rhetoricians to consider at intersection with environmental justice.

Olfactory Rhetoric focuses on mediated relationships between public, sensory, and embodied ways of ontological knowing juxtaposed against scientific, technical, and legal epistemologies. Ontology grapples with existence or philosophies of being and layered world-making: It asks what exists in the world and beyond and how we live. Ontological inquiry informs how ideas about reality vary and depend on sociocultural, languaged, and materially embedded processes. Epistemological inquiry informs us of what is knowable and seeks truth and facts. The book puts ontological approaches to sensing the existence of environmental harms and risk through material bodies and mediated texts in conversation with epistemological approaches to scientific quantification of environmental damage and risk through machine sensing and technical expertise because the debate informs how environmental risk is characterized, understood, and addressed. Physiological sensory signals, of which olfaction is but one signaling device, work as indicators of environmental damage, yet those with the power to do something to redress the damage and risk often dismiss said signals and privilege machine-based quantification and profit.

"Risk characterization" is an "interpretation of a certain limited body of evidence," which includes sense perception (Leiss and Powell, xiv). Risk communication scholars William Leiss and Douglas Powell suggest an essential "combination of creative scientific research, sound risk assessment, enlightened government policy, and good (responsible) behavior on the part of citizens" works best to address environmental risk (xv). Responsible behavior of a public (citizens or residents) includes response to, and reportage of, sensory signals set off by specific environmental hazards in their midst because they can share knowledge and inform risk assessment and how it is addressed in local landscapes (Besley and Nisbet; Walwema 246–47). As Kristin Arola (Finnish/Anishinaabe)[4] puts it, "Knowledge is the relations between our sensate experience, our memory, all of which are inextricable from the land upon which we have these experiences. Yet the concepts of land and experience are not fixed" and change (203). Evaluating environmental changes from a mediated and embodied perspective supports better analyses of environmental damage and risk exposure in a given place.

---

4. Whenever I first cite an Indigenous-identifying person, I bracket the cultural affiliation they have noted to draw direct attention to it to make it visible to readers. This is part of my citational practice that aligns with situating Indigenous peoples and ways fully in the present.

FIGURE 1. Cuyahoga River fire, 1952—Jefferson Street and West Third. Original photograph by James Thomas. Image credit: The Cleveland Press Special Collection, Michael Schwartz Library, Cleveland State University.

As an example, some readers may recall the now infamous, toxic legacy of the Cuyahoga River in Cleveland, Ohio. In 1920 residents told city engineers that local tap water smelled foul and "tasted 'medicinal' or like chlorine or carbolic acid"[5] (Ellms and Lawrence 463). After extensive study, engineers reported that the Cuyahoga's toxic water had indeed breached public waterworks intakes in Lake Erie, causing the foul taste and odor in residents' tap water (471–73). The initial dismissal of residents' sensory-data claims protracted the problem, which meant people ingested contaminated water for much longer. The lead crisis in Flint, Michigan, presents a contemporary example of the same type of dismissal and delayed response (Sanburn). Hegemonic power structures privilege short-term profits over people or nonhuman entities affected by long-term damage in both Cleveland and Flint (Hesford 1–4).

The Cuyahoga's oil-slick surface so bubbled with pestilence that it occasionally burst into flame (see fig. 1). The river's surface caught fire at least ten

---

5. Carbolic acid was a disinfectant rendered from coal tar and was commonly used in the 1920s.

times between 1868 and 1969. The 1969 fire made the cover of *Time* magazine. In December 1970, *National Geographic* featured the river's ecological mess (Boissoneault). The Cuyahoga became a symbol of public concern and skepticism about industry and industrialists. The Cuyahoga "fire object" was significant and generative within a growing environmental movement (Law and Mol; Law and Singleton).[6] In 1970, US president Richard Nixon created the Environmental Protection Agency (EPA) to address such exigencies alongside the welter of confusing and often ineffective local initiatives that shunted problems downstream or downwind. The 1970 Clean Air and 1972 Clean Water and Pesticide Control Acts were among the first EPA duties, which included monitoring of municipal and industrial wastewater and air pollution. By the mid-1990s, the EPA enforced at least twelve major statutes, which included uranium mining by-products, drinking water safety, school asbestos abatement, and ocean dumping, and the 1980 Comprehensive Environmental, Response, Compensation, and Liability Act (CERCLA). Also known as the "Superfund," CERCLA addressed abandoned waste dumps. Efforts, though infused with environmental injustice and racism (Bullard et al.; Bullard and Wright; Chavis and Lee; Gilio-Whitaker; Weidner), improved the nation's waterways, airways, and smellscapes as environmental cleanup ensued (Billets and Dindal). Five decades later, despite adding more than 140 million people to the US populace, emissions and "common pollutants as measured by weight [fell] 71%," and individual automobiles produce 99% fewer emissions (Biden).

Such successes result in people who forget why environmental protection laws exist, which, in turn, allows subsequent administrations (at state, federal, judicial, and international levels) to rescind so-called "job-killing" regulations, favoring polluters' interests over public health.[7] Pollution then resurges and negligent behavior regarding public health and safety recurs, leading to environmental crises that capture public interest and result in renewed cleanup efforts, starting the cycle again. Such cycles align with Rice's view of "memory claims" that both "create . . . possibilities for engagement" with environmental issues and "serve as a way for subjects to write themselves out of public

---

6. Drawing upon Law and Mol, organizational communication scholars John Law and Vicky Singleton describe the incendiary nature of fire objects as sociomaterial conditions bound to objects that represent the comingling effects of language, materiality, and power. I elaborate on the fire object concept in chapter 1.

7. For instance, on June 30, 2022, the conservative majority on the US Supreme Court ruled against the EPA's authority to regulate carbon emissions, which does not bode well for de-escalating global heating. In her dissent, Supreme Court Justice Elena Kagan protested the decision and characterized the implications thusly: "The Court appoints *itself*—instead of Congress or the expert agency—the decision-maker on climate policy. I cannot think of many things more frightening. Respectfully, I dissent" (Kagan 32–33; my emphasis).

debate" concerning environmental change (103–4). People who have no living memory of the Cuyahoga ablaze reflect "subjects of nonmemory," yet they still live in relation to "narratives of memory" (104). Evoking a sense memory through an odorant, photograph, or sound helps to interrupt vicious cycles of nonmemory.

The Cuyahoga example highlights complex interactions between how publics come to sense a place and how agencies like the EPA gather data to prove both harm and success (see, e.g., US EPA, "Cuyahoga"). The complicated meshwork relies on the ability to ascertain environmental risk and the political will to redress problems affecting public health. In the next section, I provide an approach to consider environmental issues like the Cuyahoga through an intersectional ecofeminist lens attuned to sensory rhetoric. Then, I converse with literature that informs the approach (e.g., intersectional ecofeminism, Indigenous material rhetorics, sensory studies, and environmental rhetoric).

The Affordances of and Audiences for a RISE Approach

First, I want to zoom out and discuss the sensory rhetorical approach and why I use the broader term when olfaction is the cynosure of the book. A sensory rhetorical approach complements existing work and methods in material rhetoric studies examining material spaces/places/conditions that intersect with identity (e.g., Blair, "Reflections"; Druschke; Hesford; Middleton et al.; Propen; Schmitt et al.). A sensory rhetorical approach attends to the role the senses and embodiment play in assessing an environment and allows for what surfaces in the textual and mediated public sphere as a result. *Olfactory Rhetoric* resists a material/discursive dualism that puts the body and language in opposing corners and "foregrounds the material and discursive as co-constitutive" (Hesford 22). It attends to how environmental concerns emerge in and through publics and how people address issues that affect their lived experiences and health. Occasionally, I consider my immediate sensory experiences with olfaction as a feminist rhetorical style of anecdotal witnessing. I do so to underscore analysis of textual and mediated artifacts of people's lived experiences. Debra Hawhee instructs, "Perhaps the best we can do as critics or as theorists is to toggle back and forth between sensation and criticism or theory" and consider how "other attachments matter for rhetoric—political, bodily, technological, and sensory, and [how] these intermix and move recursively" ("Rhetorics" 13). Such toggling involves "constitutive roles of sensation in participatory, rhetorical acts," including how mediated sensations circulate in rhetorical ecologies (13). The book bypasses autoethnography and autotheory related solely to my sense perceptions and instead focuses on environmental justice. Aspects of my embodied experiences create concrete analogies to illustrate the book's more abstract concepts.

While I could have narrowly named the approach an olfactory rhetorical approach, I assume rhetoricians' interests in the broader sensorium beyond olfaction. The idea opens the conversation to include a wider array of categories, cares, and critiques of sensation. Rhetoricians interested in a sensory rhetorical approach can then use it to analyze non-scent events such as noise, eyesores, radioactive menaces, or overlapping sensory concerns (e.g., when eyesores, noise, and stench comingle). Thus, a sensory rhetorical approach offers a way for multimodal, visual, sonic, haptic, or gustatory rhetoric scholars to extend it to their own research or teaching interests if these interests pertain to a different sense perception or synergies of perceptual activity affecting networked "relationships of discourses, political agency, and bodies" (Blair, "Reflections" 273). This includes the role sensory ecologies play across different life-forms. Sensory ecology pertains to the study of how organisms (human and nonhuman) gather, perceive, exchange, and respond to their surround and the animate and inanimate matter and energy in it (Nevitt; Müller et al.; Stevens). While "rhetorical ecology" refers to feelings, "effects, enactments, and events" and mediated works that circulate in rhetorical publics (Edbauer 9), "sensory ecology" recognizes how sensory systems inform and change human and more-than-human communication processes (Stevens 4). For example, in the Salton Sea case study (chapter 3), I discuss how birds use olfaction to locate specific chemical compounds in the scentscape to find food like krill or decaying fish, how trees and soil fungi communicate through chemical exchanges, and how this differs from yet complements human sensory ecology. Conceptually, sensory ecology builds from and expands existing material rhetoric studies interested in posthuman inquiry because it addresses how different organisms, humans included, use sensory filters (our own and others') to make sense of the world and myriad environmental settings. While other scholars have taken up how materials and matter in our rhetorical ecologies shape us and public memory (e.g., Bennett; Blair, "Contemporary" and "Reflections"; Cerulo; Jenell Johnson; Middleton et al.; Rice; Senda-Cook), no published work touches on how sensory ecology physically and rhetorically informs these processes. Incorporating a broader view of sensory ecologies deepens how we understand patterns of behavior and communication across human cultures, as the broader view illustrates care for nonhuman and more-than-human entities (see Eduardo Kohn's *How Forests Think* or Anna Tsing's *The Mushroom at the End of the World* for detailed beyond-human examples).

A RISE approach addresses matters of materiality, relationality, and embodiment that emerge from bodily experiences and perceptions and languaged, mediated aspects of the experiences. In "Sensate Regimes," sociologist Kevin McSorley writes, "It's important to state . . . there is no such thing as raw sensation—particular bodily ways of knowing and sensory experiences always emerge and are developed within specific environments and social worlds, are made culturally and politically meaningful, and become enlivened through particular material and media assemblages," a recursive Moebius strip (156). In this book, mediated events stem from embodied sensory experiences happening within historically minoritized and marginalized US communities that disproportionately contend with environmental hazards, including the worsening effects of global heating. In chapter 1, using RISE as an approach, I provide a heuristic for analyzing and evaluating composite sensations that emerge through publics' mediated artifacts. The heuristic provides a way to analyze sensory-rhetorical tactics communities use to address environmental risks. Tactical success has patchy characteristics and is often recursive, involving intermittent progress and persistence. In chapters 2 through 4, I apply the heuristic to place-based case studies where olfactible events impacted communities' perceptions of environmental risks and how to rectify them.

One RISE goal engages how human and more-than-human bodies transform matter and material experiences into language that emerges in the mediated public sphere. Philosopher Susanne Langer informs how words connote "the things from which our sense-experiences originally derived . . . [and] the context in which they were derived" (144). Accepting a "thoroughgoing empiricism" that privileges scientific quantification and the "little shivers and wiggles of our apparatus" fails to account for the "surprising truth that our *sense-data are primarily symbols*" (21). Langer expands the idea: "Symbolism furnished by our [senses] . . . is a *nondiscursive symbolism*, peculiarly well suited to the expression of ideas that defy linguistic 'projection'" (93). Sense data have inherent rhetorical projections because they persuade and create what Langer might call "feeling structures," though I pluck the term from the philosopher's treatise (xix, 83, 97–102). Applying the idea of feeling structure and sensory appreciation to olfactory rhetoric, imagine how a pleasant odor can move one and evoke an associated memory one has of the experience, which one can articulate to another. The same applies to an unpleasant odor, like the example I shared in the preface's opening scent event in which neighbors and I exchanged olfactory rhetoric about the hog factory's asphyxiating effects on our mutual lungscape.

How one regards and uses sense data like olfaction creates meaning and shapes how one interprets an environment, be it "natural" or otherwise.

Implicitly addressing environmental rhetoric, "nature," Langer declares, "speaks to us, first of all, through our senses; the forms and qualities we distinguish, remember, imagine, or recognize are symbols of entities which exceed and outlive our momentary experience" (93). Odor molecules we breathe in are persuasive and can leave lasting impressions. On an overt level, body odors reflect the emotional states of stress, anxiety, or calm others may consciously or unconsciously perceive. Olfactory cues provide snootful evidence of emotional states long before visual or verbal signals register. As Sara DiCaglio corroborates, "The unknown within the sensorium, the aspects of our senses that may be outside of control and even easy perception, [are] vital for rhetoric itself" (58). For example, we exude fear and happiness pheromones others in our midst detect, inducing mirroring suasive effects (D. Chen and Haviland-Jones; Lübke and Pause; Endevelt-Shapira et al.).

Incorporating more-than-human or nonhuman entities in analyses emphasizes how nonhuman agents and agency operate in the case study chapters. Intersectional ecofeminist and Indigenous approaches to posthumanism are foundational. Intersectional ecofeminist Norie R. Singer writes, "Posthumanist approaches decenter and disperse agency from any human or more-than-human individual" and situate "agency [as] intermeshed and networked across shifting ecological linkages" (269). The world consists of "dynamic and agentic" enmeshed actors (270). Yet, Amanda Booher and Julie Jung caution that "too often" mainstream posthumanist and object-oriented studies "fail to ask questions of race, culture, gender, disability, or other features," which "underhumanize[s]" different groups of people and allows some posthumanists to "throw off [their own and others'] bodily compartments" (2). This move "risk[s] reinscribing a privileged position that allows one to minimize the body—its agencies, variances, e/affects" embedded deeply in differing loci of power (3). Put otherwise, to focus solely on nonhuman matters or objects without espousing and enacting an ethical commitment to consider power differentials elides the bodies—human and nonhuman—deemed not to matter, and that is antithetical to intersectional ecofeminism and to me.

In terms of nonhuman agents or nonhuman agency, I prefer an Indigenous materialist concept of connected animacy in which living organisms and inert materials like rocks or the water cycle or the jet stream exert a lively suasive force that affects humans and nonhumans (Kohn; Ravenscroft; Z. Todd; Tsing; Watts; Yates et al.). For example, a hurricane as an agent has animacy (liveliness) and therefore agency to move people in its path and wake. Addressing an expansive sense of liveliness, Indigenous feminist Zoe Todd (Red River Métis, Otipemisiwak) elaborates on *Sila* as an Inuit concept referring to a sense of both climate and breath "that circulates into and out of every living thing" and an idea that connects "environment to knowledge" (Qitsualik qtd. in Z. Todd, par. 2, pars. 2–6). Similarly, Diné (Navajo) refer to wind as *nilch'i,* or "holy wind," as an interdependent life force, a breath that connects all of Earth in its entirety (McNeley 1). Indigenous concepts of animacy contrast with Western ideas about intentionality tied to human agents and agency because webs of relation extend far beyond an anthropocentric frame. Similar to the concept of *Sila* as both "climate *and* a life force" (Z. Todd, par. 8), Shoshone and Paiute American Indians name the energy of sacred places like Yucca Mountain in the desert Southwest *puha* because a place "possesses energy, vitality, [and] life" (Kuletz qtd. in Endres 49). As animate relations, places deserve the same respect one might hold for a revered elder. Unbounded fluidity between what is considered alive or lively is comprehensive in many Indigenous worldviews. Boundaries are unbounded and unfounded, which changes one's perspective about how to value "all our relations" (LaDuke).

Interdisciplinary rhetorical labor births mutable disciplinary boundary work and induces a "critical gerrymandering of rhetorical inquiry" required to push problems like environmental injustice into the spotlight (Graham 4–10). To give readers a sense of this labor, *Olfactory Rhetoric* draws from and is indebted to a variety of literatures: Indigenous materialisms, rhetorical new materialisms, anthropology and sociology of the senses, intersectional and ecofeminist theories, environmental justice scholarship, technical and environmental communication, and philosophy. This book's primary audience will be environmental rhetoricians interested in the senses and more-than-human materiality that intersects with environmental justice. Secondary audiences include technical communication scholars, feminist rhetoricians, intersectional ecofeminists, and multimodal scholars interested in how nondiscursive and discursive rhetorics collaboratively influence. Tertiary audiences include people who study risk at intersection with environmental issues and environmental communication scholars trained in communication studies departments. *Olfactory Rhetoric* builds upon scholars' interdisciplinary intersectional approaches to agency, rhetorical sensation, human and more-than-human enmeshments, and structural inequities that negatively impact environmental conditions in historically minoritized and marginalized communities.

Of course, this book will impart interstitial spaces bound to one's intellectual genealogy, training, and more. Openings should prove useful to other rhetoricians, particularly those attentive to "discourses happening outside of the rock-star arenas of Euro-Western thought," though I draw from those resources too (Z. Todd 8). Concomitantly, Scott Graham asks, "Is rhetoric a *what* or a *how*?" (10). Graham notes how "English and speech rhetoricians" come at rhetorical inquiry and analysis from different perspectives (11). Speech rhetoricians—scholars interested in public address—have an "artifact canon," and English rhetoricians tend not to privilege an artifact canon. Graham considers the English approach to rhetoric a "*how*" instead of a "*what*" (11). Rhetoric as a how takes note of how and why senses like olfaction, touch, vision, taste, or hearing work to persuade. Rhetoric as a what considers objects emerging from sensory experiences articulated as olfactory, visual, haptic, or sonic rhetoric that circulate in the form of textual or mediated artifacts. Like Rice, I am interested in what happens when we blend the two subfields and approaches, for they are not mutually exclusive (21). Both emphasize public and civic engagement.

Another purpose of the book expands topoi in feminist-oriented material rhetorics to include how olfaction informs environmental decision-making and risk assessment. As Alain Corbin points out in *The Foul and the Fragrant*, "Abhorrence of smells produces its own form of social power, [and] foul-smelling rubbish appears to threaten the social order" (5). Consider an example of municipal garbage workers on strike in a metropolis like New York City. The refuse piles up on curbs, dumpsters overflow, shared air reeks, and a public health crisis looms. Rats, mice, cockroaches, and bacteria may find the largesse beneficial, though these nonhuman population booms bear with them their own hazards. While the refuse in the example spotlights throwaway culture and human overconsumption of finite resources, the material in the trash bags or dumpsters is more-than-human and exerts a suasive force. Stinky pileups highlight crucial work trash collectors do, which can result in a raise or other employment concessions the workers ask for, like safer working conditions, stable pensions, or whatever striking workers in a union-friendly state hope to achieve.

The example above relates to another purpose of the book, offering an approach to olfactory rhetorical analysis. Environmental rhetoricians can use the approach to examine environmental problems that surface when people notice an unusual or rank odor circulating within a given environment and the "visceral . . . relationship between bodily boundaries and intense feelings" that emerge as a result (Jenell Johnson 3). In the case study chapters, I use the approach to analyze textual and mediated artifacts related to site-specific, ephemeral scent events that I did not, and could not, personally experience. However, this approach is not, as Roland Barthes notes, a "zero degree" writing practice or an aloof thought experiment (48). My family's and community's visceral exposure to the nauseating stench and biohazards associated with hog manure and industrial agriculture inform and introduce the book project in the preface. The people who own and built the pig plant do not live in the community and reside in the neighboring state of Iowa, where confined animal feeding operations have had caustic environmental impacts. Legal pushback in Iowa now encourages agro-industrial corporations to find places with laxer siting rules, which resulted in the facility smothering my community. Community experiences of trying to resist the factory's construction and the nauseating after-effects led me to research and better understand historical patterns of where confined animal feeding operations and other environmental hazards are typically placed, which is in poorer urban and rural communities and usually BIPOC communities (Bullard and Wright 67–72; Weidner 241, 245). Informed by capitalism, lax regulations, greed, and self-not-collective interest result in hellish environmental consequences for people, animals, plants, soil, water, and air.

My community's unsuccessful grassroots activism and failure of our "visceral public" to move policymakers in the hog factory context encourages me to actively seek examples that have met with better success, though success is sometimes murky, mired in recursive complexity, takes time, and is less straightforward than one might hope (Jenell Johnson 2). Struggle and hope are fertile, though they often remain incremental and aggregative. Sniffing out success stories begins with gut-wrenching sensations, the intensity of which can lead to a visceral public who discusses and leaves records of those discussions in the mediated public sphere. Olfaction contributes to minded and embodied states. The nose sniffs out, deliberates, evaluates, and comprehends environmental problems. The translated mediated effects circulate.

Rhetorician Carole Blair recommends we "consider the material conditions of discourse," focus "upon the lived-in body as a condition and consequence of rhetoric," and expand "the domain of rhetoric to include cultural practices and artifacts beyond spoken or written word . . . as well as understandings of extra-linguistic rhetorics" ("Reflections" 273). The points Blair elucidated more than twenty years ago are enmeshed in how an environmental rhetorician identifies sites, objects, and artifacts to analyze (rhetoric as a what) and how they understand their own bodies in relation to other bodies (rhetoric as a how), which extends to the concept of material rhetoric, ethical posthuman inquiry at intersection with Indigenous approaches, and a politics of how (288). Blair indirectly informs how one might approach textual and mediated experiences of ephemeral, evanescent events and how we read these messages informed by our own lived experiences and sensory ecology even when not proximal to the object of study. Scent events are "nontraditional targets" of rhetorical criticism, though the textual and mediated evidence of them likely is a traditional target (273). Though I did not conduct field-based participatory studies based on in situ "toxic tourism," I do consider issues of embodiment and materiality in the case study chapters, as these inform both how and why the environmental concerns highlighted in the case studies emerged as informed by human olfaction and by extension through sensory rhetorical ecologies (Pezzullo 4–8).

It is not always possible to have an in situ experience of a scent event. It depends on the situation under review or analysis. Sometimes, it is simply impossible. This is particularly true of ephemeral scent events with limited duration or intermittent characteristics. Scent events are by their very nature *volatile*, a Latin term meaning to fly, fleeting, evaporating rapidly, flighty, or fickle. The "aura" of an original scent event may be "subsumed" in the act of examining the textual and mediated evidence of the event, but the beholder can "with the aid of certain processes . . . capture images [or scenes] which escape natural vision" or other sensual interactions (Benjamin 4). We and our fleshy and fibrous nonhuman companions are permeable bodies enmeshed within the circulating fluxes and flows of a given environment, including that which circulates in textual or mediated forms.

Critiques of "ocularcentric and scriptocentric" approaches to environmental hazards and their impacts on bodies include how a focus on visual and textual evidence of a/effects has a distancing effect that can further marginalize BIPOC bodies (Pezzullo 30). Discussing in situ environmental ethnography, Phaedra Pezzullo underscores multisensory partaking with "people who have been pushed to the margins" and opted to go on "toxic tours" led by community activists to develop "sensitivity to a much wider range of communicative symbols, practices, and effects" in BIPOC communities where the results of environmental racism are present (30). The purpose of Pezzullo's "toxic tours" is to "invoke the uglier sensualities of our world: the disgusting and the grotesque. Tourists are asked to expose themselves to the costs of human greed: poisoned air, polluted water, degraded land, and bodies that are diseased, deformed, or dying" (10). Facing such uglier sensualities in my own community informs my ability to imagine other sites where noxious odors indicate environmental damage, as does my insider understanding of EPA monitoring and cleanup efforts. Readers, even if you do not have an insider's understanding of EPA efforts, you also have the capacity to sense and imagine.

Drawing on cognition research, the capacity to imagine olfactive scenarios like those presented in this book relies on what sensory sociologist Karen Cerulo describes as "embodied simulation" and "iterative reprocessing" and their roles in "olfactory meaning-making" (366). Through embodied simulation, we can begin to understand situations by mentally simulating experiences others describe. This involves fusing worlds lived and imagined. Practice by imagining the taste of chocolate ice cream on a hot summer day or how it feels to open a car door after it has been parked in the summer sun for a few hours. Now, imagine the smell of sauteing onions. Did you close your eyes and inhale? Importantly, we build a mental image of the scenario steeped in our past experiences, and embodied simulation "shows that most of us not only visualize these experiences—we feel [or sense] them" (Cerulo 367). Reflexively, in our mind's "mouth," we can feel the cold and taste the chocolate in our mouth, or we feel the blast of hot air and the steering wheel's heat on our hands, and it has an observable impact (375). For example, you might have pursed your lips and rolled your tongue in your mouth when thinking of the ice cream or curled your fingers and winced when recalling the hot steering wheel. Importantly, embodied simulation "makes use of the same parts of the brain dedicated to directly interacting with the world," meaning that simulation draws upon prior experiences and "brain patterns" based on "previous perceptual and motor experiences" (Bergen 14; Clark). Embodied simulation also applies to things we have not experienced, and language helps us to parse relevant experiences and engage in meaning-making and to tap "olfactory experience" (Bergen 17; Weidner 240). Thus, extradiscursive, nondiscursive, and discursive elements all reside in the body/mind. Embodied simulation interdependently links the extradiscursive, nondiscursive, and discursive as meaning emerges. As Cerulo articulates, "Olfactory meaning-making . . . [involves] people's 'know how' experience and their 'know that' declarations" (367). A combined extradiscursive, discursive, and olfactory meaning-making results in olfactory rhetoric people use to describe their lived experiences, and embodied simulation allows us to empathize and have feelings and sensations of compassion for other people and entities.

Iterative reprocessing links extradiscursive, nondiscursive, and discursive elements because after people have an initial response to stimulus, either in situ or through embodied simulation, they revisit the experience and add reflective and reflexive components to their sense-making in a "repeated toggling between automatic and deliberative cognitive" acts (Cerulo 368). The first occurrence may involve a gut reaction to a visceral experience. Reflecting on the experience and discussing it with others is part of this toggling process. The initial evaluation is immediate and may or may not be accurate. When we reprocess our own and others' experiences through embodied simulation, we do so informed by our sociocultural locale, and iterative reprocessing plays a role in what we perceive.

Pezzullo notes that "toxic tours are negotiations of power" and as such require an intersectional ecofeminist researcher to be circumspect about how their body moves to or in a space deemed ruined. One can learn from olfactory injustices even if one is not present because one can imagine them (Weidner). Through iterative reprocessing one can also come to new conclusions about what these communities face. People, primarily community activists, conduct "toxic tours" to spotlight environmental issues, and while I understand and find merit in the approach, I have trod a different path to evaluate how visceral publics use olfactory rhetoric in the mediated public sphere to mitigate or alleviate environmental damage (Pezzullo 5). In addition, a short-term scent event that emerges and recurs sporadically may not afford one the opportunity to nose it in the flesh. However, Pezzullo's account of "witnessing as a tactic of resistance," in which "one can take action afterward, reporting, testifying, and relating to others that which has been witnessed," resonates in terms of embodied simulation and iterative reprocessing (146). Pezzullo's purpose and ethical commitments and mine align. Next, I frame my arguments and purpose in scholarly literature that informs them.

Framing the Book's Ethical Commitments and Arguments

Indigenous views about webs of relation and materiality, including nonhuman entities and enmeshments, undergird RISE and my analyses throughout the book. Jennifer Clary-Lemon explains, "Rhetoricians who study new materialism . . . [should] note that a holistic [relational] ontology and an emphasis on the non-rational, the embodied, the affective, or the power of things not only resonates with Indigenous knowledge, but it is emerging directly from it in non-attributed ways" ("Gifts" par. 8). Work to "unseat the colonial attitude" situates Indigenous peoples and ways fully in "the present, the political, the rhetorical, and the material," crushing a "vanishing Indian" mythos (Clary-Lemon, "Gifts" par. 8; Maroukis). Indigenous cosmologies, knowledges, and relational ontologies value and teach how human beings are materially, socially, and spiritually entangled and networked within all Earth's processes, creatures, effluvia, and beyond (Arola; Cajete, *Look* and *Native*; Clary-Lemon, "Gifts" and *Planting*; Deloria; Driskill; Druschke; Druschke et al.; Haas; Houdek and Ore; Itchuaqiyaq, "Iñupiat" and "When"; Jack; Kimmerer; L. King et al.; LaDuke; Z. Todd; Wildcat; Yates et al.). Zoe Todd advises we "[credit] Indigenous thinkers for their millennia of engagement with sentient environments, with cosmologies that enmesh people into complex relationships between themselves and *all* relations, and with climates and atmospheres as important points of organization and action" (7–8). In contrast, Western cosmologies typically privilege a Great Chain of Being that places a medieval God at the apex and bottoms out with minerals, metals, and a sin-riddled punishing underworld, which is a hierarchical structure that conceals rhizomatic, webbed relations key to a RISE approach (Rowland 19–20, 143).[8]

As an environmental rhetorician, the material and sensorial turns in rhetoric studies excite me. As an author and uninvited white settler on unceded Indigenous lands, restorative justice choices in this book spotlight Indigenous voices and BIPOC perspectives. Mindful of my positionality as a US citizen and middle-class, cisgender, heterosexual white woman who has primarily benefited from harmful power structures, I also think about transparency, reciprocity, and how "citation lists [are] gifts that we carry forward in ways that distribute the agency of the sole author . . . and decentralize who is speaking at any one time" (Clary-Lemon, "Gifts" par. 22). Emphasizing the voices and scholarship of BIPOC and other marginalized groups means learning from and listening to their perspectives as I work to decolonize mine. Engaging with Indigenous ontological traditions starts with Trinh T. Minh-ha's ethics in mind: "not to speak about [or for] but rather to speak nearby" Indigenous ontologies (qtd. in N. Chen 87). Such conversations require reflexive practice and do not lay claim to it or seize it but seek to usher in "an attitude in life" that positions one in "relation [with] the world" and other worldviews (87). Intersectional ecofeminist approaches to environmental justice like mine attend to overlapping axes of oppression, and I recognize that my positionality has both advantages and constraints tied to my race, gender, class, abilities, institutional placement, sociopolitical upbringing, viewpoint, and more. Like "co-conspirators" Matthew Houdek and Ersula J. Ore, I ask, "What might it mean to embrace conspiratorial acts against a world that denies far too many the right and capacity to breathe, and what is the role of white folks therein . . . , and what might it mean [to] . . . inaugurate an Age of Breath suited to Black and Indigenous survival and liberation?" (85). Conspiratorial acts include taking up anti-oppression work in ways that "take on the responsibility of injustice and breath[e] with as opposed to hoarding the air for [oneself]" (88). Thus sensitized, rhetorical awareness ought to extend to our most foundational streams of sensorial suasion, including that which circulates in the very air we breathe.

Embracing webbed relations, *Olfactory Rhetoric* offers two main arguments. First, a RISE approach to environmental case study analyses and the artifacts and experiences associated with them expands to a range of sense perceptions including and beyond olfaction, informing the methodological

---

8. By "Western" here I reference a "style" of inquiry rather than one based on region (Yates-Doerr and Mol 48).

argument. Rather than bequeath readers a hidebound methodological jewel, RISE instead conveys a multifaceted code for conduct or a sensitizing approach to thinking and writing about mediated material sensations regardless of the sensory categories involved. Informed by a RISE approach, the topical argument takes olfaction and its mediation function seriously when addressing environmental concerns. Intense olfactive experiences influence public policymaking and other behaviors. A RISE approach to olfaction and olfactory rhetoric equips readers with a topical and methodological repertoire that builds alliances designed to serve socioenvironmental justice goals while disrupting ableist notions of what it means to make sense, be sensible, and become sensitive to life on Earth.

When people experience a disgusting odor, it elicits a visceral response that persuades. Odors move people to respond to and address perceived environmental hazards. People may consequently deploy olfactory rhetoric to discuss those experiences and to mitigate damage. Examining how people use olfaction and its mediation rhetorically supports us to understand, analyze, and redress troubled and troubling environmental conditions. Since smells along with "affect and emotions are ephemeral, subjective phenomena, we only have access to the feelings [and smells] of the past through their recorded expression—the same textual [and mediated] traces that tell us *a public was here*" (Jenell Johnson 3). How a public senses and responds to an environmental hazard connects with Jenell Johnson's description of "visceral publics" (2). Johnson explains that visceral publics have two primary characteristics: They "emerge from discourse about boundaries [bodily or otherwise], and they cohere by means of intense feeling" (2). "Visceral *issues*" that appear in the public sphere may emerge because they are indeed "*visceral* issues"—matters of the flesh, sensation, gut instinct, and emotion (2, 4). Olfactory persuasion relative to the intensity of perceivable environmental hazards epitomizes this because visceral publics often form in response to intense odor experiences. Visceral publics tap into gut feelings. "Gut feelings," Johnson elaborates, paradoxically both suggest an "absence of reason" and "reveal a primal truth outside of language, culture, or history," and they "guide deliberation about controversial issues in science and medicine" and environmental policymaking (5). Johnson makes clear that "disgust in particular" involves "emotional expression of deep wisdom, beyond reason's power fully to articulate it" (Kass qtd. in Johnson 5). Connecting matter to meaning, visceral feelings like disgust have embodied stickiness that hangs around in a mediated visceral public. Matter and meaning are co-constitutive, and what they create—language, material entities, sensations, and political a/effects—is built from a weave of relations and socioenvironmental inter- and intra-actions. When considering the weave, we must address how intersecting axes of oppression affect different groups.

In 1989, legal scholar and civil rights advocate Kimberlé Crenshaw created the concept of intersectionality to recognize how overlapping axes of oppression inform the experiences of Black women, which helped promote polyvocal approaches within and to the feminist movement, a movement that historically focused on issues that affected white women and neglected to parse inequities among different groups ("Mapping"). Crenshaw explains, "Any analysis that does not take intersectionality into account cannot sufficiently address the particular manner in which Black women are subordinated," and this extends to how other historically excluded groups of people are subordinated in different contexts ("Demarginalizing" 140). Building upon Crenshaw's scholarship, Black social theorist Patricia Hill Collins notes how an intersectional approach "[sees] social [and environmental] problems caused by colonialism, racism, sexism, and nationalism as interconnected," which "provide[s] a new vantage of the possibility for social change" across intersectional convergences of oppression, sensations, and visceral publics (1). Hence, intersectional ecofeminist approaches to environmental problems allow for a broader understanding of how different groups and communities build and sense their agency based on identity markers to which a group may identify or disidentify. It also supports us to understand and analyze how different groups of people respond to and redress environmental hazards that have inequitable impacts. For example, in the Flint, Michigan, water contamination crisis, white women were frequently shown as the public face of the issue in mainstream media outlets, though the crisis has had a much larger impact on BIPOC Flint residents (Bates, "Activist" 210). Intersectional ecofeminist approaches to analysis work to rectify these inherent injustices.

In this book, I take an intersectional ecofeminist approach to sociohistorical constructions of race, gender, and other power relations in public perceptions of nature, culture, and environmental health. Ecofeminism is a philosophical approach to feminism that merges ecological care and gender equity concerns to confront patriarchal approaches to environmentalism. Historically, white male-identifying environmentalists (e.g., Leopold; Muir; Thoreau) focused their efforts on paternalistic stewardship, wilderness preservation, rugged individualism and resilience, and class-based issues. They failed to consider gender, race, or other intersectional issues. Ecofeminism draws from a diverse array of theoretical and political perspectives that includes animal rights, environmental studies, feminist science studies, feminist activisms, women's and gender studies, queer studies, and beyond. Common threads among the weave of ecofeminist writing are "critique of patriarchal science," concerns about environmental degradation, and "the making of links between these two and the oppression of women" (Molyneux and Steinberg 86). Early ecofeminists highlighted how the domination of nature, women, and animals were related (e.g., Aviva Cantor; d'Eaubonne; Gaard, *Ecological* and "Misunderstanding"; Singer; Warren). For example, in *Ecological Politics*, Gretta Gaard notes connections that provide a foundation for ecofeminism, which include attending to "ecology, animal liberation, and feminism" and resisting patriarchal constructions of the environment and masculinist domination paradigms that seek to tame something or someone for domestic, recreational, utilitarian, or nefarious use (3). Some ecofeminists attended to gender, race, and the Global South (e.g., Mies and Shiva). In the foreword to Maria Mies and Vanda Shiva's now classic 1993 book *Ecofeminism*, Ariel Salleh writes, "With ecofeminism, the political focus turns outwards . . . to [build] global political alliances with workers, peasants, indigenous peoples, and other victims of the Western drive to accumulation . . . under the stranglehold of global neoliberalism" (xi). We suffocate under this stranglehold and its sociohistorical "rhetorical infrastructure" (Koerber).

One constraint of the gendered binary in ecofeminist discourse regardless of geographical location is a "motherhood trope" that positions women as "the most natural caretakers of the earth," which suggests that women "are best suited to clean up men's ecological mess[es]" (Singer 275; Stearney). This echoes domestic sphere rhetoric about women's second-shift roles in cis-het partner households where women do the majority of childcare and household chores (cleaning up messes) above and beyond any paid employment they may have. Second-wave ecofeminism, however, often used these overt characterizations of women and women's roles in environmental carework to make visible the labor once obscured by masculinist discourse (Gaard, *Ecological* and "Misunderstanding"; Mies and Shiva). I do not want to undo that work of visibility, even as I acknowledge its limitations. Singer situates intersectional ecofeminism as "an anti-essentialist heuristic [that] overtly rejects any singular, universal categorization of identity as a covering explanation of agency and experience . . . [which] helps to account for variables of experience and power" that extend to both "human [and] more-than-human" entities (269). In a similar key, I strive against hegemonies such as ableism, racism, sexism, ageism, and classism that attempt to discredit olfaction and other embodied experiences. The case study chapters of *Olfactory Rhetoric* illustrate how these hegemonies impact visceral publics working to remedy environmental problems. I contextualize why the hegemonies are at play in chapter 1, in which I fully explicate my methodological and topical arguments. Throughout, I focus primarily on environmental justice issues affecting BIPOC communities that "historically have been segregated from elite centers of power," as this orientation aligns with my values, intersectional approach, and commitments to redress environmental damage that impacts the world's most vulnerable (Pezzullo 5). Similar to Donnie Sackey, I see an intersectional ecofeminist positionality as one that is "value-sensitive" in its approach to research design and implementation such that environmental justice becomes "integral to planning processes" from the outset (39). Put another way, webs of relation, visceral publics, and how we examine and address intersectional power inequities matter as we seek ways to combat wicked environmental problems.[9] Such intense problems burrow under the skin and up the nose.

Scent events are ephemeral, unique, unduplicable experiences influenced by the source's conditions and the environment in which the source and receptor are located. This makes field-based study of an in situ event hit or miss, informing why I privilege textual and mediated evidence of olfactible events after they occur. Insisting that the researcher have direct, personal experience can minimize the experiences and reporting of those directly impacted and is an artifact of a hegemonic hierarchy that elevates documentation by credentialed researchers and experts over that of impacted populations (Koerber 255, 257). It is one of the root causes of environmental injustice. My focus on environmental injustice cases also shapes the heuristic I developed and why I selected scent events and sites located in historically minoritized communities (i.e., Irwindale and Salton Sea, California, and Pearland/Fresno, Texas).

Why Olfaction Matters

Because our sense of smell is typically undervalued, readers may not have a good sense of how it works or what it does to our mental and physical health. With every breath we take, we inhale vaporized bits that enter us and become part of us, whether it be a lover's or stranger's skin, a pine tree, a pet, or hog manure. Troubling thought, no? Little wonder we involuntarily suspend breathing when we smell something disgusting.

Far beyond "a simple physiochemical process," olfaction is a "plastic process that is strongly tied to memory," and we "learn to smell" (D. Wilson and Stevenson 1). However, unlike our other sensory systems (e.g., vision, hearing,

---

9. Design theorists Horst Rittel and Melvin Webber introduced the concept of "wicked problems" in 1973 and listed key characteristics: They are difficult to define. They do not have a clear stopping point or overt solution. They do not have a true/false solution dichotomy but do include good/bad outcomes. Solutions cannot be tested. One wicked problem usually stems from another, which adds to the complexity.

taste, and touch), our olfactive sense does not require a "thalamic relay," meaning that our olfactive sense involves no perceptual gatekeeping and an odorant's effects go straight to areas of our embodied mind that drive perceptions and behaviors associated with smells (Shepherd 166). Scent marketing and branding firms are wise to this (Henshaw et al.). Leslie Albrecht puts it this way: "Odors function like mood music for your nose," and companies like ScentAir that design and manufacture custom fragrances for theme parks (Disney), hotel chains (Hyatt), and stores (e.g., Starbucks, Abercrombie and Fitch, Apple) persuade consumers and build brand identities by leading people through the nose (par. 5). For example, Disneyland has patented devices known as "smellitzers" that shoot scents at theme park visitors designed to cement the experience in people's memories and to evoke nostalgia for the place (Spence 6–7). *Smellitzer* is a portmanteau of *howitzer*, a World War II artillery shell launcher, and the word *smell*. The militaristic assault on the senses is literal and rhetorical. The technology patent suggests orchestrated scent narratives consisting of odorants "presented sequentially to be congruent with sequential elements" in a theme park "story" to make it more memorable to visitors and to build brand loyalty (6). Understanding such information can support readers to better evaluate the claims I make throughout this book about the "embodied rhetoricity" of olfaction and odors (McKerrow 319–23), or what Caroline Gottschalk Druschke might identify as "a more capacious, physical, and equivocal version of rhetoricity" ("Trophic" par. 39). In terms of rhetoricity, olfaction is a speedy sense, indeed. With no need for thalamic relay, the fastest sensory-related synaptic processing that most humans possess exists between the moment we inhale a scent and the moment our neurons respond (Drobnick 348; Feldman Barrett 121). Odor response happens in less than 100 milliseconds in mammals (D. Wilson and Stevenson). A key function of human olfaction is "hedonic" in that human animals are excellent at articulating whether a smell is pleasant or not (Yeshurun and Sobel 219). Moreover, inhaled smells take a direct route to the amygdala and hippocampus (Yeshurun and Sobel). The amygdala and hippocampus are deep in the middle of the brain and are part of the limbic circuitry of the brain—the "lizard" bit of our brain that is responsible for basic survival responses (Feldman Barrett 107; Lübke and Pause). Both the amygdala and hippocampus are key to emotion and learning-memory. The quantity of sense receptors associated with the sense of smell is second only to those associated with vision. Olfactory processing also begins with "odor images" analogous to visual images, meaning that in addition to a mind's eye we also have a mind's nose that we tap into in terms of embodied simulation and iterative reprocessing (Haberly; Shepherd 167; D. Wilson and Stevenson). While olfaction is known as the "affective sense" in the West, outside of that tradition it remains free of thousands of years of "disqualifications" and "assumptions" about its "cognitive value" (Howes, "Olfactory Art" 7; Corbin 7–8). In India, olfaction is a spatial sense with capacity to push or pull that informs navigation irrespective of memory or nostalgia (Howes, "Olfactory Art" 7–8; McEvilley). We follow our nose, tracking scent markers and navigating nosewise like a shark to prey or an ant on a scent trail.

When functional, our sense of smell is both speedy and shrewd. A groundbreaking 2014 study published in the journal *Science* asserts that humans can distinguish around a *trillion* different odors (Bushdid et al. 1372), challenging a decades-long assumption that humans can only distinguish about 10,000 different odors (1370; Gilbert 10–15). The speed with which we process odor experiences can help save a life or lives when seconds matter. One's body reacts to a scent before thought kicks in. The odor of "smelling salts" serves as an example. Smelling salts, an ammonia compound, rouses the inert body because it irritates the nose and lungs, causing the body to inhale.

Besides spatial navigation—letting the nose lead to someplace (un)savory or sweet—the emotional processing olfaction fosters is crucial to different aspects of one's mental and physical health. Cultural traditions train one's sense of smell to appreciate different aromas and scentscapes (Herz xvii). Olfaction's close link to emotions makes olfactory rhetoric powerful when evoked effectively. Apprehending the "osmocosm," a portmanteau of the Greek term *osme* for smell or odor and the material "cosmos," hints at the magical complexity of the "invisible nimbus of flying molecules" we breathe in and notice on a spectrum of both ability and attunement (McGee xi). A closer type of cosmos refers to a system of thought. Olfaction is crucial "to survival and the apprehension of dangers, and particular smells can evoke such vivid, whole-body sensations and emotionally charged memories that its political significance should not be dismissed" (McSorley 157). Following Debra Hawhee, such intense experiences constitute a "felt rhetoric," and evoke rhetoric as an "art of intensification" (*Sense* 15, 4, 19, 79). The following presents an example of evocative, effective olfactory rhetoric: "'The forgetting of breathing' haunts Western thought and has led to an impoverishment in our relation to the earth and each other" (Škof and Berndtson qtd. in Houdek and Ore 86; Škof and Berndtson x). Even if anosmic (unable to sense any odor), we do not breathe without taking in odorants, so Škof and Berndtson's words exemplify powerful olfactory rhetoric used to persuade people to reconsider the a/effects of this forgetting. The effect is a type of collective rhetorical anosmia that allows people to ignore both olfaction's affects and environmental issues. Another example tied to environmental impacts: Consider one of my neighbor's "hog smog" reports to the Illinois EPA. "Friday, July 10, 2020. Wind came out of the southeast. It was very humid. The afternoon stench of hog manure clawed the back of my throat. Vomit crept into my mouth with a copper-y tang. Eyes watered and stomach lurched between the hours of 5:31 PM and 8:25 PM. The toxic cloud just lingered around for hours. I'm so sick from this. Can't you do right by us?"[10] My early-middle-aged neighbor died two months later. The family did not indicate a specific cause of death. When we breathe in a pleasing odor, it affects our mood and mental health. Unpleasant odors, as my neighbor attested, do the same thing but to ill effects. Our response to such stimuli affects our choices and emotions both consciously and subconsciously in osmocosmic relation (Han et al.).

Olfaction also exposes our vulnerability to sensory extinction. How we direct our attention over time shifts our capacity to notice, be sensitive to, and, ultimately, be persuaded by the rhetorical force of one sense as it comes under the influence of another. Consider how, on the one hand, a functional human olfaction system becomes inured to a persistent scent relatively quickly—something named "extinction" or "conditioned stimulus" in olfactory research circles (Gilbert 114). On the other hand, as olfaction expert Avery Gilbert argues, "bad smells are natural candidates for Pavlovian conditioning" (117). When constantly exposed to malodorous events, we can become habituated (insensitive) to the odors and may come to ignore their suasive power to make us act differently in certain situations and environmental settings (118). The US military trains soldiers under this rubric. For example, maneuvers at the Fort Irwin Training Center in the Mojave Desert include "sensory inoculation" exercises designed by "olfactory engineers" (McSorley 158). The exercises habituate soldiers to the smell of "Middle Eastern villages," which includes the simulated odors of "'Middle Eastern cooking,' 'hookah,' camel droppings,' . . . [and] the viscera of 'vomit,' 'corpse,' and 'burning flesh'" (158). These drills preexpose soldiers before they encounter warfare smellscapes. The drills desensitize soldiers' responses "to particular smells" in the "service of military efficiencies" (158). Sensory extinction or "inoculation" depends on intensity too. A really noxious odor maintains its hold on us. For example, when exposed to the stench of hog manure on a hot, humid summer day, I cannot tune out the unrelenting odor and become a veritable prisoner inside my home.

---

10. Laypeople cannot access reports made to the Illinois EPA, but we often share our logged entries to understand what to do and where to report, and to compare notes on whether the agency officials acted on our reports. I'm omitting my neighbor's name to protect her family's privacy.

While sensory extinction involves risk, its inverse or enduring sensation in response to noxious or seemingly agreeable olfactive stimuli has serious health implications as well (Schiffman and Williams). Because olfaction prompts emotion, when we experience a personally negative or overtly harmful smellscape, we must respond. Often the emotional response is visceral and sometimes long-lasting. Sara Ahmed writes, "Emotions are what move us, and how we are moved involves interpretations of sensations and feelings. . . . Focusing on emotions as mediated rather than immediate reminds us that knowledge cannot be separated from the bodily world of feeling and sensation" (171). Encountering an odor can evoke antecedent pain, cause panic attacks, stimulate nausea and vomiting, trigger depression, kindle stress, and more. For example, abused people burned with cigarettes or tortured near cigarette smoke may be triggered into a debilitating panic attack simply by smelling secondhand smoke (Hinton et al. 156–58). Embodied responses to trauma can also emerge through words and media people use to articulate the experience to others.

Defining Olfactory Rhetoric and Its Importance to Environmental Justice

Emerging directly from odors' suasive appeals, people use mediated olfactory rhetoric in different situations for myriad purposes, like redressing environmental injustice. Olfactory rhetoric is the mediated translation of odors' persuasive impacts. A conceptual apparatus like olfactory rhetoric, then, assists environmental rhetoricians to ask critical questions and resolve problems people have sniffed out. Hence, olfactory rhetoric offers topoi (topics, spaces, places, and themes) that pertain to olfaction and suasive scent events. Olfactory-rhetorical inquiry also entails a nondiscursive pursuit that exceeds the domain of language because it tendrils around embodiment. The concept helps us analyze how peoples, institutions, genders, and others are reductively written through signifiers referencing scent, which I address in chapter 1 (see also Smith).

That olfaction informs how we both perceive and rhetorically construct our past experiences and judge people, places, and memories begs the question of how our culturally informed sense of smell shapes our language, composing, and embodied practices. Such inquiry into our sense of smell encourages us to reexamine rhetorics of personhood, race, class, gender, space, place, and (dis)ability as they are tied to odor and olfaction. Olfaction is an important means of persuasion. How "olfactory effects . . . work in concert with the other sensory channels to reinforce meaning" or "conflict with the other channels" matters because the effects extend to who or what is deemed valuable, offensive, or disruptive (Banes 70). Focusing on olfactory a/effects discloses different layers of meaning-making at work in environmental discourse.

The interdisciplinary reach of olfactory rhetoric makes new questions possible. We can ask how scholars in different disciplinary domains are rhetorically and sensorially trained to interpret stimuli as they represent a given environment or concept to an audience (Murray). For example, a cognitive neurobiologist can represent an odor by describing the synaptic process involved in smelling and memory enhancement—a matter of mirror neurons and limbic responses. Perfumers can represent odorants and aldehydes by writing down the specific chemical formulae associated with specific odor compounds. A gas chromatograph allows a chemist to represent the molecular signature of an odorant from its constituent, separable parts. For a poet, an odor can evoke a particular feeling for a love lost or interrupt a moment in time. Craft beer brewers will tell you about their favorite esters and phenols. For an Indigenous hunter, fisherperson, or forager, an odor can mark seasonal changes associated with the optimal and responsible gathering of foodstuffs. For a judge, an odor may be enmeshed with, and impinge on, someone's right to be unperturbed by another's aroma or a pungent industrial process. For a rhetorician, an odor will be imbricated in a specific, embodied, mediated, and relational context.

The complex nature of environmental change that we uptake and translate with our sensory perceptions into mediated language makes a constellation of methods, or conceptual apparatuses, essential to helping people make sense of facts among an array of outcomes (e.g., economic, political, short- and long-term environmental impact, human and nonhuman health risks). That is, facts and concerns surrounding environmental change need to be sensible and translated across myriad cultural, embodied perceptual modes and frames in order to create change in public response and action (social mobilization) regarding the risks inherent in the denial of catastrophic environmental changes, be they local or global in nature. Olfactory rhetoric, and sensory rhetorics more broadly, tap the imagination to make such change possible and may foster social movements, building political pressure to redress ecological damage and the material effects thereof.

Intersectional ecofeminists are attentive to material effects on bodies created through power differentials, and they critique simplistic binaries (e.g., nature/culture, masculine/feminine, human/nonhuman) while working to redress inequities (Booher and Jung). Sensory studies and disabilities studies scholars show how cultural interpretations of otherness, ableness, and environments manifest and impact different human and more-than-human populations. Yet, despite the implied ethical imperatives in these areas of scholarship, few have considered the role of sensory ecologies—differentiated biological sensory systems—in environmental rhetoric and public policy discourse related to environmental justice and healthy bodies. Fewer still have examined olfaction's role in environmental discourse. Attending to how odor and smell are suasively experienced, written about, and mediated in different domains allows us to identify how people and nonhumans use olfaction to evaluate potential environmental hazards and to what effects.

Olfactory persuasion matters for environmental justice because unpacking its impact helps confront and combat environmental *in*justice—inequitable access to healthy environs and excessive exposure to toxins within communities of color. Many of the toxins smell, taste, look, sound, and feel bad, so people notice their presence (Alaimo; Pezzullo). Thus, a RISE approach recognizes sense data (like olfactive inputs) and encourages us to analyze persuasive appeals drawn from the data to prevent or rectify hazards. Environmental rhetoric and interdisciplinary scholars, such as Robert Bullard and Beverly Wright, Winona LaDuke (Anishinaabeg Ojibwa), Catalina de Onís, Rob Nixon, Phaedra Pezzullo, Donnie Sackey, and Daniel Wildcat (Yuchi Muscogee), note how crucial a sense of environmental justice is to grasp how discriminatory the exposure rates are. In the US, more than 60% of Black, Latine, and Indigenous peoples live near hazardous waste sites.[11] When empirical data analysts factor smaller units (like tract and block group versus city and county aggregated data), then the exposure rates climb to more than 80% (Banzhaf et al.). This book responds to these injustices, and olfactory rhetoric is one appeal used to redress problems.

Configuring Chapters

Olfactory Rhetoric is an environmental justice project that offers an account of human and more-than-human sensory rhetorical ecologies as they surface across mediated visceral publics. Chapter 1 reviews the historical categorization of the senses in Western contexts and exposes a patriarchal sensory hierarchy that values vision and hearing over smell, taste, and touch. The chapter

---

11. I use the more gender-inclusive term *Latine* that resists the binary dualism inherent in the *o* or *a* *Latino/Latina* construction. Christina Cedillo notes that the commonly used word *Latinx* in academia is a contested term because different people may prefer a more culturally specific referent (par. 1). *Latine* is made for and by Spanish speakers in a manner that *Latinx* is not (Kamara pars. 7–8; Epstein).

orients readers to a broader sensorium and sensory rhetorical ecologies, explicates affective intensities that circulate in visceral publics, and points out the sociohistorical political construction of the senses as these are tied to race, gender, class, ability, and more. The chapter provides a theoretical and methodological repertoire for evaluating and analyzing how sensory rhetorics are at work in public discourse about environmental matters. The chapter then provides a heuristic for examining how composite sensations emerge and inform visceral publics' persuasive tactics to move policymakers and other agents to mitigate environmental risk and degradation. I focus on olfaction as a throughline in this book because I recognize that a sensory rhetorical approach cannot address everything simultaneously in one book project. While RISE will apply aptly to other sense perceptions, the theoretical and methodological approach I take here supports readers to examine environmental justice case studies through a RISE lens that homes in on olfactory rhetoric as defined in this introduction.

The three case studies of this book (chapters 2, 3, and 4) share three important commonalities. All contain environmental justice exigencies, and all are situated in historically marginalized and minoritized communities where the people represented are majority-minoritized folx. All case study chapters involve olfaction, olfactory rhetoric, and textual and mediated materials associated with the different smellscapes' environmental concerns. All are situated in the contiguous United States. The case studies also have important differences tied to regional geography and population density. This is purposeful and illustrates how RISE-informed olfactory rhetoric works across an array of mediated visceral publics and the "trans-corporeal in which the human is always intermeshed with the more-than-human world" (Alaimo 2, 112–13). Each case study plumbs olfactory rhetoric and then expands to consider how RISE-informed analysis is useful to both examine and intervene in public perceptions (and policies) related to environmental injustices for human and nonhuman life.

The first case (chapter 2) is rife with intersectional food politics that span Latine and Asian food traditions. The Huy Fong Sriracha sauce factory in Irwindale, California, is the study's locus.[12] In the chapter, I analyze olfactory rhetoric related to hot pepper emissions that nearby residents described as making them sick. I evaluate the effectiveness of olfactory-rhetorical appeals made in a court case and in the visceral public sphere. I also consider how e-nose technologies (digital sniffers) impacted argumentation in the court

---

12. Because sriracha is a generic term like salsa, I differentiate the variety produced by Huy Fong foods and capitalize the word *Sriracha* throughout to distinguish it from other products in the marketplace.

case, which addresses the more-than-human interplay between scientific measurement and quantification and what people can naturally sense in an environment. More broadly, the case underscores connections between unsustainable Western agro-industrial practices and public health risks and juxtaposes these with the Indigenous concept of webs of relation, or relationality. The case contributes to the book's methodological argument about how a RISE approach draws attention to historically minoritized and marginalized communities, discloses deep-seated environmental racism, and reveals how our sense of smell is wrongly marginalized and neglected relative to our well-being. The topical focus on olfaction and olfactory rhetoric allows readers to consider the impacts on and responses by residents, local government, and private-sector manufacturing companies.

The Salton Sea, adjacent to California's Imperial Valley, shares connections to unsustainable agricultural practices and public health risks as illustrated within the Sriracha sauce case. In the Salton Sea case study (chapter 3), however, agricultural water use is the key concern. The Salton Sea is the largest inland sea in California and a primary flyway for migratory birds in the desert region. The current sea came into being due to record flooding of the Colorado River and a catastrophic 1905 engineering mishap and has since been maintained by agricultural runoff. As it evaporates, the sea's primary fish (tilapia, introduced by humans) die en masse and release pungent plumes that can travel through the air for many miles. The case study also highlights nonhuman agents at circulation in the atmosphere and on the ground. As the sea evaporates, the shoreline recedes and exposes toxin-laden soil, which is the result of decades of chemical runoff. The dust that blows around in the air is dangerous to people, animals, and plants. In the chapter, I use olfactory-rhetorical analysis to evaluate how Salton Sea scent events inform local action and public policy measures intended to ameliorate deteriorating environmental conditions.

The third case study (chapter 4) moves east to the massive Blue Ridge Landfill located by Pearland and in Fresno, Texas. Both majority-minoritized communities must contend with the landfill's effluvia (airborne and liquid). Deploying a RISE approach to the case, I use olfactory-rhetorical analysis to evaluate how citizen/resident scientists and community leaders developed and employed an "Odor Task Force" to combat the poorly managed landfill's emissions problems. The task force included training options for residents on how to collect and record olfactive sense data in a consistent manner. The results show how residents' lived experiences of noisome odors associated with the landfill provided identifiable patterns and evidence necessary for legal intervention. Like the Sriracha sauce case, digital sniffing technology was employed to quantify and verify what residents reported, though the technological interface in this instance included human-augmented digital sniffing tools named field olfactometers (informally known as "Nasal Rangers"). As with the former two case studies, this chapter highlights sustainability issues and environmental injustices, but it focuses on waste rather than agricultural issues.

In chapter 5, *Olfactory Rhetoric* concludes by providing a summary review of the RISE approach and extending the approach to consideration of global environmental concerns. The chapter opens with a discussion of climate change, or more accurately global heating, and how we and our nonhuman companions sense it. In the chapter, I assemble transdisciplinary ecorhetorical alliances, recap the goals of a RISE approach to a range of sensory rhetorics, briefly compare aspects of the case study chapters, describe some limitations of the project, and suggest how others can move forward from my points of departure, including ideas for bridging academic–activist tactics.

In sum, visceral publics and environments are rife with sensory rhetoric, but we (rhetoricians and everyday people) may not be attuned to how hierarchical categories of the senses cast light or shadow on how our "sense-data as symbols" unfold in textual, mediated, and embodied experiences (Langer 21). The RISE approach supports readers to pay greater attention to the suasive nature of our senses and what circulates in a sensory rhetorical ecology. Moreover, spotlighting olfaction and how visceral publics deploy olfactory rhetoric in the public sphere to inform risk assessment of perceived hazards in the environments can impart additional modes of analysis used to remedy environmental injustices.

CHAPTER 1

Proposing a Sensory Rhetorical Approach to Environmental Problems

> The sheer materiality of sensation travels into meaning itself: stirred air stirs meaning.
>
> —Debra Hawhee, "Rhetoric's Sensorium"

Mistreating the environment and those othered by society is directly related to how we write about, speak of, perceive, and believe the value of different kinds of sensory stimuli. In this chapter, I define and describe an approach designed to support rhetoricians to understand and evaluate how and why "noseworthy" composite sensations emerge and circulate in mediated visceral publics when environmental risk is involved. How a visceral public articulates and documents composite sensations varies and can include myriad genres, like social media or public commentary posts, technical reports that incorporate quantitative analysis, lay witness testimonies in legal cases, journalists' interviews, policy reports and recommendations, news broadcasts, field investigation reports from both scientists and citizen scientists, and narrative "counterstories" by minoritized folx (Martinez). Some genres and media pertain to qualitative human experiences. Others are enmeshed in scientific and legal domains where quantitative verification is privileged over experience reports. This chapter shows how our senses are segregated and categorized in Western contexts, describes what the hierarchical construct does, explains why it exists, and proposes alternatives for rhetoricians interested in complex sensory-rhetorical relationships and their consequences. I then feature concepts that inform the RISE approach by highlighting examples of different sensory ecologies, situating affective intensities, defining the sensorium, examining relationality, and considering embodiment. Finally, I introduce a heuristic to evaluate how composite sensations emerge in the sensorium and have the capacity to transform embodied experiences into mediated visceral publics that influence policymaking and direct action to improve environmental conditions. The same heuristic can also help us understand where and when things go wrong or efforts stall and fail to instigate change.

Sensory Categorization in Western Contexts

In Western contexts, human beings are traditionally understood (and taught) to have five sensory categories (sight, hearing, smell, taste, and touch). Our five senses have been named the "Aristotelian or Kindergarten" senses (Rubin 11). Five categories of sensation present an oversimplification given the convivial complexities of our sensory ecology. Scholars in anthropology, sociology, biology, cultural studies, cognitive science, medicine, psychology, and philosophy confirm myriad senses exist. Anywhere from ten to thirty-two senses are involved in cognition and physiological function, and how we prioritize and categorize sensation as qualia (sense datum combined with introspection and analysis) is deeply cultural and ideological (Classen, *Color*; Classen et al.; Corbin; Jenner; Langer; Low; Manning; Mason and Davies; Panagia; Pink; Rubin; Sauer, "Communicating"; Smith; Tuan, *Passing*; Vannini et al.).

Beyond the five senses with which readers are likely familiar, we have a vestibular sense that helps us to maintain our balance. We also engage a more generalized somatosensation—a whole-body sense of touch—that includes a variety of sensory modalities, such as proprioception, interoception, and chemoreception. Proprioception results in our ability to navigate our way to the light switch in the middle of the night. Interoception allows us to sense our own heartbeat, breathing, and internal activity related to our emotions. Chemoreception allows us to perceive chemical stimuli and is foundational to interactions among living organisms and the environment. Olfaction relies on chemoreception.

Every breath you take involves chemoreceptors that help you make sense of chemical signals circulating in the environment—the veritable "prickle in the air" (Hawhee, *Sense* 2). For example, when you walk through the woods, the scent receptors in your nose pick up and respond to chemical compounds like terpenes (essential oils) emitted from the trees and plants around you. Your brain processes these scent signals, allowing you to smell and differentiate the earthy forest smells from the aromas of various flowers, trees, and other vegetation. This olfactory chemoreception allows you to sense and make sense of the living ecosystem you are moving through in a way vision alone cannot. The chemical signatures circulating in the forest air carry information used by your nose and brain to perceive the environment. So, with every huff and puff taken up the trailhead, chemoreceptors tap into organic compounds released by the life-forms around you, helping you achieve olfactory-based chemoreception of your natural surroundings. For those less inclined to outdoorsy recreation, imagine walking into a kitchen and smelling freshly baked cookies or bread. The scent molecules from the baked goods travel through the air to chemoreceptors in your nose, which detect and recognize the smell, sending an immediate signal to your embodied mind: "Mmm, something smells delicious here!"

It is easier to record sights and sounds, and there are often legal requirements to block unpleasant sights or sounds. For example, walls built next to freeways block the sights and sounds of traffic, though they have little to no mitigating effect on air pollution. Requirements to block or limit other offensive stimuli that assault our noses, our tastebuds, or even how we are touched and by whom are deemed more subjective, which is tied to power and the sociohistorical construction of the relative worth placed on different sense perceptions. Treating our senses of smell, touch, and taste as less important than sight and hearing is directly related to how humans treat Earth's resources and othered humans and nonhumans as unimportant or dispensable.

Importantly, the "specular" and "the dominance of looking" elide other sensory rhetorical ways of meaning-making (Dolmage and Lewiecki-Wilson 32; Banes 69). Disability studies scholars Jay Dolmage and Cynthia Lewiecki-Wilson invite researchers "to imagine how other senses (hearing, touch, smell) might provide different metaphors and ways for making knowledge" (32). Though the call is epistemic in nature, it hails researchers, students, teachers, and other publics interested in myriad intersections among rhetoric, materiality, affect, and nondiscursive sensation. The call should not discourage those interested in visuality or visual rhetorics or sonic rhetorics. Nonetheless, it can—and I argue should and does—inform approaches to the critique of both visuals and ocularcentrism and aurality (Berger; Classen, *Worlds* and "Witch's"; Jay; Kerschbaum; McClanahan and South; McSorley; Mirzoeff; Smith; Sturken and Cartwright; Tuan, *Landscapes* and *Passing*; Zelizer). Expanding our perception of what matters and why within the sensorium is one goal. Developing more capacity for rhetorical intervention aimed at socio-environmental injustices is another.

Rhetoric scholar Debra Hawhee also suggests we build on and expand the kinds of approaches we take to the sensorium, particularly when marginalized senses are involved, as they shape our knowledge and meaning-making and "other attachments [that] matter for rhetoric," which include the political, bodily, and environmental and how these "intermix and move recursively" ("Rhetoric's" 13). Researching marginalized senses formed within Western contexts (e.g., smell, taste, touch) can build on work devoted to the study of images, image-making, vision, visual rhetorics, hearing, sonic rhetorics, and so forth. They coexist, and Dolmage and Lewiecki-Wilson reveal that an ocularcentric paradigm implies a kind of limited perspective one might have toward our othered senses, an a/effect rhetoricians should consider. Valuable research openings result. If one teaches and researches visual rhetorics, which is what inspired my own journey to consider other senses, then calls to expand what we investigate in the sensorium inform why we might wish to do so for social and environmental justice. Olfaction's indexicality contributes to the endeavor, for it contributes to public memory.

The traditional five sense categories that we learn about today began with Plato and Aristotle, and these categories continue to persist despite overwhelming evidence indicating more than five (Rubin 11–13; Synnott 129–32). A few scholars interested in links between affect and sensation argue the two are so entwined with material stimuli that they are de facto meshworks, inseparable (Damasio, *Descartes'* and "Feeling"; Ingold 47, 157–59, 166–67; Murray 6–7; Pink; Vannini et al. 7, 20). Sensory uptake is as complex as the perceptions we build of our lived environments. Western worldviews construct taste, touch, and smell as less important sensory categories than sight and hearing because they are proximal (close-up) senses. To elaborate, senses that generally require proximity to help us understand and perceive a situation do not provide a rhetorical sense of distance historically important to the masculinized idea of objectivity. Hence, proximal senses (olfaction, taste, and touch) are feminized and/or animalized, in part, because they are rhetorically deemed more intimate and therefore too subjective to provide a sense of physical or emotional distance. That sight and hearing are considered distal (faraway) senses contributes to their hierarchical positioning as masculine, more objective, and in some cases sublime senses (Irigaray; Classen, *Color* and "Witch's"; Howes, *Sensual*; Tuan, *Landscapes* and *Passing*).

Our senses of taste, touch, and smell also problematically owe some of their philosophical categorization to gendered activity (Classen, *Color* and "Witch's"; Corbin; Jenner 337; Muchembled 218, 476; Panagia 130–31; Reinarz 21, 113–45). Culturally informed decisions made about who or what to value and why exist across hierarchies. Of the "European hierarchy of the senses," sensory studies scholar Constance Classen explains:

> Both men and women [and those outside the binary] were understood to make practical use of all of their senses: men could touch, women could see.

Nonetheless, touch, along with taste and smell, was imagined to be essentially feminine in nature: nurturing, seductive, dissolute in its merging of self and other. Sight, and to a lesser extent hearing, was essentially masculine: dominating, rational, orderly in its discrete categorization of the world. . . . The symbolic division of perception into masculine and feminine territories carried [and carries] immense social weight. . . . The feminine sensory sphere consisted of labors associated with the intimately corporeal sense of touch, taste, and smell. ("Witch's" 70)

The gendered sensory categories Classen notes inform how taste is often associated with food preparation, feminine refinement (think of old-fashioned "finishing" schools), gentrification, or, by contrast, deviant witchcraft, class-based judgment, and herbal remedy (Bourdieu; Classen, "Witch's"; Panagia 128–33; Reinarz 21, 113–45). Touch is both intimate and a source of contamination—think of how a woman's or a person of color's touch can be dually configured as a symbol of kindness and a source of possible contagion (Classen, *Deepest*; Douglas; Manning 85–89; Muchembled 253–58; Smith). Erin Manning's discussion of the "politics of touch" is particularly relevant here (86–90, 102). Manning emphasizes how we "touch hierarchically," which delineates the position of the "one who chooses to touch," yet touch also "functions as a medium of open-ended exchange" when we "reach out" toward another (88, 89). Both Classen and Manning contend with the gendered complexity of our tactile sense and its place at the bottom of the five-sense hierarchy.

Western cultures tend to represent olfaction—like the construct "woman"—as feminine, baser, primitive, and emotional, implying a sense closer to the ground or "nature," though its position in the extant hierarchy is more liminal because of its association with religious rituals in Western and some Middle Eastern cultures (Brennan; Classen, *Color*; Classen et al.; Gaard, *Ecological* and "Toward"; Harvey; Jenner; Jütte; Smith). Systems of power also inform situational shifts in the sensory hierarchy. For example, "gastronomic craftsmanship" (food preparation) in high-end restaurants is male dominated (e.g., chefs) (S. Parrish; Scander and Jakobsson). Likewise, touch can carry wanted or unwanted sexual connotations embedded in power dynamics.

In *The Color of Angels*, Classen articulates the "ranking of the senses . . . in their traditional order of importance: sight, hearing, smell, taste, and touch" and provides context for this ranking schema as it is steeped in Western theology and Christianity (1). Classen notes that "the visualist regime of modernity, [has] in fact, pride[d] itself on its transparency: everything can be seen, everything can be known, nothing is withheld from our inquisitive and acquisitive eyes" (1). The gaze penetrates. Classen rightly points out that the "visualism of modernity . . . [throws] a cloak of invisibility over the sensory imagery of previous eras," making it difficult for the contemporary reader to "even recognize that there might be something worth [interrogating] underneath" (1). Classen examines approaches to the senses in both spiritual and physical capacities, referring to St. Hildegard of Bingen[1] and German philosopher Jakob Böhme.[2] Despite their historical divide, Hildegard and Böhme both addressed the complexities of sensation, yet Böhme emphasized "vision" in both physical and spiritual contexts. For example, related to both senses of vision, Böhme notes that "Jesus is the light, . . . the Holy Ghost is the 'glance or splendor,'" and "the Devil . . . made the creation of light impossible" (qtd. in Classen, *Color* 13). The ability to see light is both a physical sense and an interior one connected to spirituality. It only takes a small leap of imagination to understand how this demonizes people who lack or resist spiritual vision or sight in an ableist manner because, as the passage implies, the "Devil" is responsible for a spiritual and, by extension, a physical sense of darkness. Classen explains Adam and Eve's failures as failures of the flesh attached to their senses and sensuality. In both a metaphorical sense and a literal sense, Eve found the apple "pleasing to the eye" and did not turn away (Gen. 3:6). The original sin, however, was one based in touch, taste, and smell once Eve and Adam decided to take a bite (Classen, *Color* 3). The eyes tempted, the ears persuaded, yet touch, smell, and taste ultimately led to the downfall.

The feminized hierarchy of sensation correlates with how some humans treat Mother Earth as an object to be mined, used, abused, and discarded, though our very existence relies upon her. Greedy eyes take stock of what can be extracted. Tone-deaf ears ignore damage reports. However, one cannot ignore the taste, smell, and touch of collateral damage when it impacts bodies placed in harm's way. Environmental studies scholar and intersectional ecofeminist activist Tzeporhah Berman explains how patriarchal Western metaphors and common phrases such as "virgin forest," "Mother Earth," "Gaia," and "rape of the land" reify "hierarchical traditions which continue to objectify women and Nature" (258). However, understanding "gender-nature relations as intersectional" and "gender-nature relations as resistance" to a "malestream lens," I intentionally position Earth-as-mother to highlight

---

1. Hildegard was a nun and Benedictine abbess in medieval Europe lauded as a visionary and mystic. She was born in 1098 in Bermersheim, Germany. She had a "profound reverence for nature and placed great importance on our relationship with the earth" (Overweg).

2. Jakob Böhme was born in 1575 and was a German philosopher, Christian mystic, and Lutheran theologian. He wrote several treatises on the nature of divine light and free will. In 1624, he wrote *The Supersensual Life*, which is written as a dialog between a disciple and a master theologian.

intersectional ecofeminist and environmental justice work, spotlighting links between gender, race, class, ethnicity, and neoliberal policymaking (Singer 274–75).

In Western contexts, vision is associated with masculinity, scientific instrumentation, rationality, scalability, observation, and reason (Howes, *Sensual* xii–xiii; Tsing 50–55). Sight is the one sense most people say they do not want to lose. Our metaphors for sight are legion. Olfaction does not draw the same breath. We may wonder why blindness is a feared disability and anosmia is not (Blodgett). Many of us can recall the challenge of enjoying a meal while dealing with a nasty cold. The lingering loss of, or changes in, the olfactive and gustatory senses will also now be familiar to a great number of people who experienced the COVID-19 coronavirus (Patel; Soler et al.). While many can imagine the dangers vision loss might pose, fewer may imagine trying to escape from a room filled with colorless, odiferous fumes (e.g., butane, propane, formaldehyde, methane). For rhetorically persuasive purposes, manufacturers add smelly, sulfurous additives—thiols—to liquid propane and natural gas used in homes and businesses to warn us of a dangerous gas leak. Thiols are the same chemicals skunks use to defend themselves against threats (Stewart184). People with anosmia cannot smell the warning message, which means they would need a different signaling device, like a digital detector connected to a light fixture or to an audible alarm, to make sense of the danger posed and to assess risk.

Some non-Western and pre-Western cultures offer alternatives for sensing what is afoot in our world that we ought to consider (Kimmerer; Ríos, "Cultivating" and "Performing"; Tuan, *Landscapes* and *Passing*). Robin Wall Kimmerer (Potawatomi) notes how "cosmologies are a source of identity and orientation to the world" that shape us, help us understand ourselves in relation to others, and support us to sense and make sense of the world (23). Kimmerer relates a story of Skywoman—a celestial being who fell to Earth, was rescued by animals, and formed land on top of a turtle's back, which created the Earth, or "Turtle Island" (15–20). Skywoman created "a garden for the well-being of all" and became "cocreator of the good green world" (23). Skywoman appeared on Earth after other entities and relied on these esteemed relations in a reciprocal manner. Skywoman constellates a different orientation to the Earth and provides a guide for reciprocal relations and responsibility for our shared life support system. Other Indigenous groups express similar ideas. For example, the Māori have a concept of *ka mua ka muri*, which roughly translates to walking backward into the future. Māori relationships to chronoception (having a felt sense of time) are influenced by their greater cultural consideration for past events in relation to future consequences.[3] The Andaman Islanders construct their calendar based on distinct odors emitted by flowering plants at different times of the year (Reinarz 87). The "calendar of scents" closely attunes the Andaman to the environment and its changes (Classen et al. 95). The Desana of the Colombian Amazon rainforest specifically reference olfaction in their worldview. *Máhsa seriri* translates as both "tribal odor" and "tribal feeling," or "sympathy" (98). The Desana liken the idea to knowing one's territory as it is marked by the scentprints of the people who live within it and their interdependent environmental entanglements. Feminist anthropologist Anna Tsing notes, "Smell draws us into the entangled threads of memory and possibility," and such scent threads simultaneously involve indeterminacy, elusiveness, and some certainty because, while we know another is there, we may have difficulty describing where the smell takes us and what relational impacts of the smell involve (56). Tracing scent threads across porous skin boundaries requires emanant nose-how that supersedes visual perception.

In the West, our *undervalued* sense perceptions—smell, taste, touch, and more—have the capacity to help us disrupt hegemonic ideology about harmful environmental impacts and conditions. Attending to olfactory, gustatory, and tactile senses can shift our perceptions of who and what we are in webs of relation because they do proximal work, which differs from our distal visual and auditory senses. Our proximal senses help us to understand how completely we are enmeshed within and dependent upon a healthy environment to survive and thrive as an interdependent species. Paying attention to all our senses and embodied affective reactions to sensory stimuli has value and provides useful insights as we seek to maintain a healthy relationship with our environment.

From Sensory Ecologies to Affective Intensities

The rhetorical and material forces of sensation and their embodied cousins perception and intelligibility support us to recognize and contend with environmental damage. Hawhee explains that "the binding together of sensations . . . produces meaning and perception," and by extension eases intelligibility

---

3. Concepts expressed in a language influence perception, and different languages inform how and what we perceive. To illustrate, George Lakoff and Mark Johnson examine the front-back organization of time in the English language. Metaphorically, English speakers often structure "TIME AS A MOVING OBJECT" (137). The "future is moving toward us," or "the time to act is now," or we have "put that behind us" demonstrate how language shapes our sense of time, which informs chronoception (137–69).

("Rhetoric's" 7). Perception is the neurophysiological process that moves us from inchoate feelings to awareness through the senses. Sensation is to perception as root is to tree, an essential, rhizomatic conduit that communicates, innerves, and feeds. Perception is to rhetoric as bud is to leaf, wherein the second necessarily relies on the first and grows from it. Our networked perceptions of an environment and what circulates within it and within us are materially constituted through sensory rhetorical ecologies, activity, and relationality within said environment. That is, our material senses are rhetorical because they persuade us to act based upon what we sense and consequently perceive and make intelligible to others. Intelligibility is comparable to a mycorrhizal network—a "wood wide web"—that allows trees to gather and communicate suasive news about the environment using their sensory ecology, which relies heavily on syncopated chemical communication (chemoreception) in underground and airborne networks of interspecies relations (Grant; Kimmerer 49–51; Kohn; Tsing 133; Wohlleben 35, 207, 413).[4] Trees communicate, and "communication is very much the norm amongst almost all species on the planet, whether it be between animals, insects, plants or bacteria, . . . [and] humans also have communication systems that aren't language" but are persuasive (A. Parrish 43). For example, we use gestures to let people know when we want them to come closer or move back, and we may use body language to show interest in something or someone by leaning toward the object or body. Our bodies also produce pheromones or "infochemicals" that encourage or discourage interaction, which is a form of chemoreception (Müller et al. 981). Collectively, we exchange shared air, and all species take part in this planetary breathing and chemical reciprocity through molecular exchange. Most things emit and intake a mix of entangled molecules, many of which are volatile or airborne.

In a process known as "masting," pecan trees and pine trees use chemoreception and share chemical signals through the air (pheromones) and through their root networks to signal when to produce flowers (Kimmerer 34; Tsing 159). If only a single tree were to produce flowers or cones, cross-pollination with another tree's genetic material is unlikely to occur. Moreover, squirrels or other opportunistic species (humans, mice, raccoons, etc.) could take most of the single tree's nuts, which limits the ability of the species to sprout a new generation. Pecan trees use masting to produce a suasive effect that results in mass flower production across a region. Botanists do not know precisely how this happens, but the unison of response is consistent (Kimmerer 32–35). Ants

---

4. Mycorrhizal networks are co-constituted by hairlike root tips of trees and microscopic fungi that join in symbiosis in a "wood wide web" to share resources and exchange information and nutrients (Simard et al.; Wohlleben 10).

also use pheromone secretions to communicate and persuade. Entomologists have identified a couple dozen chemical phrases with specific meanings like telling other nestmates danger is near, food is around the corner, whether they be friend or foe, and so forth (E. Wilson 74–77).

People also exude and breathe in pheromones and other suasive volatile combinations (Mostafa et al.), so Johnson's educated inference that "perhaps smell" informs human feeling tracks (3; Brennan 9–11, 68–69, 94–99, 136–37). We may not be able to see the molecular mix of smells and chemicals we inhale, but imagine clouds or fog. Clouds and fog consist of water molecules that clump together, resulting in a range of forms, shapes, sizes, and combinations. Now, imagine if individual odor molecules were "somehow color-coded to reflect their tremendous diversity" (McGee xiii). Like McGee, we would figuratively "see rainbow odor plumes constantly forming and dissipating, puffs and swirls and masses moving, disappearing, reappearing, blending," from the lilac and lavender in the yard, from the iridescent detritus in the dumpster next door, creamy bakery and gray car exhausts, yellowed sweaty joggers, and beyond (xxii). When we inhale, the rainbow plumage becomes a part of us. While chemoreception differs from verbal, textual, and mediated human communication, the examples show webs of relation, sensation, and sensory ecology that we and nonhuman entities rely on for food, shelter, species survival, and social bonding. A species' survival includes a spectrum of activities ranging from attraction to a potential mate that can result in offspring and forms of pheromonal attractions that go beyond mere reproduction to include friendship bonds, queer attractions, and other "social chemical" connections people and other entities need to survive and thrive (Friesen et al. 26).

Feminist philosopher of affect Teresa Brennan proposes that "what is at stake is rather the means by which social interaction shapes biology," which begs us to consider how someone's "affect, if it comes across to you, alters your anatomical makeup for good or ill" (74). Affect as a noun pertains to emotion or desire, as either influences behavior or action. As a verb, affect is about making an impact, touching the feelings of another, or moving one to respond or act. Hawhee makes a distinction between affect, emotion, sensation, and feeling. For Hawhee, affect and emotion ride "a line of cognitive awareness where knowable concepts of emotion organize otherwise inchoate though no less visceral affective intensities" (*Rhetoric* 6). Affective intensities can be individual or group characteristics that reflect the relative concentration or dilution of emotional response to a given set of sensory stimuli based upon our sensory ecology's "intensity modulation mechanisms" that function as a kind of "volume control" informed by the central nervous system (Moore et al.; McDavid Schmidt and Beucher). When a group experiences something unpleasant (or pleasant) in the sensorium, affective intensity can ramp up and result in a visceral public. For example, if a community is exposed to an extremely noxious smell like a major spill of crude oil or ammonia after a train derailment, then the affective intensity people feel and later articulate reveals a traumatized visceral public (Le Rouge; Phillips). Affective intensities that arise from "communal sensations" vary from entity to entity—yet the idea of communal sensation does "take seriously the participatory dimension of the sensorium" (Hawhee, "Rhetoric's" 13). If we go back to the pecan tree example, there is a communal sensation, an affective intensity enhanced by the wood wide web, that transfers among networked individual trees and their worldly entanglements with underground fungal relations. Of course, any given tree will likely have different levels of sensitivity or production of pheromones, but the holistic effect still results. In the human realm, communal sensations can circulate in a visceral public inspired by emotional responses to pollution or another stimulant.

Affective intensity, and by extension a visceral public, begins with sensation. Sensation pertains to the "faculty of perceiving through the senses . . . [that] binds together all animals . . . all living beings" and feeling that "stretches from pleasure to pain" and extends to "emotions" (Hawhee, *Rhetoric* 5–6). Sensation is of limited duration and specific. Feeling is broader than emotion and may entail longer duration. For example, a public feeling can persist for a while and be shared and recirculated through different communication channels like social media, podcasts, and news broadcasts, which can reverberate in a rhetorical ecology or ecologies.

Emotions are short-term and often directed at a source. For example, when I experience the intense odor of hog manure when the wind direction is unfavorable, I am overcome by nausea and emotion derived from sensation. The emotional result is fury at the distant white men from Iowa who funded the facility, and the local white man who allowed it to be built without regard for anything but personal gain and profit. My emotional response to the odor has names attached. Affect works with emotion and encompasses how sensations, moods, and emotions circulate within public feeling and visceral publics both short- and long-term (Hawhee, "Rhetoric's" 12–13).

The materiality of the senses is rhetorical in that material inputs into our senses exert suasive appeals that inform actions in word and deed. Similarly, Brennan writes, "When the senses succeed in producing conscious awareness of this or that, they produce [embodied] knowledge that can be communicated either to oneself or another in language," and the senses, "as vehicles of attention, connect the supposedly higher cognitive faculty of linguistic thought with the fleshy knowledge or codes of the body," which results in "sensations that find a match in words" (137, 136, 140). To illustrate, when I feel the wind shift direction from the south to the southwest near my Illinois home, I know through embodied experience that I will be assaulted by the stench of hog manure within seconds, and I make haste to go inside and shut windows if I left them open in otherwise nice weather. If I am too slow, then visceral waves of nausea, retching, and fury will course through my body due to the odor molecules and associated particulate matter that enters my nose. The result encourages me to move faster next time the wind direction changes because my embodied memory of the olfactory experience is so persuasive, and it encourages me to report the incident in writing to the appropriate authorities at the Illinois EPA who log community complaints and may act upon those deemed most hazardous. In my experience, Illinois EPA authorities have not acted on smellscape issues but have acted when manure is spread too close to residential wells. There is visual and soil-bound evidence of the latter, and the former is deemed less hazardous, though odor nuisances cause more immediate illness (Hinton et al.). As Brennan notes, "Rapidly moving olfactory knowledge is regarded as inferior," though this is a result of "foundational fantasy" that "results in the disposition to see [olfactory] activity as mindless [and] passive," when the opposite is more accurate: Olfaction is a speedy sense (136).

Like plants and other more-than-human entities, people respond to perceptible, qualitative, and quantifiable signals at work in their environments (Itchuaqiyaq, "When"). For example, when there is a forest fire or flood that people can smell, see, or otherwise sense, then the situation garners attention and action. People determine the source and cause of the hazard and decide how to address it. Because people pay attention to and act upon sensory signals, we need to understand how the signaling works and support people to become more attentive to changes in environmental conditions. Some scholars suggest that our very thought processes necessarily rely upon an environment to function, meaning that human sensory perception and by extension our thoughts (intellection) are deeply informed by material environmental conditions (Brennan; Clark; Hutchins; Reid 70, 76; Ríos, "Cultivating"). Brennan names the senses "seneschals of attention," meaning that they govern and steward our decision- and meaning-making activities (136).

Defining the Sensorium

Sensorium has several meanings across disciplinary contexts that suit a variety of needs, interests, and purposes laid out in this book. While an exhaustive definition is impractical, acknowledging the variety for those new to the term provides context. On one hand, a sensorium constitutes the totality of how one's embodied mind receives, processes, perceives, interprets, and articulates sensory stimuli. Referencing Lauren Berlant's work on the "historical sensorium," Ben Highmore helpfully characterizes the sensorium as "patterns of feeling as they are materialized in sensorial forms," which operate at the register "of all that can't be incorporated in conscious cognition and reflective reason" (49). This register "requires attention not just to a range of affects and feelings," but also to "different ways of perceiving the world" and paying attention to "waves of responses" that include myriad modes of attention (50). Berlant directly explains that the sensorium is "a space of affective residue that constitutes what is shared among strangers," a place of "collective experience" (194). I liken this to composite sensations that visceral publics intensify. Communication scholars Emily Winderman and Robert Mejia also elaborate, "The sensorium refers to an analytic and affective experience. As an analytic, the sensorium situates the senses—hearing, vision, smell, taste, and touch—as an assemblage of political, economic, social, cultural, technological, and physiological processes" (23). The affective experience connects sensation to our larger perceptions of the world. "Because a sensorium assembles political, economic, cultural, and physiological processes, interventions on one axis—such as the emergence of [an environmental problem]—affect an entire sensorium" (23). Gilles Deleuze and Felix Guattari characterize the sensorium as a "body without organs," meaning that our sensing body is an assemblage and part of the world's meshwork (4). Think of our astronomical position as an analogy. Each planet exists in relation to another in a larger configuration we call the solar system. Our solar system is part of our galaxy, the Milky Way, and our galaxy is one among countless others that constitute the osmocosmic universe. Like planets in a solar system, each person's sensorium is composed of multiple sensory modes that work together in our sensory ecology to produce our material response to sensory stimuli. That personal response breathes within the larger constellation of our societal galaxy situated in our ecological universe. This second, broader meaning of *sensorium* relates to the galaxy and universe contexts. If one person's sensorium is akin to a stellar system, then a larger view of *the* sensorium means that a bunch of people's "sensori" equal the sensorium. At a minimum, the second meaning of sensorium creates a more public galaxy of perception—one we can all tap into in some manner. Concurrently, it means that we can become more attuned to nonhuman sensorial responses and sensory ecologies when we pay attention. The sensorium depends on relationality. Moreover, as we share our perceptions with others, we have a relational impact that informs our reactions and responses.

Joseph Dumit describes how the sensorium helps us evaluate our senses and sensations, as both work together to build, make, and author in our reciprocal relations with a variety of publics. "[The] sensorium," Dumit writes, "is the sensing package that constitutes our participation in the world . . . [and] this assemblage of sensory inputs defines our boundaries, making the world present to us and by subtraction making us present to ourselves as beings in the world" (182). The sensorium features a mode or place of embodied relationality in a complex ecology. I imagine it this way: The sensations we experience—our "sensing packages"—shape who we are and provide knowledge about phenomena at work in any given environmental setting. Further, political theorist Davide Panagia describes sensation as a "heterology of impulses that register on our bodies without determining a body's nature or residing in any one organ of perception" (6). At the core, the two scholars' discussion of the sensorium and sensation suggest points of rupture between what we register about our environment and what we can represent to others in our midst. Rupture reveals relationality. Bodies rupture in relation to environmental conditions—glacier to boulder, volcano to lava flow, grass to drought, insect to dew, icecap to heat, human to famine, and brush to fire. Paradoxically, perhaps, we can tap into a larger sensorium to create a better understanding of global conditions. For example, the continental scale of Australian bushfires in late 2019 and early 2020 killed at least half a billion animals and created tornado-like smoke/fire storms that inundated the sky with smoke, blocking out the sun in many places and entering unprotected sinuses and mouths many miles downwind. The same thing happened in 2021 on the northwest coast of the US and Canada. An unprecedented heatwave in the same geographical region during July 2021 killed "more than 1 billion sea creatures" (Yurk). The massive fires and marine "graveyards" generated a collection of sensory experiences that could not be ignored (Harley qtd. in Yurk). If we can imagine human perception as a sensorium in the Australian or Pacific Northwest fire contexts, then we might consider how those events constellated, circulated, and impacted public policy.

The sensorium is an aggregate system that suggests the possibility for intermittent spontaneous combustion between our sensate understandings of an environment and our enmeshment within a larger ecological system. Spontaneous combustion happens when there is no obvious ignition source, yet a fire erupts anyway. For example, if one places a pile of varnish-soaked rags in a paper bag and leaves the bag in a hot place, then the bag can burst into flame without anyone setting a match to it. By extension, unprompted perceivable events in the sensorium (e.g., major forest fires, toxic spills, extreme weather events) can unite people because they understand that they need to collaborate to redress an ecological harm and bodily threat. Maurice Merleau-Ponty describes this as perceptual "[plunging] into the things perceived" that is instrumental to our becomings in "the flesh of the world" (Merleau-Ponty and Lefort 38, 144). The sensorium allows for a segue between internal becomings and some sense of exteriority—a hypothetical, invisible bubble of perception.[5] Hawhee describes the sensorium as "the corporeal limn that guides sensory perception," as she explains that it "names a locus of feeling" not confined to "presumed bodily boundaries" because it "includes sensation ecologies" beyond the human ("Rhetoric's" 5).

The sensorium is a "fire object" because it is complicated and defined differently by different actors in a network (Law and Mol 616–18, 620; Law and Singleton 344). Borrowing from concepts relevant to science, technology, and scholarship that embraces actor network theory, John Law and Vicky Singleton contextualize a "fire object" as something that is "energetic and transformative," "depends on difference" (what is absent and present), and acknowledges that "otherness is generative" (344). Fire is the "element of passion, action, energy, spirit, will and anger," and fire implies "creative destruction" and sensuality (Law and Mol 615). Conceptually, a fire object's emergence entails complex interactions among matter, agents, and the agentive potential of nonhuman actors to coalesce into something perceivable like a scent event that sparks human action. Fire objects are "messy," meaning that they are complex to interpret and are defined differently by different people because their perspectives, needs, locations, and knowledges differ (Law and Singleton 333). Analogously, the sensorium is a relational ontological fire object, meaning that it depends on interdependence, a sense of beingness, and linkages among individuals' sense perceptions and "patterns of relations of conjoined alterity" that extend to more-than-human entities (Law and Mol 616).

The sensorium is a fire object because it too is energetic and transformative, depends on difference, and acknowledges the generative nature of otherness (Law and Singleton 344). Law and Singleton situate "absent and present" as "fuel or cinders" and "flame," respectively. In the case of the sensorium, "absent" is the form of stimulus response and "present" is the (non)sensible object. "Generative" implies emergence and creativity, but it can also conjure rupture and violence. Imagine how a forest fire destroys mature trees and life in its path as it replenishes soil and makes way for the emergence of new seedlings. A sensorium destroys the notion of an isolated sense while it

---

5. Temple Grandin is my inspiration here. She writes about how cattle go through a chute on their way into a slaughterhouse, and she explains that to ease the animals' discomfort one must limit their capacity to see what is ahead of them. To my mind, a "perception bubble" works like this.

replenishes the idea of relational ecological enmeshment and makes way for the emergence of new becomings.

When we study intersectional embodied material a/effects of sensation rhetorically, we must do so relationally. Thinking about relations helps account for how human responses to stimulus stem from cultural, social, ethical, and political commitments within a larger, shared sensorium.

Relationality within Our Sensorium

Relationality is tied to key ideas described in American Indian studies and Indigenous rhetorics about our ethical obligations to each other, the land, and to Life on Earth in a holistic sense. Relationality pertains to "all our relations" and "life itself" (LaDuke 2). It involves an acknowledgment of our interdependencies and connections to other life-forms and Earth's vibrant materiality that provides a foundation for all living organisms now and into the future (Bennett 58–60; Ríos, "Cultivating" 65; Tsing 28–29; Voyles 12). Situated within this book's argument, relationality is decolonial in nature and the opposite of a Western-centric transactional stance, where the goal is to maximize personal gain. Such greed neglects larger community concerns at the expense of future generations. Relationality imparts an approach that highlights and builds reciprocal, ethical connections that embrace the social good. Reciprocity informs how we understand our relationships with all life. Relational thinking orients one toward maintaining a sense of environmental interdependence without subsuming an individual person to an entirely collective sense of self. That is, there is room to address individuals' intersectional ecofeminist concerns and to maintain a crucial sense of connectedness to the larger world and a breathable future.

Many Indigenous peoples approach understanding ecological and political interdependencies from a "seventh generation" vantage point. The seventh-generation model asks people to consider how today's actions might impact their grand-, and great, great, great, great, great, great-grandchildren, or great-niblings if one has no offspring. The kincentric model also assumes that all our relations extend to nonhuman entities that form much larger, longer kinship systems. Kairos, an immediate sense of necessary action, and *chronos*, an imaginatively expanded sense of the future we face together, comingle in kincentric models based on seventh-generation thinking. Such temporal regimes suggest ecological entanglements that posit how environments are part of our family and insist that we care for them appropriately rather than abuse and abandon them when they seem no longer useful to our immediate concerns or purposes. The same holds true for our political enmeshments. When a visceral public emerges in response to a composite sensation tied to environmental harm, we might also investigate how long the visceral public has been contending with the situation and what failure to address the situation today might look like in, say, 140 years. For example, had nuclear engineers thought about the disposal of waste at the Hanover Nuclear Site in Washington State using a seventh-generation model, it could have saved lives and the enormous amount of money spent to mitigate or slow the damage from leaking drums and poor site risk management. The same holds true for global heating, and island nations already suffer the disproportionate effects of sea-level rise. This longer-term view requires us to imagine and connect our current activities to future lived experiences of ourselves, our descendants, and our nonhuman kin.

To foster connectedness and relational thinking, Daniel Wildcat's concept of "indigenous realism" and Cana Uluak Itchuaqiyaq's (Iñupiaq) explanation of "kincentric" thinking inform the value of relationality within the RISE approach constructed in this book, for the concepts draw us back into the natural world and the physical environments thereof (Wildcat 9; Itchuaqiyaq, "When"). Think of it this way: To be Indigenous means that one is historically, culturally, and decolonially connected to a place and space. Realism involves an attitude or practice of understanding and evaluating a situation as is and addressing it accordingly, preferably foregrounding social and environmental justice that unearths the systems of power at play in a situation. Indigenous realism as Wildcat builds it, and I draw upon it, has "respect for relationships and relatives that constitute the complex web of life" (9). Indigenous realism is key to "accept[ing] our inalienable responsibilities [and obligations] as members of the planet's complex life system" (9). In other words, we have a responsibility and obligation to pay attention to and sense ecological changes in our surround and to avoid "ecological amnesia" that is brought on by "human fascination with technology," which tends to "isolate us from the natural environment" and, I would add, from one another (Wildcat 9). Realism suggests a kind of sincerity and unidealized approach to an environment or subject that is unconcerned, and, in fact, rejects conventional or idealized impressions of beauty that circulate in white Western "aesthetic economies" (G. Böhme). Thus, Indigenous realism values all landscapes, not simply ones that are naturally beautiful like the Rocky Mountains, the Louisiana bayou, the Amazon, Angel Falls, or other geophysical marvels one may find visually compelling in their imagined wildness. A gritty cityscape also has value for its human and nonhuman inhabitants.

A question relationality begs is one of ethical impact in a RISE approach because inequitable systems of power inform relationships, distributed agency, what circulates in mediated publics, and coalition building and action. Relationality also wonders what might happen if we remake our current sensory hierarchy into rhizomatic, intersensory connections rather than an anthropocentric, hierarchical linear progression from vision to touch, evoking a reconfigured sensorium that is more inclusive to somatic (bodily) cognition and sets aside dualistic thinking in favor of an expanded ethical capacity. Relationality summons a *"sensorium commune"* wherein a "body and its senses [become] a *topos* for a counterethics" that "challenges" the sticky Enlightenment "notion of Pure Reason" and informs how "so-called rational thought performs in the service of the sensuous ruler . . . [and] the *kairotic* instant" (Herder 139). That is, topos based in reason is transfigured and replaced by a topos of embodiment, or as Diane Davis puts it, "reason, then, is a function of the *body's* will" in relation to what is around and within it, which includes mediated texts (*Breaking* 37). Relationality also underscores how Western rhetorics of sensation are hierarchically scaffolded and historically mapped onto different bodies writ large and suggests a different approach that is more rhizomatic, entangled, and lively.

Relationality and emplacement are embedded in how we evaluate a sense of belonging to (or being alienated from) a given setting because we often imagine and contextualize our relations to place, space, and embodied sensation. We build rhetorical sensation out of a material, embodied attunement to our surround, which happens through emplacement fastened to relationality. We also create textual and other mediated responses to these scenes that subsequently circulate in sensory rhetorical ecologies. Emplacement as I use it here refers to a principle of geology where something is set in place or is being set in place. For example, a glacier gradually moves large boulders over long distances, far from their place of origin. The boulder is bound to the glacier as it moves, but when the glacier melts, the boulder becomes set in place. If it is deeply coupled within a soil substrate, then the work of erosion and frost heave help the boulder to emerge and make a rupture in the soil. The boulder, glacier, and soil demonstrate relationality in slow-motion action. An explosive volcanic eruption, on the other hand, has the same principle of emplacement but is an example of rapid-action rupture in relationality. Slow and rapid acts are akin to Jean-Jacques Rousseau's ideas about people's tolerance for discomfort in relation to a threshold point that forces action (Silvestrini 280). That is, a problem must reach a critical point to force action. The critical point is often referred to as a threshold event because some line is crossed that demarcates the entrance of something new and signifies the closure of something else. The connection to environmental concerns such as catastrophic climate change is evident because threshold events can be physically sensed when we interact with changing environmental conditions, illustrating a "felt magnitude" (Hawhee, *Sense* 12–15). The question of what is tolerable and what the threshold is remains to be seen, but the RISE approach suggests that we pay attention to sensory rhetorics and sensory ecologies to identify points of tolerance, threshold, and rupture that emerge in the mediated public sphere.

Fluidity, turbulence, and the potential for change rely on relationality. Consequently, relationality adheres to the emergent potential of sensation to (re)shape behavior for good or ill. For example, if I enter a room inundated with the smell of smoke, the implication of fire may cause me to exit the room, pull the nearest fire alarm, and warn others of the danger. If I were anosmic, I may have a different response, notice burning eyes, and feel for heat. If I were an apartment dweller familiar with the secondhand scent of marijuana smoke, I might recognize the residual hijinks of my neighbors and think no more of it, or if I were not familiar with the odor, a companion's familiarity and subsequent dismissal might be transferred to me—the smoke's potential danger to my health is of a different kind than a residential fire. To understand how one embodied sensation may relate to another alters our path to perception because our sense perceptions are networked. Because they are networked, one sense impacts another, building a larger sense of what is happening around us. For example, our senses of smell and taste are closely linked, so if our sense of smell is interrupted, then we cannot fully taste food. If our sense of smell is disrupted for a long period of time, then it leads to depression because our enjoyment of everyday things like meals or the aroma of food preparation is muted (Croy and Hummel). People also broadcast their experiences in mediated publics. The COVID-19 virus and how it has impacted people's sense of smell is an example. Many people started reporting their loss of olfactory function in the mediated public sphere. That reporting emerged as a useful indicator to alert people to quarantine when testing kits were scarce or not yet available. Embodied responses to the virus's early stages became a sensitizing vehicle that drove others' actions.

Embodiment in Our Environments

Embodiment is a noun fraught with complexity. The word can represent a tangible form of an idea. *She is the embodiment of liveliness, vitality personified.* It can represent the role of the body in (re)shaping cognitive habits. *After the accident, he built a new sense of embodiment informed by the height of his wheelchair.* It can represent the braided nature of mind as indistinct from bodily perception. *She relied on her embodiment to navigate the dark, smoke-filled room*. For conceptual framing, Abby Knoblauch differentiates three ways that the rhetoric and composition communities "talk about embodiment as it relates to knowledge production and writing" (50). She unpacks "embodied terminology" through three categories, "embodied language," "embodied knowledge," and "embodied rhetoric," while demonstrating that the three concepts overlap and inform each other. First, embodied language entails the use of "terms, metaphors, and analogies" referencing the "body itself" (52). In the case study chapters, residents exposed to noxious odors often use embodied language to discuss their experiences, referencing the impact of scent events on their sinuses, eyes, and lungs. Embodied knowledge is the "sense of knowing something *through* the body" (52). In the case studies, visceral publics discuss knowing when something harms their bodies because they physically feel the effects of environmental hazards. Embodied rhetoric is a "purposeful decision to include embodied knowledge and social [position] as forms of meaning-making with a text" (52). In this book, I discuss how, when, where, and why BIPOC community leaders use embodied rhetoric pertaining to their senses to persuade policymakers and others to address environmental concerns. I also use my embodied experience anecdotally to flesh out points for readers. All three definitions are important to a RISE approach and to archival activism because they collapse the mind/body, nature/culture, and mediated text/personal experience dualisms that may circulate in descriptions of environmental and social injustice zones. Moreover, the last concept, "embodied rhetoric," informs RISE, as it contends with emplaced, ecosystemic embodiments reflected in mediated environmental rhetorics.

A RISE approach recognizes how complex, embodied entanglements inform relationality, including how people communicate ephemeral sensory experiences. As a concept, embodiment works to braid our lived experiences to an exterior mediated materiality that informs our uptake of sensations—a "realness" we inhabit, "incorporate and inscribe" on ourselves and other forms of life (Hayles, *How* 193).[6] Embodiment is rhetorical, and rhetoric is embodied. Knowledge stems from these facts of being. My body differs from another person's in how it projects, feels, reacts, and senses, but humans can share how (and what) we sense to describe what persuades us to act in a given situation.

---

6. Hayles introduces the partnered concept of inscription and incorporation in her book *How We Became Posthuman*. What emerges for Hayles is "a certain kind of subjectivity" that can offer "a new, more flexible framework in which to think about embodiment in an age of virtuality" (193). This flexible framework consists of two intermingled "polarities" that function, according to Hayles, as a heuristic: (1) a culturally constructed body that feels and interacts with its environment and (2) "a dance between inscribing and incorporating practices" that are "in complex syncopation with each other" in cahoots and coupled with "body and embodiment" (193).

For example, I will leave a room or a conversation if the room starts to smell of electrical smoke and go pull the fire alarm—my sensing body will react to the agentive potential of smoke as an actant in my noetic/somatic field, persuading me to take immediate action as I assess the risk posed and contend with a perceived threat.

A RISE approach necessarily considers relationality between types of bodies and embodiment, and a posthuman appeal is a crier to issues before and after the human. To wit, our nonhuman counterparts have the embodied capacity to share what they sense in gesture, expression, or other modes (e.g., pheromones, scent-marking, posture, gaze, proximity, vocalization, sensitivity to touch; see Armstrong and Botzler; Bugnyar et al.; Hawhee, "Rhetoric" and "Toward"; Kennedy; Propen). Even plants respond to each other and us through embodied response (Chamovitz; D. Davis, "Rhetoricity" 437; Kimmerer; Wohlleben). For example, upon touch the "sensitive plant" (L. mimosa pudica) will fold its leaves inward to better protect itself. Eyelid-like, it also closes its leaves in the dark and reopens them in the morning (Minorsky). Embodiment makes it possible to ask questions about the connections between variance in (non)human sensations and the discrimination, criminalization, dismissal, or silencing of different body types. Embodiment conceptually integrates a posthumanist sensory rhetorical stance to establish priorities that include but exceed the human. We can also analyze how embodied selective perception manifests across mediated sociohistorical, political, and cultural contexts.[7]

Embodiment is as essential to RISE as relationality is. The two are also entwined in mediated visceral publics. When we study mediated sensory rhetorics, embodiment underscores the premise that sensation is a physical-rhetorical phenomenon that affects how we are persuaded to treat other creatures, the Earth, and extraterrestrial entities (e.g., Mars, the moon, or the vacuum of space beyond Earth's atmosphere, where we deposit our satellite junk for eternity). More locally, embodiment insists that we acknowledge difference in sense-ability, sensibilities, sensuousness, and a body's need to be well-treated, sustained, and capable of life. This can be micro or macro, human or other-than-human. For example, a body can be a celestial body like the Earth, a human body, an amoeba, or a plant. A RISE perspective, however, considers

---

7. *Selective perception* refers to the idea that we may purposefully ignore something we want to misperceive. For example, white people may choose to believe that racism is over because they do not want to acknowledge their own culpability in structural oppression. A second example: Men may choose to believe that women have equal rights because women can vote, hold office, and gain employment, and men may opt to ignore inequities in reproductive rights, selecting to perceive it as a "women's issue." These examples demonstrate how I define selective perception as a concept.

the political implications of bodies that garner attention and ones selectively ignored in a particular situation in the mediated public sphere.

For example, policymakers or regional government officials may talk about a specific environmental catastrophe like a hurricane, wildfire, or chemical spill while neglecting to consider who or what suffers the most in the aftermath. The same folx may also opt to ignore longer-term results of global warming that have already resulted in longer, stronger hurricane and wildfire seasons because they have the means to remove themselves from danger when others do not have such luxury. Take as an example Scott Morrison, the former prime minister of Australia. Morrison and his family snuck away to vacation in Hawaii as the country's worst heatwave and bushfires decimated large swaths of Australia in late 2019. Only after being caught in the act did Morrison express "regret" at selecting to leave the country amid the crisis (Remeikis). People like Morrison who have the privilege to avoid crises routinely engage in selective perception and ignore structural oppressions that prop up gross inequities. An intersectional ecofeminist conceptualization of embodiment disavows that move. Instead, the intersectional ecofeminist part of RISE exposes how women's, LGBTQIA+, BIPOC, animal, insect, and vegetable bodies are sensed differently in a patriarchal culture than a human, white male body like that of Morrison or other less public examples. Nearly three billion animals died in Australia's 2019–20 fires and forty-six million acres burned, which is about the same surface area as the entire state of Washington (Center for Disaster Philanthropy). An intersectional ecofeminist sense of embodiment cares to notice things that make a difference to one's lived experiences, which tangles with the sensory rhetorical aspects of the approach. Embodiment tells stories about and through us, which makes sensation, as a rhetorical phenomenon of being/becoming, come alive with meaning-making and potential nodes of connection built into our entangled relationalities.

RISE also compels us to consider the ethics of our entanglements—political, epistemological, ontological, ideological, and so forth—when we rhetorically analyze sensational events. Entanglement is like relationality, though the concept asserts more estrangement because relationality implies kinship, and embodied entanglement insinuates a meshwork or knotty contact. This difference is relevant to RISE because entanglement's connection to embodied rhetoric advocates that we "[become] more clearly [attuned to] the purposeful effort by an author to represent aspects of embodiment within the text he or she is shaping," and the author must "attempt to decipher how [the] 'material circumstances' (Royster 228) affect how he or she understands the world" (Knoblauch 58). The stories we tell are filled with the embodied rhetorics of sensation with which we are entangled.

As an intersectional ecofeminist, I would like the sensational stories we tell to depend on the concept of relationality—the kinship bit—yet I believe our political entanglements may sometimes confuse our understanding of how we are ecologically and socially interdependent. To elaborate, if one's ideological stance is deeply tied to conservative or progressive political views, then a person may try to ignore sensory inputs that contradict the party line on a given topic. For example, people who advocate for laxer gun laws for automatic weapons like AR-15s must willfully ignore what they see and hear when a mass shooting occurs or attribute blame to some other agent or actor. In *Distant Publics*, Rice provides a rhetorical figure called the "exceptional public subject" who "occupies a precarious position between publicness and a withdrawal from publicness" (5). This vexing rhetorical figure disengages from public debate about environmental issues and avoids direct involvement, though the figure paradoxically feels involved. The figure disengages for a variety of reasons, and this subjectivity is "thoroughly grounded in *feeling*," making the "rhetorical position" of the figure resistant to or ambivalent about change (5). Feeling itself can be productive, so Rice takes no issue with pathos per se. She discusses how people distance themselves from events and situations and argues that our "current habits of public discourse and debate" cultivate publics "who are not oriented toward making sustainable interventions in rhetorical crises" (6). Instead, showing how people, nonhumans, and more-than-humans are affected by "sensible," or perhaps sentient or animate, scenes of deliberation and encouraging people to "relate differently to the world around them" aligns with a larger goal of helping people "see themselves as beings-in-the-world" or, I argue, to *sense* themselves as beings-*of*-the-world in reciprocal relation (6). Rice asserts that we need "a new rhetorical vista" that "cultivate[s] a different kind of [public] subjectivity altogether," one different in kind and character from the exceptional public subject's locus nested in the "other" divide—people who do not participate (5).

In the example I shared about Morrison, the political kerfuffle of him distancing himself and his family from massive wildfires garnered a lot of attention, and Morrison is no longer prime minister. Nevertheless, the three billion dead animals, thirty-four of which were human, and the scorched Earth leave lasting ecological and sensory rhetorical impacts. The political ideologies of folx like Morrison who withdrew from the situation informs the scorched Earth result. Aboriginal Australian voices who advocated for controlled bushland burning and environmental stewardship for decades also inform the results.

An experiential positioning system, an embodiment of place and our relations within and to it, attunes us to how our senses help us understand our environment and what we intake from it. Embodiment, as it segues to the suasive nature of sensation, suggests that a vital sense of a place ought to extend to Earth as a whole, and in an active sense, we cannot passively collect from the land without maintaining and nourishing it as we would our bodies. Just as Rice posits the rhetorical figure of the exceptional public subject, Wildcat forwards how "local knowledges" illustrate "a nature-culture nexus" born from "long standing knowledges" of places. Wildcat names this "a first-order global positioning system," or "an *experiential positioning system*" that apprehends more about one's place in the universe (55; my emphasis); he is talking about an embodiment of place. When the exceptional public subject is interrupted by an experiential positioning system via a RISE approach, she must acknowledge her own enmeshment with the Earth rather literally. For instance, when one nourishes tired soil with fresh compost, the refreshed soil contributes to the health and resilience of the plant, enabling it to produce higher-quality fruit rich in complex nutrient value that in turn sustains other life-forms. The refreshed soil smells of organic composition, in contrast to the acrid notes found in chemical fertilizers or overapplied raw manure. The feel and look of the nourished soil are experientially different from tired soil: richer in texture, nuanced in material, additive in flavor, more sustainable in nature. The fruit nourished by this soil is likely to have a richer flavor profile that is expressed through the interaction of taste, odor, and mouthfeel.

As it is tied to embodiment, we also must grapple with selective perception because it may obscure our openness to new entanglements or emergences. Selective perception might dampen a fire object. Whose perception and what fire objects garner attention have political implications. RISE aids the work of connection, meaning it can expand our conceptions of how rhetoric works within and among bodies and in the mediated public sphere. At stake is our inclusion of nondiscursive rhetoric as a cumulative force of relationality always at work on our words and material becomings.

Defining a RISE Approach to Environmental Problems

RISE tarries in this purview: When we encounter a situation, our sensations (psychosomatic responses to stimuli) persuade us to pay attention to something in or about the environment, and those sensations become part of our embodied memory and perception of the event and the setting. The responses can also be articulated and circulated in the public sphere in the form of mediated artifacts (e.g., social media posts, news broadcasts, and scientific reports). Perception of sensation is fluid, adapting details as needed to fit an ideological framework or rhetorical, material situation. Put another way, human perceptions are informed by our belief systems and imbrication in different power structures, and this can impact how individual people respond to different sensory experiences and how they choose to report those experiences to others. Composite sensations that emerge when a group of people or nonhuman entities are exposed to similar stimuli can disclose issues that bring people or nonhuman entities together to address an environmental or other social problem. For a nonhuman example, elephants can generate vocal vibratory sounds that fall well below the level of human hearing, yet other elephants can feel the vibrations through their extremely sensitive feet over many miles. The tactile sensations, a form of "seismic communication," can disclose the proximity of another group of elephants and allow them to detect earth vibrations so they can move away from impending danger ("Elephant"). Composite sensations form a constitutive function in that when combined they have the power to establish or give organized existence to something once inchoate. Hence, composite experiences can merge to provide a more developed sense of what happened or is happening in a given situation and why. As a human example, when visual and auditory video evidence of George Floyd Jr.'s murder circulated globally online, the composite sensations and resulting perceptions sparked visceral publics' mass protests against the police officers' brutality, which, along with video footage and eyewitness accounts, led to a form of justice for Floyd's family.[8] Audiovisual sensation in this example was thus rhetorical in both immediate embodiment (human response to the in situ scene) and mediated relationality (people protested across the globe against police brutality in their own communities and in Floyd's community). Sensation's a/effects stick to artifacts that circulate in a rhetorical ecology.

A RISE approach exposes environmental and social injustices because it allows us to describe and evaluate relationships between sensation, perception, intellection, and community. The approach also encourages rhetoricians to analyze (re)actions, actants, and distributed agency and unearth rupture or emergence in conceptual viewpoints. In simplest terms, sensation is rhetorical because it is persuasive. To research sensation rhetorically thus requires that we develop appropriately complex conceptual approaches for doing so. Debra Hawhee argues this point in her 2015 article "Rhetoric's Sensorium," positing that

> as scholars pursue sensation as a useful category for theorizing rhetoric, they are likely to reach for or develop theories or methods, e.g., ethnography, memoir, or transdisciplinary explorations . . . that will avoid the pitfalls of

---

8. George Floyd Jr. (age forty-six) was a Black man who was brutally murdered by a white police officer in Minneapolis, Minnesota, on May 25, 2020.

generalization even as they consider more deeply the constitutive roles of sensation in participatory, rhetorical acts. (13)

Hawhee builds from feminist work performed two decades earlier (1994) by Sonja Foss and Karen Foss. Foss and Foss argued for a more-than-visual perspective and advocated for a "multi-sensory version of rhetorical style" (qtd. in Hawhee, "Rhetoric's" 11). Both Hawhee's and Foss and Foss's arguments indicate that the point of a multisensory perspective is to expand our range of invention, as we expand our ideas of what rhetoric is and can do (rhetoric as a how). RISE is designed to encourage rhetoricians to pay attention to a wider array of sensations that circulate in the sensorium, ones that we may not have bothered to notice much, like olfaction and chemoreception, and thus dwell upon a multisensory prospectus in rhetoric studies. RISE also must address how wider structural and intersecting relations of domination render some people's and more-than-human others' sensations to be unworthy of attention.

In *Bodies That Matter*, Judith Butler "makes clear [that] a gendered matrix is at work in the constitution of materiality," and specifically asks feminists to "[conduct] a critical genealogy of its formulation" (8). Intersectionality vis-à-vis Crenshaw and Hill Collins from the introductory chapter makes apparent overlapping axes of oppression that white feminism historically neglected to address effectively, like BIPOC voting, reproductive and property rights, access to equitable economic and educational opportunities, and the impacts of environmental racism. Intersectional ecofeminism in RISE addresses these oversights and spotlights how embodiment, media, materiality, and power relations impact human and nonhuman subjects and objects differently based upon sociohistorical constructs steeped in white supremacy, colonization, and neoliberal patriarchy.

I do intersectional ecofeminist work through the vehicle of the senses. That is, when intersectional ecofeminist objectives like gender equity, redressing racialized environmental hazard placements, and more are deployed to address environmental injustices, we can direct attention to how BIPOC communities and others use their senses to respond to and redress these inequities and hazards. The term *sensory rhetorical* that I use throughout this book underscores how mediated rhetoric shares a covalent bond with what we physically and materially sense going on around us. The term *sensory rhetorical* thus

- signifies that our senses shape our rhetorical choices and vice versa;
- makes explicit that nondiscursive and extradiscursive sensations shape how we understand different environmental and social settings, allow-

ing us to better analyze a rhetorical situation by considering our sense-makings of an experience, place, person, or object;
- focuses our attention on the relationships—relationality—between rhetoric, sensation, and mediated publics;
- permeates mediated artifacts that pertain to socioenvironmental concerns; and
- reconfigures an ableist hierarchy of sensation that tends to privilege vision and hearing, preferring instead a complex sensorium that values different ways of knowing, being, and reflexive meaning-making.

To build on the last point, a RISE approach asks that we use a broader range of sensation to create a climate that values multiple modes of sensing the world rather than rendering the blind, deaf, or otherly-abled body as deficient. RISE invites us to question commonplace assumptions about how we sense and what we sense and destabilizes separate sensory categories and hierarchies. Our material embodiment exists in relation to an environmental setting, and some settings pose more risk than others. Finally, material embodiment rhetorically informs and shapes mediated artifacts that people share and circulate in a variety of rhetorical ecologies. In the next section, I provide a heuristic and process rhetoricians can use to analyze how, when, where, and why composite sensations emerge and how they work to shape public perceptions of environmental issues. I illustrate each aspect of the heuristic with a brief example to assist readers' understanding. Then, I procedurally apply the heuristic in chapters 2 through 4.

Outlining a SCENT Heuristic for Sensing and Analyzing Environmental Injustices

S—Sensing and Searching

First, identify specific sensory experiences for analysis, such as foul odors, toxic fumes, or other olfactory, auditory, visual, or other sensorial cues related to environmental hazards or pollutants. Next, use thick description to describe specific sensory experiences or composite sensations under analysis. The opening paragraphs of the preface serve as an example of what thick description involves when one has direct experience of a scent event. If one cannot be proximal to a location, or for people with sensory-processing or mobility differences, then identify and describe mediated sensorial impacts associated with *N* below. Then circle back to context.

C—Context

Using the RISE approach, evaluate the geographic, historical, and sociopolitical context in which the sensory persuasion emerged alongside an environmental concern. Look for historical and ongoing patterns of environmental neglect. Identify whether the site context includes a disproportionate number of polluting industries in marginalized communities and investigate local activism, advocacy, and regulatory oversight or enforcement in the area. RISE focuses on BIPOC communities, though one can apply the SCENT heuristic in non-BIPOC communities for different purposes. For example, the hog factory near my Illinois home is in a majority-white community, though the area is both rural and predominantly working class. Both represent historically neglected communities but benefit from white privilege.

E—Emplacement and Embodiment

Examine emplacement and embodiment of specific entities within the site context under analysis. Evaluate embodied experiences and composite sensations of individuals or communities exposed to harmful sensory stimuli associated with the environmental hazard. Include potential health impacts; physiological, psychological, and rhetorical a/effects; and disruptions to daily quality of life. If one has the necessary means and mobility to do so, go conduct fieldwork (e.g., Druschke; Rai and Druschke Gottschalk; Pezzullo; Senda-Cook et al.). If one cannot, then ethically deploy embodied simulation and iterative reprocessing to consider the lived and mediated experiences of residents exposed to environmental hazards. To do so, conduct qualitative interviews with local actors in the network or gather narratives from publicly available resources like social media posts, news reports, meeting minutes, or other materials. Depending on access to resources and time constraints, use qualitative mixed methods inquiries that involve a combination of embodied simulation, iterative reprocessing, archival and digital research, interviews, and field visits. If warranted, use quantitative methods to triangulate results (e.g., text mining for sentiment analysis and statistical analysis). Prioritize based on access, time, anticipated audience, and purpose.

N—Narratives

Select narratives to evaluate. Identify vernacular exchanges, stories, testimonies, and social media of those affected by the sensory experiences. Seek research partners or interview participants based on measured priorities and constraints. Evaluate and analyze these narratives and testimonies of community members describing their sensory experiences. Compare and contrast them with scientific, bureaucratic narratives or corporate rhetoric that downplay or deny the existence of environmental hazards and the embodied sensory experiences or composite sensations of a visceral public.

T—Tactics and Transformation

Select and categorize suasive tactics. Evaluate sensory-rhetorical tactics employed by different stakeholders, such as activists and community organizers, and counterstrategies of corporations or government entities in transforming the experiences, discourses, and responses surrounding the sensory experiences and environmental injustices.[9] Analyze how, when, where, and to what a/effects the rhetorical tactics used by activists, community organizers, and environmental justice advocates raise awareness, redress problems, challenge and transform dominant narratives, and demand accountability from polluters or regulatory bodies.

Use a procedural approach to apply the SCENT heuristic to systematically evaluate sensory-rhetorical dimensions of environmental injustices and their effects. Focus most on those related to sensory experiences, like foul odors. Readers can apply the heuristic and process to other aspects of the sensorium.

A Procedural Approach for Applying the SCENT Heuristic

Stage 1—Begin with Sensing and Searching for Emergent Problems and Assess the Context

Conduct analyses of environmental injustices to understand, disclose, and redress them. The first step in the SCENT heuristic involves the analyst identifying when, where, and how people or other sensing bodies notice something "off" in an environment—the *S* and *C* parts of the heuristic. A rhetorician might have an in situ experience in a place or space (akin to Pezzullo's "toxic tourism"), or one can identify an emergent problem because of mediated

---

9. In *The Practice of Everyday Life*, Michel de Certeau makes an important distinction between "tactic" and "strategy." The former is deployed by ordinary people who have less power to subvert strategies imposed by powerful institutions and systems. Strategies are the preserve of the powerful. Tactics are the improvisational, resourceful ways that folx with less power resist domination in subtle and overt ways.

encounters, witnessing accounts of nosesay or other sensesay that circulate afterward. With either approach, humans and nonhuman entities like dogs, birds, plants, insects, or machine sensors like e-noses, pressure sensors, or other apparatus sense an environmental risk. Physiological senses are inexpensive equipment analysts can access. Additionally, textual and mediated artifacts people or other entities produce in sensory response to a specific environmental concern, such as local meeting minutes, social media posts, public and government reports, and news broadcasts, are readily available and inexpensive. A RISE approach dictates stage 1 of heuristic application include historically excluded or marginalized communities' concerns to work toward socioenvironmental justice goals. The RISE framework recognizes how multiple axes of oppression routinely delimit attention to BIPOC communities' concerns about environmental hazards and works to redress those injustices. History and universal design principles also tell us that when we improve living conditions for the most vulnerable, it can result in better living conditions across the board (Kerr et al.).

Use the heuristic to identify communities dealing with environmental injustices related to olfactible or other sensible events. If focusing on olfaction, first scan the internet and a variety of social media sites for examples of nosesay and nosewitness accounts of unusual or offensive smells. I elaborate on both nosesay and nosewitness in chapter 2, the first case study chapter, but both neologisms relate to *hearsay* and *eyewitness,* respectively, yet disturb the associated hegemonic ear-centric and ocularcentric paradigms. Enter search terms like *stench, stinky, disgusting odor, reeking, nauseating smell, foul air, rank, fetid, funky, dank,* and so on. This process disclosed the scent event sites I analyze in this book's case study chapters. One could do a similar search for inflammatory skin reactions, dysgeusia (impaired sense of taste or taste aversions associated with environmental toxins), eyesores, noise pollution, or another sensorial stream associated with environmental hazards. Look up US Census Bureau data to determine whether the context meets the RISE constraint of a majority-minoritized community. Then, search for federal EPA and state or local environmental hazard placement databases to understand if there is documented evidence of extant environmental risk. "EnviroMapper" and "EnviroFacts" are two tools one can use. A host of agencies and academic institutions use the Environmental Systems Research Institute's (ESRI) Aeronautical Reconnaissance Coverage Geographical Information Systems (ArcGIS) StoryMaps to document and communicate information about environmental hazards, which is also useful in context assessment and beyond (Stephens and Richards). GIS stands for *geographic information systems,* which includes Web-based global satellite positioning for hazard mapping accuracy. ArcGIS story mapping combines maps, multimedia content, and narrative text to engage and inform audiences about complex environmental hazards. The Federal Emergency Management Agency, National Oceanic and Atmospheric Administration, US Geological Survey, EPA, many state organizations, non-government organizations like the Nature Conservancy and World Resources Institute, and myriad academic institutions use ArcGIS StoryMaps to communicate complex information about environmental hazards. The Salton Sea case study, chapter 3, highlights a few examples for readers. To assess context, start at a larger scale (e.g., the United Nations Environmental Programme, the EPA, or, for a non-Western example, the National Environmental Management Authority in Kenya). Then, identify state and local environmental data for additional granularity. For example, the Blue Ridge Landfill case study, chapter 4, includes material derived from EPA data, Texas Commission on Environmental Quality data, and county and municipal data.

Using this process, I identified the majority-Black community of Brunswick, Georgia, which is home to a number of Superfund sites per the EPA database. Scent events happen frequently in Brunswick because of the community's proximity to four active noxious polluting industries, which include a paper mill, a resin factory, a water sanitation plant, and a waste and recycling facility. Scent events shift with the wind direction, the heat of the day, and the pollution produced, which is tied to the intensity of residents' lived experiences of the event and their exposures to airborne toxins.

Stage 2—Evaluate Emplacement, Embodiment, and Narratives

By stage 2, the sensorial scene is set and the context assessed. Under the RISE framework, the scene and context affect a majority-minoritized community. Next, analyze more specific emplacement and embodiment of humans and nonhumans facing the environmental concern—the *E* part of the heuristic. Move from macro to micro. Identify places and spaces where people or other sensors have lodged complaints about the smellscape or sensescape, which could be official or unofficial, like e-nose reports, town hall meeting minutes, state-based EPA complaint portals, or social media postings—the *N* part of the heuristic.

Bearing in mind that "nothing is in the intellect that is not first in the senses," in stage 2 analyze how an environmental problem has been sensed and perceived in intellection with others (Cory 110). Evaluate how messaging about the problem gains traction and circulates in a sensory rhetorical ecology. If someone, something, or a multitude senses something amiss within an environment or social scene and does *not* communicate that sensual experience, then composite sensations are unlikely to emerge in the public sphere or circulate in the form of mediated artifacts or narratives. The reverse is also accurate. When people or other entities do communicate sensual experiences, then composite sensations emerge in the public sphere and circulate in the form of mediated artifacts and narratives. An intersectional ecofeminist approach underscores when, where, why, and how BIPOC communities' mediated composite sensations circulate in response to environmental risks and to what effects. Having access to a broader audience can support BIPOC communities contending with environmental injustices because the messages circulate in the public sphere and spotlight problems to be addressed. For a famous example, residents of Hinkley, California, experienced foul-tasting and -smelling water in the 1990s, before internet or social media platforms were broadly available. Then a legal clerk, Erin Brockovich, looked deeper into the situation and uncovered evidence of hexavalent chromium in the local water supply that created long-term health problems for residents, more than 40% of which are Latine, according to US Census Bureau data. Brockovich smelled a corporate rat, sniffed it out, and took action, and the 2002 film bearing her name and the story still circulates. The Pacific Gas and Electric Company agreed to a $333 million settlement—one of the largest payouts in US history (Banks).

To return to the Brunswick example, in 2019, frustrated Brunswick residents created a Facebook group named "Smell Something, Tell Something!" Residents who experience unpleasant scent events report their experiences to others in vernacular communication that circulates on social media. The olfactory persuasion Brunswick residents engage results in translation of personal sensory experiences to the group, and residents often share data that corroborate their lived experiences using scientific data to warrant their emplaced, embodied claims. For example, on January 10, 2023, one resident explained their difficulty breathing and attributed it to exposure to odors from a nearby paper mill, which the resident then associated with air quality index data on a local weather app (Smell, "I was awoken"). The group also shares ways to report their experiences to authorities, log the effects of "slow violence" over time, and work to elicit action to address myriad environmental problems (Nixon 2). Rob Nixon characterizes slow violence as a "violence of delayed destruction, [and] attritional violence that is typically not viewed as violence at all" (2). Slow violence takes place over decades or even generations.

Stage 3—Examine Tactics of Visceral Public Using and Broadcasting Sensory Experiences to Elicit Action and Transform Outcomes

In stage 3, analyze the sensory-rhetorical tactics a visceral public deploys to address an environmental problem and how these are broadcast into the mediated public sphere to evaluate how, if, when, and where they are amplified by external actors like journalists, advocacy groups, coalitions, scholars, or conscientious government agents. Evaluate how a noxious odor functions as a rhetorical device, evoking visceral reactions, emotions, and associations. Consider how the smell's intensity, pervasiveness, and unpleasantness shape a sensory rhetorical ecology and influence or transform public perceptions and responses. What tactics do visceral publics take to communicate the impact, and what circulates as a result? In stage 3, evaluate the broader reach and circulation of sensory rhetorical appeals. Analyze what people and nonhumans do to address environmental problems they sense. What role does sensory persuasion play in their tactics? For a brief nonhuman example, cockatoos in Australia have lost natural habitat due to human activity and have increasingly taken up residence in Sydney. The birds' tactics now include opening many kinds of trash bins, which they show their offspring and other cockatoo community members how to do (Klump et al.). Cockatoo tactical communication is not mediated in the same manner as human communication, yet it represents information-sharing on how to address an environmental issue that circulates in a sensory rhetorical ecology. In the cockatoo example, that is access to food and adapting to habitat loss. In RISE and human terms, stage 3 of the analysis process includes evaluating mediated responses to composite sensations that sometimes fizzle out because those with the strategic power to address an emergent environmental problem may opt to ignore or suppress the situation out of ignorance (a problem this author seeks to address) or for a host of unethical reasons (e.g., financial, racist, sexist, ableist, and classist). For our cockatoo friends, tactics resulted in a variety of strategic human policy measures designed to keep them from dumpster diving and ideally provide more suitable habitat (Kirksey et al.).

Illustrating human tactical response, a January 10, 2023, Smell Something, Tell Something! post involved one resident telling other residents how, why, when, and where to report odors to regulatory agencies. To officially complain to state and local environmental protection and regulatory agencies in the Brunswick area requires residents to log in to an online portal that has a form designed to capture the location, intensity, duration, and description of an odor and its embodied impact. The poster explained how odor nuisance reporting alone was an insufficient report category because, as the poster put it, public officials lump "all of [the] community complaints in an 'odor' category which requires NO action" (Smell, "I was awoken"). Subsequently, the poster explains that residents need to file a "health" complaint and provides information on how to do so. Hence, residents deploy olfactory persuasion and support the poster's claim about human health impacts but use olfactory rhetoric as an indirect, tactical appeal to transform a negative environmental impact into a better outcome.

Stage 4—Determine How or if Broadcasted Sensations Transform Policy and Cultural Attunements

Finally, in stage 4, analyze how visceral publics' broadcasted sensations and tactics mitigate environmental damage and positively impact public policy. Evaluate effects circulating across sensory rhetorical ecologies that amplify environmental concerns of residents and other communities. Identify forms of cultural attunement that emerge as a result. For example, between March 2023 and September 2023, record-setting wildfires occurred across Canada, and the effects were both sniffable and visible across much of North America. While I was in Illinois, I could smell and see the burnt-orange smoke and experienced it comingling with the smell of hog manure from the local concentrated animal feeding operation. In 2023, a massive wildfire on Maui had devastating impacts broadcast both in the air and on the airwaves. In late February and early March 2024, the Texas Panhandle's massive wildfires were also sniffable and visible to me several hours away in Lubbock, Texas. Since massive fires occurred in Australia in 2019–20 and on the west coast of the US in 2018 and elsewhere, visceral publics across the globe have demanded that forestry management agencies examine and use Indigenous approaches to landscape health, which is happening and represents an important ideological shift tied to sensorial suasions (Bardsley et al.; Hessburg et al.; Lake and Christianson).

However, the shift also involves analyzing intersecting axes of power that affect who or what receives a more immediate response. RISE can account for cultural shifts that are not simply enshrined through policy or law. Readers with different analytic skill sets and backgrounds can use the heuristic and process differently to analyze other aspects of environmental justice like direct action or means irrespective of law and order. Chaining oneself to a tree is a very tactile, tactical response with which readers are likely familiar. Staging an unsanctioned public protest is another. Taking a bottle of one's smelly tap water and upending it on a public official's head is a third.

When analyzing settler-colonial approaches to environmental concerns, the last stage of analysis involves evaluating different kinds of genres based in quantitative analysis and scientific and/or legal inquiry. The analyst can assess the rhetorical and material effects thereof to understand how and when cultural attunements and environmental policy shift to address BIPOC and other communities' sensorial appeals and environmental concerns more effectively. For example, stage 4 analysis reveals incremental and iterative success for Brunswick, Georgia, residents. A visceral public is present and active in Brunswick and has been for a long time. In 1990, Brunswick community members formed the Glynn Environmental Coalition, which consists of a mix of residents who wanted to understand why their community "became so polluted" and to develop a plan to address it (Glynn Environmental Coalition, "Who"). The coalition includes residents who have scientific training who provide "technical assistance" and focus on "governmental oversight and environmental justice," which helps residents and local government build anti-nuisance clauses and preventive measures into any new business development or expansion plans for existing industry settings, among other things ("Who"). Odor nuisance clauses are just one facet.

Procedurally applying the SCENT heuristic supports analysts to gauge sensible changes in behavior, attunement, and remediation of environmental injustices. Relative success or failure of sensational suasion among a visceral public is a matter of analytic interpretation and should be related to environmental justice goals. Rhetorical analysis is a way to unpack both "actions implied" and "the interests represented" (Wander 18). Applying the heuristic can disclose incremental improvements of the living conditions and long-term health outcomes of a given human community and, by extension, nonhuman entities in its midst, though the two may be at odds occasionally (e.g., the cockatoo dumpster divers). The applied heuristic can also pinpoint places that need more attention and solutions. Acts of sensory rhetorical analysis should serve the communities presented.

When applying the heuristic, one can showcase places where immediate relief and positive long-term environmental health improvements unfolded for all involved—ideal breathable futures. Other applications show efforts that are incremental and may involve multiple iterations of analysis to determine why one community's efforts work and why another's may falter. BIPOC communities face intersectional challenges that warrant recursive analysis when the environmental concern is complex. Applying the heuristic can also disclose the dismissal of sensory suasion that results in worsening environmental conditions. If a mediated visceral public successfully draws attention to an environmental problem and policymakers both dismiss the problem and retaliate to make matters worse, then an analyst can identify why, when, how, or where in the process that occurred. Imagine a Black community that complains about ineffective trash removal. Shortly thereafter, white city leadership opts to cut funding to municipal services yet allocates funds to build a park in a different neighborhood. It may be difficult to prove that the act was vindictive, but the applied heuristic can disclose important details.

A RISE approach and the heuristic apply to any sense perception or overlaps among them. For example, in the introduction, I noted how people *visually* witnessed the surface of the Cuyahoga River ablaze, though on-site witnesses could also have smelled it, heard it, felt the heat, and even noted a taste in the air, depending on their location (see fig. 1). Stage 1 analysis reveals visual (and other sensual) proximity to the fiery scene by firefighters, photographers, residents, and public officials. In the 1952 photograph of the scene, we see only white men on the bridge, either fighting the blaze or conferring. RISE emphasizes why the masculine focus reflects power imbalances that persist more than seventy years later. Now the visual evidence of the Cuyahoga's environmental damage is no longer visible, though there is still widespread sediment contamination. In contemporary Cleveland, Ohio, the top polluters remain located primarily in minoritized communities (Kumar et al.).

Composite sensations that circulated in Cleveland's mid-twentieth-century sensory rhetorical ecology intensified the a/effects on public policymakers. The results led to environmental regulations and cleanup, including ongoing efforts to redress damage to the sediments through dredging and other remediations. Analyzing how BIPOC and other communities develop anticipatory language based in a "precautionary principle" in permitting processes that address things like odor nuisances, pollution controls, and waste management from the outset is one affordance the heuristic offers (Bullard and Wright 178–80). For damage already done, sensible ways to intervene include analyzing mechanisms for residents' reports to be acted upon rather than dismissed out of hand when an odor nuisance or other scent event is reported (166). For example, in chapter 3, we will see how enrolled members of the Torres Martinez Nation work collaboratively with US and California EPA agencies to restore wetland habitat, plant drought-resistant plants, and develop renewable energy initiatives within and around the Salton Sea portion of their reservation. In chapter 4, we will see how Pearland, Texas, residents collaborated with local and state governments to develop a coalitional "Odor Task Force" to address a poorly managed landfill.

Nondiscursive or extradiscursive rhetoric pertains to how people and nonhumans can communicate without the overt need for words (Langer 93; Mazis 21–23; Murray). As it addresses environmental issues, this book challenges the assumption that rhetoric pertains solely to words. A noxious odor has a rhetorical a/effect and persuades people to either find and redress the source of contamination, move upwind, or otherwise escape the stench. This book evaluates how visceral publics deploy sensations like olfactory perception as vehicles for identifying and addressing environmental problems that circulate in the mediated public sphere. Deploying case studies focusing on olfactory suasion shows how theory informs analysis and how people work to improve environmental conditions. The next three chapters offer readers examples of what olfactory rhetoric involves when we sniff it out and how people use it to shape public policy or direct action to foster a breathable future.

CHAPTER 2

Is It Pepper Spray or Sriracha Sauce?

> Most plain view cases involve the sense of sight and, more recently, the sense of touch.... Note, however, that the sense of smell is one of the senses that can establish probable cause. Plain odor, however, has not been clearly established thus far as a legal doctrine by Court decisions.
>
> —Rolando V. Del Carmen, *Criminal Procedure: Law and Practice*

What happens when one mixes hot peppers, garlic, vinegar, sugar, salt, and spices in enormous quantities? In Irwindale, California, one gets Sriracha sauce produced by Huy Fong Foods, a culinary empire started by David Tran. What happens when neighbors complain about the odor? In the same locale, one witnesses a lawsuit, factory closure, and complex food politics when the scenario went viral on social media. Procedural application of the SCENT heuristic in this chapter reveals how a visceral public's sense of "civic osmocosm" worked to address an air quality issue. A civic osmocosm refers to how visceral publics engage olfactory persuasion, sniff out environmental injustices, and translate their embodied experiences of olfactory rhetoric to combat collective anosmia. A civic osmocosm, then, connects the suasive realm of odors and olfaction to the civic—how smells shape public feelings, awareness, attitudes, debates, and action around environmental risks like air pollution, industrial effluent, and more. Particles afloat in the local airstream drift and travel, as does rhetoric, both foodstuffs of osmocosmic relation. Since I was not proximal to the emergent controversy, though I did see and hear evidence of it circulating on social media and searched for more information, stage 1 of the applied heuristic begins with narrative and context. Applying stage 2 of the heuristic shows that messaging about the problem gained traction. Stage 3 application illustrates that community tactics elicited action and transformed outcomes. Finally, stage 4 application discloses that culturally informed broadcasted sensations transformed policy and how it was implemented.

Narrative and Context

In 2012 residents who lived next to the new Sriracha sauce manufacturing plant began to experience headaches, burning eyes and nostrils, irritated lungs, increased asthma, and skin rashes. Most residents in Irwindale identify as Latine on US Census Bureau data, thus meeting the RISE context criteria outlined in the heuristic. Residents' sensory experiences revealed an emergent environmental problem that reeked of pepper spray. Residents discussed their composite sensory experiences in settings like city council meetings, across the aisles in local shops, and in public parks, which resulted in mediated artifacts (narratives)—official complaints, social media posts, discussions with the local government—that spread in the public sphere. Angry residents ramped up the affective intensity, formed a visceral public, and broadcast local concerns through mediated artifacts and nosewitness accounts that circulated in a variety of places, including Los Angeles newspapers, news reports on radio and television outlets, and social media. Resisting the stale air of exceptional public subjects' inaction, residents' actions created a civic osmocosm, one attuned to olfactory persuasion, environmental harms, and civic responsibility. Inspired by olfactory suasion, government officials sued Tran based on an anticipatory nuisance clause in the factory's original permitting process, which temporarily shut down the facility during the peak pepper-grinding period in October.[1] Viral circulation of olfactory persuasion in online rhetorical ecologies put the Sriracha sauce factory air pollution controversy in national news headlines throughout the US and the globe.

The regional context and history of socioenvironmental injustices that inform the case (e.g., heuristic "Context" and "Emplacement") matter, and I will contextualize that shortly. First, interrogating Western approaches to environmental contamination controversies tied to water, though they apply equally to air, Jordynn Jack refers to "water-as-resource," "water-as-chemical-entity," and "water-as-lifeblood" from three different ontological frames of reference (329–36). Water/air-as-resources highlight how people understand safe, potable water and air quality from settler-colonial perspectives grounded in landownership that elide human responsibility toward bodies of water and

---

1. The permitting clause in Irwindale municipal code is tied to Huy Fong's agreement to operate the facility, which specifies that Huy Fong must "reduce the potential for odors." Perceived violation of that clause resulted in the lawsuit.

sky. Water/air-as-chemical-entities privilege the scientific expertise of technicians who test water/air quality in laboratory spaces to determine relative purity and safety for consumption by entities that rely on both for survival. Water/air-as-lifeblood pertains to Indigenous perspectives that consider water and sky as relations demanding care and relational reciprocity in a constellation of relations, which involves a more holistic, intergenerational sense of care for environmental matters that transcend limited human and nonhuman lifetimes. Drawing upon Jordynn Jack's explication of water/air ontologies and how different approaches to valuing water/air shift notions of expertise, I characterize air-as-resource, air-as-chemical-entity, and air-as-lifeblood as ontological frames affecting how people characterize and narrate air pollution in Irwindale (e.g., heuristic "Narrative" and "Embodiment"). Importantly, air-as-lifeblood challenges the dominant paradigm of quantitative approaches to air-as-chemical-entity and air-as-resource prevalent in Western models of risk assessment and works toward environmental justice because air and elements suspended in it circulate everywhere in the planetary lungscape.

Regional History of Environmental Injustice

The Sriracha sauce factory in Irwindale, California, is in a mixed residential and industrial setting in the Greater Los Angeles area (see fig. 2). The factory's emplacement (sociohistorical context), odor, and inadequate pollution controls coalesced to expose more complex relational, intersectional, and legal ruptures. The relational and intersectional ruptures resulted, in part, from the history of environmental injustice in the San Gabriel Valley, where Irwindale is located.[2] The region has an abysmal record of industrial pollution and corporate malfeasance that exposes less-affluent people in the Greater Los Angeles area to toxins in the surrounding air and water. The necropolitical landscape creates a zone of existence for a form of "living dead," people who desire sovereignty over their own bodies and embodied inhalations but have little (Mbembe 40).[3] Necropolitics is a sociopolitical framework used to examine how people live and die based upon power structures that dictate the conditions of their existence. Dire conditions confer entire groups to a

---

2. The San Gabriel Valley encompasses forty-seven working-class neighborhoods in a 284 square-mile radius. The 1.4 million residents are of mixed ethnicities. Latine represent approximately 45%, Black 2.5%, Asian 26%, white 25%, and the category of "other" 2% (US Census Bureau, "Irwindale"). Irwindale is the least diverse of the neighborhoods, with 92% Latine.

3. Achille Mbembe defines "necropolitics" as the "subjugation of life to the power of death" (39).

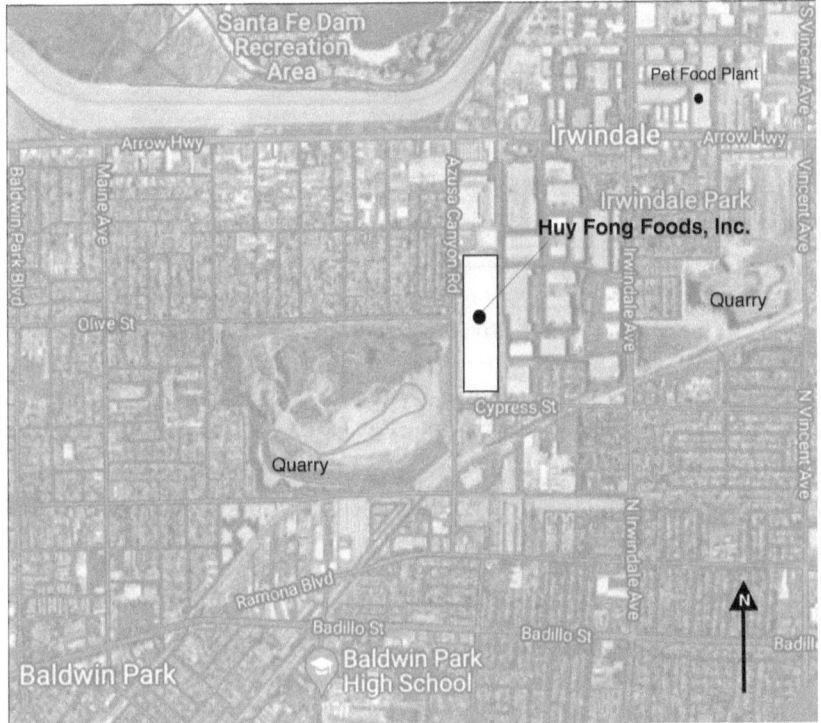

FIGURE 2. Map of Irwindale, California, featuring the location of Huy Fong Foods in an industrial park adjacent to two quarries, a pet food plant, and residential neighborhoods. Image credit: Lisa L. Phillips.

status Achille Mbembe labels the living dead, and while the Irwindale scene may not on the surface appear as stark as those Mbembe references (e.g., the Holocaust, Palestine, South African apartheid, the Kosovo war), "slow violence," gang violence, and police brutality reveal a different sort of "deathworld" still steeped in structural oppression (Nixon 2; Mbembe 40).

Intersectional and relational ruptures of a living dead are tied to complex interactions among class, race, ethnicity, languaged identities, immigration, foodway politics, and settler-colonial frameworks that reinforce cultural and other divisions. The legal ruptures resulted from the difficulty of using legal language and machine-sensing systems to characterize and address the elemental effects of pungent odors on human mental and physical health.

In 1979 the EPA placed Irwindale and forty-six neighboring communities on the San Gabriel Valley Superfund site due to high levels of groundwater contamination found in area wells (US EPA, "Pacific"). Historical and living dead understandings of how environmental racism, classism, and sexism determine which communities receive better, or any, cleanup shape residents' attitudes and health outcomes. Ethnically the least diverse of the San Gabriel region, Irwindale's small residential community of about 1,500 people is 92% Latine and occupies approximately 1% of the incorporated municipality's landscape. Industrial facilities dominate the other 99% (City of Irwindale, "2008 General Plan" 24). Despite the urban sprawl that surrounds Irwindale, it is one of the few places in the Greater Los Angeles region with space to build large-scale manufacturing plants because the area's former sand and gravel pits were remediated (cleaned up), smoothed out, forested, or commercially developed as part of the Superfund initiatives during President Reagan's era (1981–89).[4] Though Irwindale's political profile is small-town-like in nature—everyone knows the mayor, the city council members, and the local ne'er-do-wells—the municipality exerts significant influence on policy decisions that impact local (though globally influential) businesses and thousands of employees. (See Hernández-López for a more complete discussion of the historical and political context.)

Atmospheric Elements and Odor Surveillance

Sriracha sauce production generates about $60 million annually for the family-owned business. Tran, a Vietnamese refugee of Chinese descent and US immigrant, started the company in the mid-1980s in a different Los Angeles neighborhood and built the 650,000-square-foot facility in the middle of Irwindale in 2010. An increase in formal odor complaints registered at Irwindale city council and mayor offices is consistent with a 40% increase in Sriracha sauce production over a two-year time span (Ferdman).

As odor complaints increased at city hall—civic osmocosm's central depot—Irwindale hired Soil, Water, Air Protection Enterprise (SWAPE) to test air quality at the plant on the city's behalf, which is an example of a tactic I identified using the heuristic. While Irwindale officials believed residents' composite olfactory rhetoric, they juxtaposed their belief with scientific, technical, and legal epistemologies in response to the odor problem. This is a common ontological move that privileges technical expertise, machine sensing, and Western approaches to science. Segregating composite sensations and ignoring the complexity of circulating shared airspace bypass human

---

4. Ronald Reagan was a California governor before he became the fortieth US president, which influenced how, where, and when Superfund monies were initially distributed. President Jimmy Carter's administration brought greater attention to environmental issues, which inspired the creation of the Superfund Act and its origin story.

experiences, but the US judicial system privileges an air-as-chemical-entity model.

Elements are small, abstract things or essential characters, members of a set. As chemicals, they refuse further simplification and are distinguished by atomic number—the number of protons in a given nuclei. On an interdependent scale, people, nonhumans, and odorants all wind together as different elements in a scene. To feel the atmosphere on one's skin, its wrath, its calm, its nip on one's nape, is to be out in the elements. A different sort of element transmogrifies electric current through wire, resulting in sensible heat. Elements carry stories. Atmospheric elements include clouds, gases, and odor molecules—air-as-chemical-entity.

After processing SWAPE's air-as-chemical-entity evidence in mid-October, the city of Irwindale sent a notice of violation to Tran and officially declared the Sriracha sauce factory's odor a public nuisance. Layering another aspect of air-as-chemical-entity, government-based South Coast Air Quality Management "odor surveillance" officials also tested the air. Officials concluded odors emanating from the plant presented a nuisance because capsaicin—the chemical element responsible for the "hot" sensation associated with a variety of spicy peppers—can cause pervasive odor-related headaches, burning eyes, sore throats, inflamed asthma, skin rashes, and nosebleeds (Atwood qtd. in Becerra and Shyong). In an air-as-lifeblood move, one Irwindale resident noted the sensation felt "a little like pepper spray," both suggesting an attack on residents' ability to breathe freely and implying a form of known and policed brutalities loosed in the scentscape (Bracamontes qtd. in Shyong et al., "Some"; Solar News Group). Though no Irwindale resident was likely to die immediately from exposure to the factory's pungent emissions issue, contact with airborne capsaicin does tap into an elemental fear of death most people possess. Whenever one experiences something that burns the eyes, skin, and nose, it will trigger a fight-or-flight response in the limbic system. Stress responses of this nature have cumulative a/effects.

Residents' official complaints (sixty-one across approximately twenty households) did not reflect all community outcry circulating in the civic osmocosm, according to Mayor Mark Breceda, but enough residents were willing to face Tran's legal team and the corporation's economic advantages (A. Cohen). In this example, air-as-lifeblood and air-as-resource took precedence among the community members and some city government officials, but air-as-chemical-entity provided quantifiable proof to inform mitigation initiatives.

Presiding judge Robert H. O'Brien initially denied the city's request to shutter the plant during peak chili-grinding season. The ruling centered air-as-resource in the necropolitical lungscape. O'Brien privileged the economic costs to both Tran and Huy Fong employees over the health concerns of a smaller number of residents who likely viewed air-as-lifeblood. After the grinding season ended in November, O'Brien ordered Huy Fong to shut down operations and install more effective filtration methods to address the nuisance (Pasadena Star-News). O'Brien set a trial date for the following year (November 2014) to hear plaintiffs' and defendants' full legal arguments. Residents' reports and quantitative methods using e-nose technologies were both to count as evidence.

Irwindale councilpersons eventually voted to drop the lawsuit in May 2014. City council member H. Manuel Ortiz recused himself from the vote due, in part, to his family's proximity to the facility, which ironically constitutes a form of expertise and credibility rather than bias. Ortiz's initial move to pursue the complaint against Huy Fong Foods was framed as a political act rather than one designed to improve public health. Fanned by Tran's public relations team, residents' critiques related to job security hit the airwaves, and then Ortiz's stance shifted to one of recusal, though not acquiescence. This is an old necropolitical tale wherein the politics of economic interests, race, and racism connect to the politics of death and capitalistic enterprise (Arendt 418). Nonetheless, Ortiz's participation in the civic osmocosm contributed to the generally positive outcome. Tran installed better filters in June 2014 and opened the factory for tours for both public relations reasons and tourism-based profit.

Emplaced and Embodied Events, Phronesis, and Foodways

While it is unusual for majority minoritized communities to meet with success when challenging a large corporation and the economic privileges the organizations have, such successes are built upon the elemental memories of emplaced, embodied harms and hard-won phronesis (practical wisdom). David Tran wields considerable economic power and culinary influence. The city of Irwindale and its people also wield unusual power in an industrial setting because a small municipality can curtail an offensive odor using permit laws to enforce air quality. This is linked to the community's exposure to a pet food plant and a massive Miller brewing facility that have been nuisances for years. Both are matters of public memory and "subjectivities cultivated" by sensation and through generative "vernacular discourse" throughout Irwindale (Rice 20).

Some Irwindale business leaders downplayed persistent nuisance issues for political and economic reasons and used olfactory rhetoric to do so. For example, Lisa Bailey, president of the Irwindale Chamber of Commerce at the time, quipped of the brewery's odor, "Most people don't consider that a bad odor. It's like, 'Oh, beer!'" (Shyong et al., "Some"). The Miller brewing facility is enormous, and the fermentation process smells more like vinegar and rotting vegetables than the finished product does. Strategically, Bailey did not discuss the pet food plant, Breeder's Choice. Rendering facilities that generate pet food reek of dead bodies, bones, and blood, giving air-as-lifeblood a vivid visceral meaning. Because the pet food plant, brewery, and Sriracha sauce factory converge within the same lungscape and come from three different compass points, residents face cumulative burdens. While an individual facility may pose an odor risk one day when the wind direction is unfavorable, a facility in the other direction will not, and vice versa. Public health expert Jill Johnson points out how this "cumulative burden" significantly amplifies negative health effects (qtd. in Barajas).

Tensions also emerge between perceptions of what constitutes a public nuisance and an individual's personal smellscape. Smells are enmeshed in memories and bodies. The public/personal impact is doubly configured through economic and other systemic structural pressures and privileges that influence people's perceptions of what a nuisance amounts to and what one can or must accept by economic necessity or by sensory design. By sensory design, consider how or what one can physically perceive in terms of an individual's sensory ecology. A person with anosmia, for example, would not sense the odor of either the pet food plant or the brewery, but they would experience the effects of capsaicin on their eyes and the effects of harmful chemicals and slow violences on their bodies more generally (Moteki 89–90; see Nixon for elaboration on slow violences).

Bailey toured the Sriracha sauce factory during chili-processing season, noting a lack of adverse reaction while in the factory itself: "[I've had] no burning eyes, no throat constriction, and I've [experienced] that while cooking chiles at home" (Shyong et al., "Some"). Bailey's olfactory rhetoric expresses how capsaicin exposure feels and smells, yet she claims to not have felt affected at the factory, which may suggest excellent indoor air removal and circulation that could travel outdoors if it were simply vented outside without appropriate filtration. Journalists confirm this was likely happening ("Some"). Sergio Garcia, a factory worker interviewed during the same tour, said he goes maskless and works in unfiltered factory air. Commenting on the indoor air quality, Garcia shrugged, "It's not so bad. You get used to it" (qtd. in "Some"). Garcia's olfactory rhetoric both indicates the odor's presence and suggests sensory extinction ensued or simply acknowledges a living dead's desire to keep his job, which affected how he spoke to reporters about the odor. In broad terms, the Sriracha sauce controversy in Irwindale demonstrates the warring language about whether (or in what manner) odor nuisance matters and whether there are ways to manage its impact on human health within a court of law.

The case also exemplifies a complex site of "law-and-foodways" that underscores how "a chili-based [odor] controversy reflects a racialized exclusion despite the application of race-neutral laws and no expressed racist animus" (Hernández-López 197). *Foodways, foodscapes,* and *foodway politics* are three terms that I will define, as they support the analysis of the case and controversy.

In anthropological and social-science circles, foodways refer to the sociocultural, political, historical, and economic practices tied to the production and consumption of food—our eating and culinary habits. Charlotte Sunseri is an anthropologist who researches intersections among ethnic and class-based identity constructions in relation to community cohesion or tension in communities like Irwindale. Sunseri describes foodways "as culturally constructed aspects of materiality related to meal selection, preparation, consumption, and disposal" that are embedded in "daily practices structured by habitus" (419). *Habitus* here refers to how a person's or a group's background (language, culture, class, gender, race, ethnicity, geographical location, etc.) informs how an individual or group perceives and reacts to the world based on said background and associated embodiment(s).

In terms of emplacement (where people live), a foodway is also enmeshed in a "foodscape," which I liken to a landscape, smellscape, or soundscape, though a different sense perception (gustation) is connoted (Sunseri 419). Sociologists extended *foodscape*'s meaning to include the "institutional arrangements, cultural spaces, and discourses that mediate our relationship with our food" (Mackendrick 16). Foodscapes in human relationships illustrate how food can invoke or evoke "rank and rivalry, solidarity and community, identity or exclusion, and intimacy or distance" (Appadurai 494). Foodscapes possess political implications too.

Foodway politics combines a group's sociocultural culinary habits with political views that are enmeshed in divergent power relations. Laws that prohibit certain kinds of food distribution, production, or consumption have been tied to foodways and racialized and/or ethnicized foodway politics.[5]

---

5. The Great Potato Famine for Irish immigrants, the influence of Italian foodways on American cuisines, and the use of the word *Krauts* to demean German immigrants are other examples.

Specific to the Sriracha sauce controversy, there were two foodways placed in conflict—the Latine foodway (heavily influenced by Mexican traditions in Irwindale) and Tran's foodway, representing a cultural fusion of Vietnamese, Thai, and Chinese foodways. Because both foodways rely on chilis for flavor and the Sriracha sauce controversy pivoted on the odor of the processed chilis, conflicting foodway politics tied to immigration and changing demographics in the United States are enmeshed in the lawsuit. Although these politics are not explicit in the court documents, a RISE approach results in a close reading of the court documents toward an analysis that includes a more holistic sensibility that, in turn, enables one to distinguish elisions (e.g., foodway politics in the Sriracha sauce controversy).

Across the street to the northwest of the Sriracha sauce factory is the city of Baldwin Park, California. Unlike Irwindale, which is 1% residential, Baldwin Park is about 50% residential and has about 75,000 residents (US Census Bureau, "Baldwin Park"). The population is 19% Asian, 39% white, and 72% Latine (the number does not equal 100% due to people listing multiple identity categories; "Baldwin"). The Asian population in the Baldwin Park neighborhood is greater in both percentage and number than in Irwindale. The average household income is higher; there are equal numbers of men- and women-identifying residents, more have health insurance, and so on. While prevailing wind patterns might make the factory odors drift to Irwindale more routinely, that would not always be the case. Santa Ana winds, for example, would likely drift to Baldwin Park. So, why did those residents not become a visceral public? Media reports contain a counternarrative indicative of foodway politics, hastening one to ask, "Is it the 'same' smell if people bring such different sensibilities to [an] encounter?" (Tsing 62). Notable is the distinction and inherent tension between a public nuisance problem and personal accounts of odor preferences that discount or interpret another individual's or community's odor nuisance problem as nonexistent or a pleasant feature of the smellscape (Poudyal and Rai). Gustatory and other sensory experiences help define and shape one's worldview and perceptions of what one prefers or finds a nuisance.

When the odor issue first garnered journalists' notice, reporters for the *Los Angeles Times* visited the surrounding area and interviewed Young Ja Whang, an Asian store owner who works just across the street from the factory on the Baldwin Park side. Whang worked from 8 a.m. to 8 p.m. most days and left the store's front door open to allow "the scent of freshly ground chiles to waft into the store," finding the odor pleasant. Whang remarked, "I'm an old lady and I have no problem with it. Actually, we like it!" (qtd. in Shyong et al., "Some"). At least two things are at work in Whang's assessment. First, Whang's age (sixty-eight in 2013) suggests that her olfactive sense may be less acute, a matter of human biology and time's effects. Olfactive acuity can change over time and with the influx of different stimuli (Tsing 60–62). Foodway politics and smellscape preferences are also at play, which necessitates translation of "cultural assemblages," or how different cultural pathways intermingle (88). Whang is likely to have sociocultural connections to sauces in the style of Sriracha, so her liking the smell could be based on her familiarity with it and pleasant memories. The "we" in her commentary likely refers to her spouse and co-owner. It could also refer to a more royal "we," as in other Asian community members, neighbors, or family, indicating a sense of community with a similar olfactive association, though it is a complex and indeterminant assemblage. The reporting shows how foodway politics can shape perceptions of a scent event in direct relation to embodied, inherently cultural ways of being and knowing.

Another Baldwin Park resident, sixty-four-year-old Thomas Serrato, used foodway references to identify the Sriracha sauce factory's emissions too, and Serrato's foodway differs in origin from Whang's. The experiential conclusion is similar, however. Serrato said the factory smelled like "someone cooking chorizo," which is pork sausage that has origins in Mexico in this context. The sausage is seasoned with dried, smoked red choricero peppers and other spices.[6] Serrato did not give a clear sense of whether the odor was offensive or pleasant but simply relayed personal experiences to reporters.

Irwindale residents were not all in agreement that there was an odor problem, either, which is indicative of tensions between individual smellscape preferences and public nuisance claims. Kathy Galaz, a sixty-six-year-old Latine woman, told reporters that she uses chilis to make "a spicy brand of salsa that makes her sister sneeze and cough," but neither her sister nor she was bothered by factory odors. This suggests that they could indeed smell it but did not take issue with it, which also discloses how individualized and visceral publics' perceptions of a smellscape can differ based on a variety of inputs like cultural context, olfactory sensitivity, proximity to the odor source, and duration of exposure. Moreover, the reporters on the scene do not appear to have interviewed younger area residents who may have more robust olfaction than their older neighbors. It may be that the interviews took place during the

---

6. There are several types of chorizo sausage. It appears to have a Catalonia origin. Spanish-style chorizo is usually smoked and is more salami-like. It is seasoned with garlic and pimentón (smoked paprika that can be hot or sweet). Mexican chorizo consists of fresh ground pork sausage spiced with hot chilis and can include vinegar. The two are not interchangeable in culinary terms (Kellogg and Acker; Morgan).

day, when retirees or store owners were available and when other workers and children would have had other commitments, preventing them from being represented in the reporters' efforts. The court documents, however, reflect a wider array of people and narratives than people interviewed by reporters, as the documents reflect parents, full-time workers, city officials, industrialists, and air quality monitoring entities.

Specific to the court documents, in the next sections, using a RISE approach enables one to probe (1) how the plaintiffs' actions were sensationally enmeshed with nonhuman agents and agency, injury claims, and food politics; (2) how one can evaluate residents' (the plaintiffs') declarative testimonies to examine the importance of proximate odor experience to human health, enjoyment of property, and class-and-race-stratified ideologies; (3) how Huy Fong's legal team and executives (the defendants) denied the importance of olfaction to human health; and (4) how one may evaluate ramifications of not having laws in place to manage olfactory perception in medical/health issues that may have led to Judge O'Brien's language in the written preliminary injunction.

Plaintiff Actions, Nonhuman–Human Enmeshments, Injury Claims, and Food Politics

The plaintiffs filing the lawsuit consisted of both the "People" and Irwindale, "a municipal corporation" abbreviated as "City" in the original court filing. The plaintiffs wanted relief from the Sriracha sauce factory's pepper-laden emissions that residents claimed burned their eyes and noses and gave them headaches, nosebleeds, and sinus-related earaches. In the opening paragraph of the complaint document, plaintiffs asserted that the Sriracha sauce factory "[constituted] a public nuisance due to the emanation of odors and irritants from the property," and the plaintiffs contended that the emissions "[were] causing physical harm and discomfort to the people of the City of Irwindale" (People ex rel. 1). To illustrate residents' narratives, Sofia Tapia noted experiences that include "severe coughing, choking sensation, and burning throat and eyes as if [she] had come into contact with . . . pepper spray" (qtd. in People ex rel. 6). Yolanda Priscilla Zepeda relayed that her asthmatic son would "severely cough when he comes into contact with the vapors" (qtd. in People ex rel. 6). Manuel Ortiz protested, "When I breathe in the fumes I feel as though I am choking, and I immediately begin to gag" (qtd. in People ex rel. 6). Arthur Tapia explained, "Although you can smell the chilies, it is the fumes that affect me" (qtd. in People ex rel. 7).

Reading plaintiffs' assertions as examples of what Rice names "injury claims" informs the "very substance through which publics come to be formed" (72). Injury claim discourse "enables people both to participate and to write themselves out of participation" when they contend with environmental damage and pro- or anti-business sentiments at work in a community (72). Injury claims "produce a collaborative site that guides our orientation to other people and to the world" (82). The plaintiffs' choice to connect public nuisance, capsaicin, and odor to embodied harm and medical/health risks links nonhuman and human enmeshments in the Sriracha sauce controversy. Nonhuman enmeshments here refer, in part, to how naturally occurring substances like capsaicin, a chemical irritant and neurotoxin, and other organic materials migrate easily across bodily boundaries. Jalapeño-based capsaicin is the key nonhuman agent in this case, as are other natural ingredients used in Sriracha sauce, like garlic. The plant growth, agricultural production cycle, and geographic locale of the ingredients are also part of the complex enmeshment between human and nonhuman elements of the case. Part of the reason Tran built the factory in Irwindale is due to its relative proximity to jalapeño- and garlic-producing regions, which thrive in the warm, dry climate of Southern California.

The Sriracha sauce controversy demonstrates racialized foodway politics—sociocultural culinary habits imbued with political views enmeshed in divergent power relations—because the Latine community and the Chinese/Vietnamese (Asian) community that Tran represents are at odds. There has been an influx of Asian immigration to some parts of Los Angeles, and some of the immigrants are very wealthy Chinese businesspeople who invest in American real estate because of China's restrictions on land and property ownership and indeterminate political stability (Sheehan). The investments have driven up prices of homes and land in Los Angeles and elsewhere in Southern California, which makes it more difficult for local Latine residents to purchase a home. In addition, Asians (as a whole) have recently passed Latines "as the largest group of new immigrants to the United States," and the new arrivals are "the most highly educated cohort of immigrants in US history" (Pew Research Center).[7] Asians are often problematically seen as the "model minority," and one fallout of that categorization is the insidious implication that Latines are not (Wu). The Sriracha sauce controversy is a manifestation

---

7. In the 2013 Pew research article, "Asian" refers to the six largest Asian American immigrant subgroups, which include Chinese, Filipino, Indian, Vietnamese, Korean, and Japanese. The information is based on 2010 US Census Bureau statistics. While this does not account for all nuance in the classification and categorization of different groups of people, it does provide insight into changing population demographics.

of racial and ethnic tensions between the two communities and beyond, and conflicting foodways provided a flashpoint. I am not alone in that perception. In "Sriracha Shutdown: Hot Sauce Lessons on Local Privilege and Race," Ernesto Hernández-López writes:

> This law-and-food conflict is an outgrowth of economic and demographic changes in suburban Los Angeles, [and the factory's location in a Latine burg shows how] the influence of municipal legal powers unveils race's role in . . . the area's local politics perpetually shaped by race and migration. (194–95)

Here, Hernández-López's interpretation of the Sriracha sauce controversy focuses on the relations between a powerful local Latine electorate, which he believes is trying to exclude a new immigrant group represented by Tran—Chinese, Vietnamese, and other peoples with Southeast Asian heritage. As I interpret Hernández-López's argument, the majority-Latine city council of Irwindale used municipal law to pester Tran to install more effective filters, yet they have not made similar moves to curtail odors from the adjacent pet food plant or brewery, which may smell worse on any given day. Maybe the city council learned to put in place stricter permit and nuisance laws based on prior odor experiences with the brewery and pet food plants, or maybe Hernández-López is correct and the majority Latine council is prejudiced against Tran's racial and ethnic background and the odors his foodway produces. Nevertheless, Tran was sued and sued again in 2016 for failing to pay city fees.

Another part of the Sriracha sauce controversy's complexity is bound to Mexican Americans' and Asian Americans' uses of chilis in particular. Transnational feminists and food justice scholars Bibhushana Poudyal and Mala Rai in "The Smell of the Other and Self-Alienation" address the "vicious relationship between rhetorical conditions and material conditions" that force people to "self-alienate" from foodways that connect them to their homes, communities, and backgrounds (73). Poudyal and Rai explain how and why food is "ab/used" to identify people based upon race and ethnicity (74). "The Others are not only othered by their food, but forced into self-othering" based on foodway aromas. Poudyal writes, "After I came to the United States [from Nepal], it did not take too long for me to realize that we [Asians] are not supposed to enjoy our cuisine without fearing its smell" (79). Discussing her Mexican American landlord's response to the aroma of food cooking in the apartment, Poudyal notes that the person made a "Whew! sound," which made Poudyal both angry and ashamed (77). That feeling of self-alienation lingered in the air and "haunted" with its "specter" of sound, as it marked for Poudyal a transition from "privilege" to becoming a "curry-reeking" Asian Other in the Mexican American's apartment complex (77–79).

Poudyal and Rai inspired me to consider how different foodways use and process chilis and whether there were associated in- and out-group intersectional connotations that overlapped with or informed cultural, ethnic, racialized, or otherwise excluded and/or marginalized concerns in the Sriracha sauce controversy. For example, classic Mexican (Oaxacan) mole poblano sauce—a dark reddish-brown sauce made from chili peppers and chocolate (usually) along with a host of other spices—is a dry-spice-based sauce that takes a lot of time and labor to prepare and is traditionally cooked slowly in a large clay pot as part of a celebratory meal ("Holy"; Timbrell). It may not be "spicy hot," as the types of chilis used in the sauce vary, and in my experience, it has a sweet aroma. This kind of chili sauce smells a *lot* different from a fermented sauce like Sriracha. Huy Fong's Sriracha sauce is a wet-based-paste sauce consisting of ground fresh chilis, garlic, vinegar, sugar, and salt that ferments in a barrel until it is bottled, shipped, and sold. The Mexican mole tradition is usually passed down from mother to daughter over generations (Timbrell). Sriracha sauce recipes also tend to be passed down among families, though it is more patrilineal ("How").

The ethnic/racial/odored and foodway identities of the defendants and plaintiffs in the Sriracha sauce factory lawsuit were essentially obscured in the court documents. Consequently, the omission becomes a matter for interpretation relationally bound to intersectional ecofeminism. That is, it is important to think across borders and bodies to evaluate how chilis are used in the Sriracha sauce factory, how they are grown in the field, and how they are collected and processed in the Latine community of Irwindale because the context likely informs why the lawsuit unfolded as it did.

For example, in each of the excerpted declarations of residents, the defendant's attorney, John R. Tate, routinely underscored the words *believe* or *belief* to devalue the residents' experiential knowledge as "hearsay," writing as grounds for objection that "no facts are provided establishing the witnesses' personal knowledge of the source of the odor" (People ex rel., "Supplemental" 2). Eyewitnessing has been granted more value than "eare wytnessing" since at least 1539, but "nosesay" is a more fitting rhetorical choice than hearsay or eyewitness testimony ("Eyewitness"). Hearsay suggests rumors, gossip, idle chatter, and a lack of immediacy and is rhetorically suspect ("Hearsay"). Olfaction's a/effect is immediate. Instead, Tate relegated residents' nosesay as "objectionable and inadmissible," privileging a one-off inspection as "expert" testimonial, which is a common move of rhetorical exclusion because "scientific and technical" arguments count and "social, political, and emotional arguments" do not (Endres 47; Collins and Evans).

Nosesay, like its parent olfaction, will have liminal qualities within an existing Western sensory hierarchy. However, due to the immediacy of olfaction's effects, nosesay more accurately characterizes residents' accounts of their experiential knowledge. People translate what the nose knows and say what they experience in a smellscape. To have a nose for something suggests a talent for detecting something (e.g., someone has a nose for fine perfume, or a nose for trouble, or a nose for news). The word *nosesay* could also play upon the unfortunate assumption that most people neither understand nor value olfaction's impact on one's overall health, though the dismissible connotation of hearsay does not work in the same way as nosesay. Nosesay has more credibility because no synaptic delay occurs with olfaction, and synaptic delay does occur with aurality. Concomitantly, the term *nosesay* could cause people to double down on their own and others' perceptions and experiences of scent events because they reject being dismissed. Hearsay also signifies an inaccurate sensory referent in the Sriracha case. To be an eyewitness carries more rhetorical weight due to dominant sensory hierarchies in Western cultures, but the word also signifies an inaccurate referent, depending on the situation under scrutiny. Thus, nosesay provides a different sensory-rhetorical perspective to think about when addressing different sensescapes and visceral publics affected by environmental hazards. Moreover, nosesay may be deployed in public debate and contribute to indecorous, yet affective, speech about environmental problems. Much public commentary pertaining to noxious odorscapes refers to open-wound "shitscapes" and those who feel shat upon though olfactory assault. The fecal focus of indecorous speech dwells within what Joshua Gunn names a "coprophilic style of public address" deployed to contend with all that stinks in environmental injustice driven by capitalism (82).

Environmental communication scholars Kathleen Hunt, Nicholas Paliewicz, and Danielle Endres examine how public participation "can become sites of radical politics when publics employ . . . indecorous voice" (65). While the scholars are concerned primarily with public hearings and information sessions designed to placate rather than redress community concerns about environmental problems, legal cases also offer visceral publics "unique rhetorical [opportunities] to bear witness and have 'rhetorical consequence'" (66). Indecorum in public hearings includes yelling, clapping, "openly defying rules," and expletives (66). Indecorum in an open court session could involve the same things. Being in contempt of the court, however, can result in legal and financial sanctions that go beyond rhetorical exclusion. One could argue that the plaintiffs' nosesay narratives deploy aspects of indecorous voice in writing to make a larger point that "contribute[s] to solidarity and community" and invoke scent "events that garner[ed] media attention" (66). Unlike a public information hearing, where indecorous voices are excluded from the official meeting transcripts, the visceral public's responses are included in the court documentation.

Rhetorical Disembodiment

The defendant's "motion to strike"—the court document that negated the plaintiffs' "supplemental materials" based in "lay witnessing" or nosesay—rhetorically disembodies the plaintiffs. After an initial rundown of all declarants' (key plaintiffs') Latine names, Tate's legal rhetoric negates their human existence by referencing only the "City" and "its bid for a temporary restraining order against Huy Fong" (People ex rel., "Motion" 1). The two-page double-spaced legal brief deploys the words "it," "its," and "City" no less than twenty-five times in the "motions to strike additional evidence" (1–2). RISE helps us understand how the word *it* is used as neuter nominative rhetoric that promotes a disappearance and/or dehumanization/animalization of the declarants' actual bodies from the site proposed for "immediate injunctive relief" of human suffering.[8] The rhetorical construction of "City" as a unified "it" helps Tate-as-rhetor disavow "respiratory complaints," for a "City-as-it" is not *ordinarily* imagined as capable of breath unless people understand a city as relationally bound to Life on Earth, which, of course, a RISE perspective absolutely avows. Tate's approach would have looked much different if it considered Indigenous ontological perspectives featuring air-as-lifeblood.

As a reminder from chapter 1, I draw upon Indigenous concepts of relationality, reciprocity, and kincentric thinking when regarding Life on Earth in a holistic sense (Itchuaqiyaq, "Iñupiat" and "When"; Kimmerer; LaDuke; Wildcat). Relationality, reciprocity, and kincentric thinking highlight our interdependent enmeshments with other life forms and Earth's vibrant materiality that includes the built environments of a cityscape. Tate's legally binding argumentative strategies illustrate the unethical impact of eliding embodied experiences and the process of emplacement that informs those embodied experiences. I also noted in the introduction how relationality and emplacement become embedded in how people evaluate their senses of belonging in

---

8. *It* is from the Old English *hit* (the *h* dropped with lack of spoken emphasis). In Middle English, *it* meant a thing or animal instead of the original use that was a masculine pronoun.

or alienation from a given setting based upon what they sense at circulation within it. Residents of Irwindale used olfactory persuasion to force mitigation efforts because their sensory experiences alienated them from the Sriracha sauce factory and, by extension, David Tran.

Judicial Response to Plaintiffs' Prayers

On November 26, 2013, Los Angeles Superior Court Judge Robert O'Brien ordered the plant to "immediately make changes to address odors or the potential for odors" pursuant to the complaint but declined the plaintiffs' suit to close the plant. The olfactory rhetoric in the judge's decision-making language is compelling, and he rejects both the defendants' "objections to the declarations" and the "motion to strike additional evidence." O'Brien enjoins:

> Although some of the [plaintiffs'] declarations contain argument and superfluous matters that the Court ignores, there is sufficient firsthand factual data requiring consideration. . . . The Court finds that the . . . initial Facility Permit requires Respondent [the Defendant] to "reduce the potential for odors" if strong odors are verified off-site. . . . The odor complaints presented to the Court are reasonably inferred to be emanating from the facility. . . . Notwithstanding a lack of credible evidence linking the complained about health problems as being caused by the odors or emissions, the odors . . . [warrant] consideration as a public nuisance. . . . The Court determines that Petitioners [the plaintiffs] are likely to prevail on their cause of action for public nuisance and irreparable harm. . . . Respondent is to immediately make changes to its site operations reducing odors and the potential for odors. (People ex rel., "Order" 1–2)

As interpreted through a RISE approach, O'Brien appears to consider "personal knowledge" or nosesay as "firsthand factual data" in supporting the idea that embodied experiences of the factory's odors and emissions do "appear as extremely annoying, irritating, and offensive to the senses warranting consideration as a public nuisance" (People ex rel., "Order" 2). Although O'Brien's language aligns with the idea that the senses provide factual raw data, the language used in his preliminary injunction also demonstrates relational ruptures between what is sensed by a human as a "nuisance" in an emplaced environment and what that implies for health: "superfluous matters" in the judicial purview vis-à-vis olfaction and actual health risk. That is, a public nuisance warrants action, yet olfaction seems to fall short on the medical risk scale, as the ruling was made after chili processing stopped. By acknowledging the emergence of "firsthand factual data" as evidence but "ignoring superfluous matters" (regarding the health impacts), the judge is employing selective perception that enables the dominant culture to ignore some bodily experiences while acknowledging others. Inundating the environment with hot sauce smog revealed corporate malfeasance, but the court did not halt pepper grinding. Instead, O'Brien ordered the plaintiffs to "prepare, serve and lodge the proposed preliminary injunction by noon on Dec. 4, 2013" (People ex rel., "Order" 1). By December, pepper- and garlic-processing season would have already been complete. Moreover, the judge set a November 2014 trial date to hear more detailed aspects of the case from both the plaintiffs and the defendants. This caused a run on Sriracha sauce due to fear of shortages, which boosted Tran's profits.

Reciprocal Relations and Building Community Connections

The Sriracha case suggests how reciprocal relationality and olfactory rhetoric may have led Tran to install better carbon filters, the city of Irwindale and its "People" to have private informal negotiations with Tran to keep the factory in Irwindale, and Tran to the decision of greater transparency, which now includes tours of the plant during peak pepper-processing season. The tours offer a way to shine the company's tarnished image, promote tourism, create profit, and perhaps quell local fire objects upon emergence (Nguyen). Rice discusses problems with public feeling and notes that "feeling too often serves as the primary connective tissue to our public spaces," and the "fallout from such feelingful relationality" can include "citizen nonparticipation" and attitudes of "exception" where people feel they are "unaffected by a scene of deliberation" (6). Olfactory persuasion sparked a visceral public's memory of past harms. Anticipatory permit language around odor nuisances addressed that memory, resulting in the opposite of nonparticipation. Tran became more open to community concerns and fixed the pollution issue. Residents sparked that action and helped to maintain a relationship that also kept jobs in the community. Although the reciprocal relationship between residents and Tran remains financially inequitable—Tran is a billionaire—it is also built upon their embodied interdependencies that necessarily rely on air-as-lifeblood over the long term.

Prior to the controversy, Tran kept the factory's interior and recipe a closely guarded secret. The factory's location and the sauce's dependence on extremely fresh peppers (four hours from pick to grind or the sauce is ruined) made relocation more complex than politicians realized, and the proximity by sea to Asian markets also made it easier for Tran to say yes to better filtration and the city to say "dismissed" to the "declarants." Since the controversy, the factory features regular tours and sells many novelty T-shirts and trinkets, and larger-than-life cardboard cutouts of Tran wearing the different T-shirts are placed throughout the factory's tourist zones. Visitors take selfies and post them when and wherever they please, with Tran's blessing.

Reflections on Emergent Phenomena and Sensational Enmeshments

In a more holistic sense, the Sriracha sauce example demonstrates how olfactory rhetorical ruptures may be used to identify, parse, and synthesize a specific, complex sociopolitical justice problem. Thus situated, olfactory rhetorical analysis becomes an important tool in a RISE toolbox because it offers a valuable analytic apparatus to help us understand how complex aspects of justice work in some settings. Nosewitnessing connected olfactory persuasion to perceivable deterioration in environmental conditions in the Sriracha sauce controversy, resulting in more effective air filtration and communicative openness. Key plaintiffs talked about Tran's new openness and stated that "they knew where to find him" if the odor problems surface again (Favot).

The Sriracha sauce case illustrates an approach to rhetorics of sensation as emergent phenomena that allows one to understand how and why some nondiscursive sensations may be more persuasive than others in rupturing environmental and/or social injustices. The Sriracha sauce controversy also shows how human and nonhuman agents and agency (sensational enmeshments and elements) are interdependent, relational, embodied, and unequal in power, which highlights our shared vulnerability as ingredients of Life on Earth. Building upon Rice's explanation of "injury claims" as "modes of production" that produce "an entry point into public discourse," the Sriracha sauce case demonstrates how olfactory rhetoric can be couched in legal writing that presents paradoxically as apolitical, persuasive, and yet somehow dismissible because the affiliated sense perception (olfaction) involved is deemed relatively unimportant, which makes ascertaining whether justice has been done complicated (83). That is, olfactory rhetoric used in the legal case both illustrates olfactory persuasion and showcases how people may look down their noses at olfactory persuasion because the sense perception and nosewitnessing language affiliated with it are devalued.

The Sriracha sauce case and other olfactory-rich examples exemplify how a RISE approach "avoids the pitfalls of generalization [as it enables one to] consider more deeply the constitutive roles of sensation in participatory, rhetorical acts" (Hawhee, "Rhetoric's" 13). The approach avoids pitfalls of generalization because applying the SCENT heuristic to understand how sensations like olfaction inform participatory rhetorical acts helps us identify, track, and determine whether a community's environmental concerns are addressed and if so, how, when, where, and why. Moreover, the approach and applied heuristic can help one evaluate when visceral publics meet with success and change policies in ways that promote positive public and environmental health outcomes.

Finally, the Sriracha sauce factory controversy underscores the effects of legislation on foodway politics at both state and municipal levels, which may help us better understand how to generate greater openness in communication and understanding between groups of people who may have conflicting needs and points of view. For example, when the air quality controversy first appeared in court and in the public eye, lax pollution legislation in Texas was strategically used as bait in an unsuccessful effort to lure Tran to relocate.

CHAPTER 3

Something Smells Fishy at the Salton Sea

> Consider the difference between an eyesore and a whiff of danger, both culturally informed judgements about matter out of place.... Smell has a history of warning of contamination linked to practices of self-preservation; its interiority, like that of taste, historically often a ground for authoritative truth-telling.
>
> —Joy Parr, "Smells Like?"

One day before the eleventh anniversary of 9/11, in September 2012, alarmed Los Angelinos' phone calls jammed emergency service lines throughout the city, constituting rapid escalation between the moment people sensed something wrong in the environment to vernacular narrative exchanges where people talked about the situation across a broad range of communities. Callers said the air stank of an unrecognizable putrescence. A visceral public affected by olfactory persuasion soon emerged and demanded to know the odor's cause and effects. People worried that the scent event of unknown origin was a harbinger of a chemical attack on the city. It was not. The odor's origin was more than 150 miles away and arose from an enormous fish kill that occurred within the Salton Sea (see fig. 3). An unusual wind pattern drove the stench north, and it lingered in the air for a couple of days. The odor was monolithic, enveloping a wide swath of Southern California in its ambit. Indio, California, resident Janis Dawson stressed, "The odor was extremely intense. We actually thought that somebody had an accident, a broken sewage main, that's how strong it was" (qtd. in Associated Press). Jose Chavez, a San Fernando resident, explained it this way: "My first thought was that maybe one of the eggs I bought was rotted.... The smell [lingered] so then I started to think it was me, so I changed my clothes. It was very pungent" (qtd. in Associated Press). Chavez informally quipped on social media, "The Valley is starting to smell like rotten eggs. In an unrelated note, Febreeze sales are through the roof"

FIGURE 3. Map of Salton Sea region in Southern California near the US border with Mexico. Top right framed image features a Salton Sea close-up. Los Angeles is approximately 170 miles (250 kilometers) northwest of the Salton Sea. Image credit: Lisa L. Phillips.

(Flaccus). Another person tweeted, "Did San Bernardino just lay a morning beer fart of biblical proportions?" (Avila). Jokes aside, a South Pasadena resident asked, "Does anyone else in #SouthPasadena smell an alarming sulfur-like smell in the air; like rotten eggs?" (Marquez). People were sensing and searching for answers.

Andrew Schlange, general manager of the Salton Sea Authority and Salton Sea local, contextualized the situation this way: "The problem I'm having is the magnitude of the area that was covered by the odor itself. . . . What happened gives us an opportunity to let people know that the Salton Sea is dying and that we need to fix it. . . . What we need is for the public to understand that this is likely to happen more often as time goes on, and we need their support to find a way to finance and pay for [Salton Sea mitigation efforts]"

("Salton Sea"). Schlange used olfactory rhetoric in coalition with a mediated visceral public who was contending with the unparalleled brute materiality of environmental deterioration. Procedural application of the SCENT heuristic in this chapter reveals how visceral publics worked to address an air quality issue. The scalar intensity of the odor spurred action. The California legislature in Sacramento took notice, which resulted in renewed mitigation efforts.

The case draws attention to a necropolitics in which life and death comingle in shared air. The zombified result confers upon the living dead a memento mori of a state-sponsored death-world for some relations, in this case, fish. Human water use throughout Southern California affects the Salton Sea's diminishing shoreline, inscribing the landscape as a contour in flux. The sea incorporates into that inscription the capacity for life support for an assortment of species. Temperature variations and urban and agricultural water usages shape embodied habits of algae that result in mass destruction of fish and birds. The complexity of international border relations and water rights makes the Salton Sea an ethical and political quagmire that makes accountability and sustainability difficult to ascertain and uphold. Such a case invites careful evaluation of how scent events work rhetorically, how they focus attention, and how visceral publics use them to address environmental damage. Applying stage 2 of the heuristic shows that messaging about the problem gained traction. Stage 3 application illustrates that community tactics elicited action and transformed outcomes. Finally, stage 4 application discloses that culturally informed broadcasted sensations transformed policy.

The 2012 nostril-stinging stench was a nondiscursive or extradiscursive call to action that forced people to consider water rights and environmental damage. Odors released en masse from alive-and-dead matter[1] in the Salton Sea exhibited a form of nonhuman agency that created a sensation and material a/effect in human social and political circles. The scent event made distant Los Angelinos and California legislators feel affected by "the scene of deliberation" at the Salton Sea in a way that disrupted the routine action of "exceptional public subjects" on this specific environmental issue (Rice 6). That is, ordinary people and people in positions of power who might otherwise ignore

---

1. The agency of alive-and-dead matter as I situate it here relies on scholarship from a range of disciplinary perspectives. Jane Bennett's *Vibrant Matter* delves into the subject of agency of material substances that are lively, though some are technically inert. For example, the ooze at the edge of a landfill may have heavy metals and other materials that impact life, and the ooze may also have bacteria in it from the landfill contents. Thus, the ooze is alive-and-dead at the same time. Karen Barad's work also pivots on the idea of nonhuman agents and agency as intra-actions among things. Diana Coole and Samantha Frost's edited collection *New Materialisms* also provides a foundation for my thinking about nonhuman agency or agentive potential in alive-and-dead matter.

the sea's deteriorating conditions could not remove themselves from the odor—"a heinous whiff of the future," as Matt Simon put it—which directed attention to the larger environmental problems at the sea. The natural world's agency disturbed urban social structures, provoking "ecophobia," a fear of natural disasters, wild creatures, and beyond embedded in a "disgust for the natural world" (Weidner 240). Dis-odor creates a form of nervous anxiety in humans accustomed to sanitized airwaves in "odor-denying" cultures like the United States (Howes, "On" 94). "Odor-accepting cultures" attend to changes in odorscapes and understand "smell as a basic arbiter of existence" such that the smell of death and life are distinct and impart a sense of one's place in the world (96–100). Disgusting odors cling to the frayed fabric of social life in environmental injustice zones. Constructing cities and suburbs to rid the world of what George Bataille names "death in the midst of things that are well ordered" is part of the colonialist agenda in the olfactory imaginary (216). In Western cultures, ecophobia plays out in human practices to rid an environment of other-than-pleasant smells, or to create a "sense of odorless bliss," or at least keep odors in their place in another's patch of land (240). Smells create an uneasy congruence between the living and the dead. The boundary-transcending nature of odors gives them a unique relationship to environmental transformation in this case study.

Patch Dynamics of the Salton Sea

The Salton Sea region epitomizes "patchiness," which feminist anthropologist Anna Tsing characterizes as "a mosaic of open-ended assemblages of entangled ways of life" for both humans and nonhumans (23). Patchiness includes "temporal rhythms and spatial arcs" that illustrate "precarity as an earthwide condition" (23). The Salton Sea also epitomizes "unintentional design" and how landscapes are constituted by the "overlapping world-making activities of many agents, human and not human" (23, 141). As Tsing puts it, "The design is clear in [a] landscape's ecosystem. But none of the agents have planned this effect. Humans join others in making landscapes of unintentional design," and landscapes that feature "more-than-human dramas" tend to decenter "human hubris" because active landscapes reveal relationality and connections among entities and places (141). Put differently, changes over time and space at places like the Salton Sea disclose how precarious ecological balance is and how complicated it is to maintain, particularly when the place is evanescent from the outset, as a flooded desert is wont to be. Situational complexity, intersectional patchiness, and unintentional design matter because wicked environmental problems do not have simple design solutions or clear origins, and the wicked impacts are inequitable. Design theorists Horst Rittel and Melvin Webber introduced the idea of "wicked problems" and highlighted how such problems rebuff efforts to define or solve them. Because wicked problems involve complex and interconnected issues, associated ripple effects obfuscate the problem-solving process. Addressing a patchwork of problems one at a time requires one to understand the bigger picture, yet focus diminishes psychological and political paralysis that can occur when facing complex problems (C. Williams, 2019).

Patching involves work to connect parts, a desire to mend. It also suggests a temporary fix, a forced disconnect, and impermanence. A patch is a place, an action, a diamond of Harlequin garb. The Salton Sea remains temporarily stitched together by geography, necro- and otherwise politics, and publics. Patchy socioenvironmental conditions of precarity at the sea inform the contiguous argument regarding how and why physical sensation rooted in material environmental conditions can act as a suasive force. Physical sensation directs human and nonhuman attention to less hospitable or precarious environmental circumstances. Thus, the associated discomfort or dis-ease can result in changes in behavioral patterns among humans, animals, plants, and the planet more broadly as anthropogenic-driven global heating ramps up. Analysis of precarity at the Salton Sea builds on patch dynamics, patches, and patchiness from ecology studies. Patch dynamics refers to how people understand ecological systems by evaluating interactions among different parts of a given environment. This includes spatiotemporal changes in complex environmental mosaics that consist of many subpatches. At the Salton Sea, the environmental mosaic includes intermittent floods, dams, desert, agriculture, migrations, industry, people, and complex interactions among them. If we extend the patchwork idea to Southern California, which produces commercial crops that are shipped throughout the world via global supply chains, then we can imagine how landscape patches might be differently maintained and managed within the agro-industrial complexities of the region.

The complex, patchy relationality between environmental conditions, historical processes, emplacement, geologic formations, biologic entities, and cultural influences at the Salton Sea site exemplify vital indeterminacy—vital in that a considerable amount of life is on the line, and indeterminate in that its state is uncertain and undecided. Roiled by atmospheric currents and global heating, Salton Sea scent events infuse the atmosphere with an audible hiss impossible to ignore with its spiky putrid top notes and sulfurous-forward approach. Odor ruptures like these create changes in human responses to environmental distress at the Salton Sea. In stage 3 analysis, think of this in terms of relations between embodied knowledge and what the 2012 scent event brought about in news media coverage throughout Southern California at the time of the event (e.g., in the *Los Angeles Times,* on local and national television and radio) and renewed interest in the sea's ecological state despite decades of intermittent government studies and patchy mitigation efforts. Scent events are harbingers of alarm that draw attention to the catastrophic effects of human malfeasance in a "zone of indetermination" as representative of the sea itself (Grosz 149). A zone of indetermination, Elizabeth Grosz contends, "characterizes both the freedom representative of life and the capacity for being otherwise that life can bestow on . . . material organization . . . [a] condition for open-ended action for living beings" (149). In essence, that life can emerge from a complex soup of nutrients and material organization helps to inform what eventually emerges, what fails to emerge, or what tries and dies.

An olfactory event is useful to understanding catastrophic environmental change because it makes an issue conspicuous and can travel through the airwaves as bio-based information technology like the infochemical exchanges between bodies I noted in chapter 1 and elements I noted in chapter 2. Information technology is often defined within computing and telecommunications domains as the study of systems for storing, sending, and retrieving information in digital/online environments. I extend the definition of information technology to include biologically based ecological systems that store, send, and retrieve direct, embodied information regarding life on Earth. Odor molecules are elemental information technology indicative of environmental change. N. Katherine Hayles writes, "Information technologies create . . . *flickering signifiers,* characterized by their tendency toward unexpected metamorphoses, attenuations, and dispersions" ("Virtual" 76). For Hayles, then, flickering signifiers introduce randomness, uncertainty, and mutation into "coding chains" of entangled bodyminds, machines, and environments ("Traumas" 138–39). The sea emits flickering signifiers of duress as a form of bioinformation technology into human and nonhuman bodyminds. The intermittent aberrations in the airwaves emphasize ecological damage better than the quiet persistent odor of smog, as smog is omnipresent in Southern California. Though different in complexity and outcomes, all three case studies in this book illustrate how bioinformation exchange works. Odor molecules travel through the airwaves abstracted, extracted, or exhaled from a body or bodies to be inhaled and absorbed into another body or bodies in a chain of complex causality. This odor exchange, or breathing complex, exemplifies relationships built on the foundation of interdependency and vulnerability between different sorts of bodies that circulate in a sensory ecology like that of the Salton Sea.

A sensory ecology pertains to how (human and nonhuman) animals "gather and use information from their environment and from other organisms," considers the role of ecological entanglements among species, evaluates how these things shape "the form and function of sensory systems [used] to best acquire and process information," and interrogates how "this influence[s] behaviour and evolution" (Stevens 4). Sensory ecology thus informs "rhetorical ecology" because what circulates in bodies immediately and over time winds up circulating in the mediated public sphere (Edbauer). When mediated visceral publics' feeling structures and affective intensities merge in coalitional policymaking efforts, then environmental problems are more likely to be addressed. Further, human beings are not exceptional or independent sensors, so we can expand our sensory rhetorical ecologies to include nonhuman and beyond-human sensing apparatuses to help us evaluate and redress environmental concerns. Tsing notes that "interspecies entanglements that once seemed the stuff of fables are now material for serious discussion among biologists and ecologists" and rhetoricians because "life requires the interplay of many kinds of beings" (viii). Crucial is Tsing's observation that "humans cannot survive by stomping on all the others" (viii). Precarity is the tie that binds, and "only an appreciation of current precarity as an earthwide condition allows us to notice ... the situation of our world" and the contemporary impacts of "patchy" capitalism and settler-colonial ideology in places like the Salton Sea (5).

In the next section, I will introduce the geographical, sociohistorical context of the Salton Sea, as it has a remarkable background (e.g., the C part of the SCENT heuristic). I specify how and why the 2012 scent event matters and put the event in conversation with the everyday impacts of air pollution. Next, I focus on documented evidence of environmental change at the sea foregrounded through olfaction—patchy scent events that act as fire objects that create rhetorical ruptures in environmental policy and motivate visceral publics. I review air and water quality data to expose the power of olfactory rhetoric to sway public policy related to environmental issues when years of analytical data had not. That is, while scientific data and reports quantify the sea's receding shoreline, increased salinity, decreased air quality, and the impact of a century's worth of toxic agro-industrial runoff, they do not always persuade because people in positions of power and other publics may not understand or value the science. Scientists, in turn, may not take the time to translate their efforts into something publics can understand well enough to make informed decisions on what to address and why (Olalde). I also follow the effects of patchy legislation and political action on the Salton Sea's ecosystem and the people who live closest to it and highlight how Indigenous peoples of the region understand the sea and their ongoing kincentric approach to changes in the sea and the surrounding landscape. While many people see the Salton Sea as a kind of unfortunate cesspool, Indigenous communities generally characterize it quite differently (Voyles 261–63). It is a paradoxical place that, like the Sriracha sauce factory case, invokes Rice's "crises of place" under development, injury claims, wound sites, and nostalgia that I will touch on throughout the chapter after sniffing out the political landscape (7).

Emplacement and Context

Lying below sea level at −227 feet, the shrinking 350-square-mile Salton Sea is a liminal space, an in-between place. Currently fifty-two feet at its deepest point, the Salton Sea is a shallow saline lake in a region that has experienced periodic flooding and desiccation for over 10,000 years, making it an intermittent mosaic of life and death (Brothers et al. 486). The Salton Sea is currently the largest inland body of water in Southern California's arid lowlands (fig. 3) in a state where 80% of water use serves agricultural purposes (Alida Cantor, "Hydrosocial" 469). Of unintentional design, it formed between 1905 and 1907 after an engineering mishap and cataclysmic flooding on the Colorado River. Geographically it rests between two deserts, the Mohave and the Sonoran; two fault zones, the San Andreas and the San Jacinto; two human-created agricultural areas, the Coachella and Imperial Valleys; three mountain ranges, the Chocolate Mountains to the east, the San Jacinto to the north, and the Cuyamacas to the west; and two nation-states, the United States and Mexico, that contend for (or with) its water. In 1999, historian William DeBuys supplied a compelling way to think about the sea: "Gravity decrees that in low places consequences collect, ... stewing with the waste of the upstream world" (DeBuys and Myers 3). Consequences collect at the sea, but they also circulate (Voyles 268).

Historically and culturally, the Salton Sea is known to the Indigenous Cahuilla as Lake Cahuilla, a former Gulf of California leftover from eons ago that features rich silt deposits from the Colorado River (Rodriguez et al. "Tribal Policy"; Laylander). The region is crisscrossed with the tracings of a mutable, impermanent sea that has had a variety of names, and the region features the storied pathways of Indigenous peoples and nations, including the Cahuilla, Quechans, Chemehuevis, Cocopahs, and Kumeyaays, who have maneuvered and negotiated the shape-shifting landscape for time immemorial (Voyles 24–28).

The Salton Sea's current socioeconomic patchwork is agricultural, rural, and racially and ethnically diverse, meeting the RISE context criteria. Now that most of California's wetlands are gone, it is a major stop for birds in the Pacific Flyway. Multispecies entanglements include migratory birds that feed upon Atlantic pileworms and tropical tilapia—both probably introduced by casual boaters through ballast, bilge, or live well water—bacteria, algae, people, plants, and other animals (Bourne; Forsman). In the century since the Salton Sea was formed, it has been fed and sustained by polluted agricultural and industrial runoff. As water does in a desert, it is evaporating, which results in episodic massive fish and bird kills and blowing dust from exposed patches of the lake bed. The rotten effects routinely threaten the health of the surrounding majority-minoritized Latine, Indigenous, and other human and nonhuman relations.

The unusual 2012 odor resulted in olfactory responses to the Salton Sea that occurred far away in Los Angeles, Palm Springs, San Fernando, Ventura, and elsewhere, initiating outcries among a critical mass of Californians, environmentalists, and some California legislators (e.g., Steve Horvitz, superintendent of the Salton Sea Recreation Area; Barbara Boxer, Democratic US senator; and Manuel Pérez, Democratic state representative for the 80th District). Taking issue with characterizations of the smelly sea as "dying," retired Salton Sea Recreation Area superintendent Steve Horvitz labeled the sea "the opposite of dead," as it takes an incredibly productive ecosystem to produce such a prodigious number of fish and other life in the first place (qtd. in Simon).[2] Horvitz asserted that the sea is, instead, "changing," and "turning into something that won't support whatever life is in it now" without human intervention (qtd. in Simon). A few months after the scent event and legislative action, US senator Barbara Boxer praised President Obama's allocation of funds to address Salton Sea mitigation efforts. Boxer responded, "It is a breakthrough that for the first time the Army Corps of Engineers is allocating funds in its budget to help restore the Salton Sea. . . . The Salton Sea is critical to the health of families across Southern California as well as the environment and the economy" (qtd. in KESQ News). Local state representative Manuel Pérez replied, "I feel like it's necessary that we do what we can to [provide] local control, local authority, to individuals who are very connected to that sea"; he added that the plan must be "phased in over time" (qtd. in Simon). An

---

2. In 2012 there were approximately 400 million tilapia in the sea (California Department of Water Resources).

epic stench persuaded people to take action. As environmental historian Joy Parr tells it, "Smell is more likely to have a phenomenology than a semiotics, to be known directly . . . to be present as an unpremeditated encounter with the environment and its features," and the "liminal material qualities of smell often, historically, have become the stuff of politics" (270). Parr asserts that we physically experience what happens in our environments (the phenomenology aspect) and sniff out danger and act to confront, translating our "sense-data" into language that circulates in the mediated public sphere. Both the semiotic and rhetorical aspects are always already politicized (Langer 21).

That the Salton Sea burp of indigestion attracted human attention in cities ordinarily inundated with the toxic smell of smog is a salient point in the case's telling because people often ignore the everyday effects of smog unless they suffer from respiratory ailments (Ghosh 5). Ultrafine particulate matter in air pollution damages the olfactory bulb over time, which has a direct correlation to lung and brain inflammation and cognitive damage (Calderón-Garcidueñas). The olfactory bulb is the structure at the front of our brain that relays information to other parts of the brain and body for processing and action. It is also the keeper of olfactory images, or the mind's nose, as I noted in the introduction (Shepherd 167). The everyday nature of air pollution in urban areas makes its material dangers less noticeable once people become insensitive to it, though some will suffer long-term effects like asthma and lung cancer that are linked to inhaling the impacts of air pollution wherever it exists (Jill Johnson et al.; Burr et al.). Given the daily pollution exposures, a scent event would have to be rather extreme for city dwellers to notice it. Los Angeles–based reporter Matt Simon characterizes the sea's odor as a "belched up fetid cloud" that emits a kind of reek that "sticks in your throat like Elmer's glue."

The 2012 scent event example also shows how people who live closest to the Salton Sea are routinely impacted by large fish and bird kills. "Then [comes] the odor," and "it's repugnant," Salton City resident Miriam Juárez notes (qtd. in Singh). Locals experience more somatic anxiety and physical effects than their urban counterparts because they live so close to the odor source, which is episodic in nature due to temperature inversions, storms, and other changes in environmental circumstances. Another Salton Sea local, Amor García, commented, "It can be a punishing place to live" due to extreme stench, toxic dust, heat, and beyond (qtd. in Singh). Maanvi Singh, who traveled to Calipatria and Salton City for work as a reporter, described the summer scentscape as "hot, grimy air [that] clings to hair and creeps under fingernails" as "the sea steams up a sulfurous stench." Startling scent events like the one in 2012 highlight how olfactory perception is rife with nonhuman agents that can inspire human actions. Those nonhuman agents in the 2012 example include odor molecules released from living and decaying entities as well as materials embedded in stirred dust that results in the highest asthma rates in California.

Nonhuman entities exhibit agency, though it may involve unintentional action on the entity's part. Agentic odor molecules in a scent event are not self-contained. They exist in relation to and emerge from site-specific conditions and bodies enmeshed in informational and political entanglements. This line of reasoning connects to Jane Bennett's explication of "the capacity of things . . . [to] act as quasi-agents or forces with trajectories, propensities, or tendencies of their own" (viii). An intersectional ecofeminist approach, however, accounts for "profound entanglements of matter and information in contemporary societies," which includes assessment of the "properties and qualities of materials and artifacts" and structural oppressions that "intersect with the circulation of information" (Lemke 39). This encompasses inequitable encounters with "vibrant matters that unsettle distinctions between near and far, presence and absence, and [what] might take place with properties and capacities closer to a liquid or gas, water or air," and how these capacious properties matter within flows of "systems such as climate that exceed intimate" and immediate "bodily presence" such as circulating flows of mediated artifacts generated by visceral publics in response to a scent event (40–41). An intersectional feminist approach must account for these things because systemic oppression informs how nonhuman agents and agency may be taken up in the public sphere, and that uptake can vary depending on the bodies impacted by the results. An intersectional ecofeminist sensory rhetorical (RISE) approach draws attention to which scent events trigger interventions that address environmental problems. The 2012 scent event composed of odorants near and far became entangled in vernacular exchanges (narratives) that led to mediated visceral publics who effected change in policy measures when the environmental problems at the Salton Sea remerged in the larger public sphere. Like the Brunswick, Georgia, example outlined in chapter 1, the use of olfactory rhetoric has been interactive and episodic. As the situation is very complex, the deployment of olfactory rhetoric has met with patchy success. There are no simple solutions to environmental problems at the sea because it is in the middle of a desert in a low place where consequences have indeed collected. Like other large bodies of water in the world, global heating is speeding up evaporation processes (e.g., Lake Mead, Lake Powell, Lake Shasta, Lake Oroville, the Great Salt Lake, the Aral Sea, Lake Good-e-Zareh, and Lake Mar Chiquita) (Yao et al.).

Situated between a desert and an agricultural area in Southern California, the Salton Sea provides an opportunity to analyze a complex set of environmental responses tied to human malfeasance and a patchwork of settler-colonialist enterprises. The case demonstrates how a RISE approach negates the human tendency to deny responsibility for ecological degradation as it critiques public policy measures that neglected the sea's water and sediment quality and a patchwork of ineffective cleanup efforts. I will also highlight success patches associated with the efforts of the Torres Martinez Desert Cahuilla Indians (TMCDI).[3]

Unintentional Design and Salty Patchworks

In *The Settler Sea*, environmental historian Traci Voyles characterizes the Colorado River as a diamondback rattlesnake that has flicked its tail back and forth across patches of the Southern California landscape for eons, creating a wallowed-out sink that rests about 300 feet below sea level and catches floodwaters (21). The Indigenous desert Cahuilla say that Cahuilla creators Múkat and Témayawet "turned up the edges of the earth" so that Colorado River floodwaters could be held in place to rejuvenate life in the desert, knowing the landscape would go through this cycle of flood and desiccation repeatedly in natural "fluctuation[s] born of the long marriage between river and earth" (Voyles 21–22). These fluctuations have historically required the region's Indigenous peoples and nonhumans to relocate or adapt in response to patchy inundation and evaporation cycles that are part of the landscape's archive (65). What is "new" about the Salton Sea is its imbrication in settler-colonial approaches to "water-as-resource" (Jack 329–36). Settlers who moved to the region were attracted to it because new irrigation canals and access to stolen land made it possible to conduct "plantation agriculture" and the associated monocultural agro-industrial crop production virtually year-round (e.g., avocados, almonds, berries, citrus, cotton, and vegetables) (Nadaraja et al.; Taylor 144–47; Tsing 53). Hearkening back to the Sriracha sauce case chapter, Jordynn Jack situates water-as-resource to characterize the importance of safe, potable water from settler-colonial perspectives, which are grounded in landowner-ship patchworks. A water-as-resource mentality elides human responsibility

---

3. As noted earlier in the chapter, there are several groups of American Indians who call this region of Southern California home. I focus most on the Torres Martinez tribe because their reservation is directly next to and in the Salton Sea. TMDCI is the abbreviation the tribe uses on its website ("Desert"). Sometimes I refer to the group as the Cahuilla, particularly when I reference older lifeways since there was more than one tribe affiliated with the name Cahuilla. Due to the impacts of colonialism, forced relocation and migrations changed some American Indian group dynamics and names over time.

toward bodies of water, which contrasts with the water-as-lifeblood perspective more common in Indigenous worldviews, where localized patchworks are part and parcel of a worldly mosaic.

Like the Sriracha sauce factory controversy, the Salton Sea case is rooted in material environmental conditions that impact olfaction and other sense perceptions, which act as suasive forces that aim attention to change in ecological circumstances. The Salton Sea also overflows with environmental injustices. Unlike the Siracha controversy, the Salton Sea context is not an industrial space where pollution controls can be straightforward to implement. In part, this is due to the "nonpoint source" nature of agricultural pollutants. Nonpoint-source pollution means that many people contribute to the problem, which makes it recalcitrant to simple summary or solution. When a factory has a pipe that dumps contaminated water into a river, or an exhaust system that vents toxins into the air, it is much easier to address and fix because there is a clear pollution source point that can be tracked and monitored. In contrast, if 1,000 farmers put various fertilizers and pesticides into their fields, flood the fields with excess irrigation water, and the results drain into the broader watershed, then no one person, business, or farm is the source point of contamination. The biocide soup emerges from a mosaic of patches. This is what has occurred at the Salton Sea. Although the case shows how the whale can be awoken from its ambivalent slumber, it is as though all the agro-industrial contributors unite to become one leviathan exceptional public subject.

The subsequent effects illustrate slow violence. Slow violence may have no obvious perpetrators, but it does have clear casualties, who are disproportionately poor people of color. Extending the conversation on racial inequities tied to environmental hazards, Bullard and Wright point out that the burden of proof for slow violence often falls on the shoulders of "victims and not on the polluting industr[ies]," which "legitimates human [and nonhuman] exposure to harmful chemicals, pesticides, and hazardous substances," and simultaneously "creates an industry around risk assessment," "delays cleanup actions," and "seldom challenges environmental racism and other forms of environmental injustice" (2–4). The Salton Sea is a clear example of how slow violence works in concert with environmental injustice, settler-colonialism, and capitalism.[4] It is also a good example to showcase how BIPOC people push back against slow violence, work to redress it in patches, and document continuous efforts among several communities to respond to environmental crises across

---

4. See Traci Voyles for settler-colonialism's impacts at the Salton Sea and Anna Tsing for late-stage capitalism's impacts on environments.

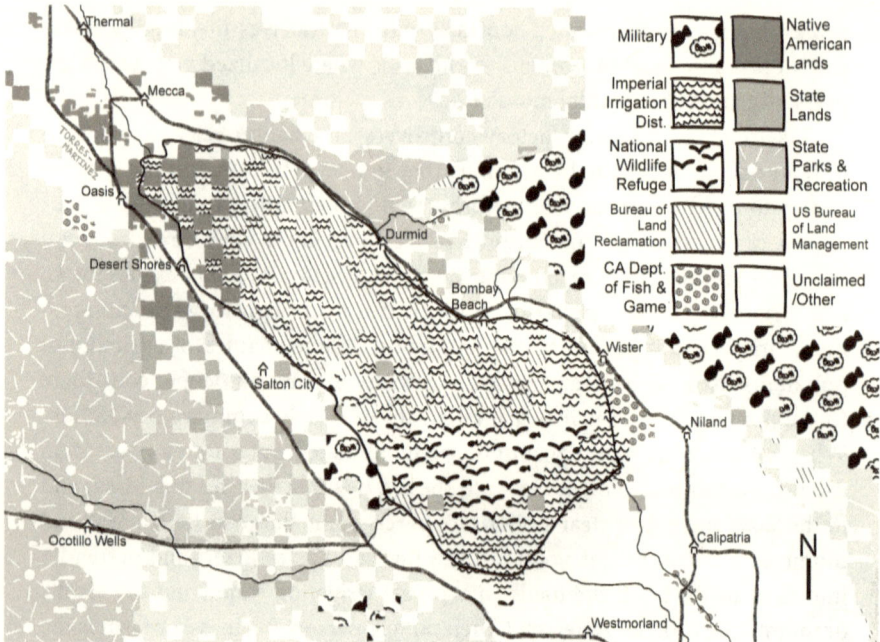

FIGURE 4. Patchy land ownership map featuring Torres Martinez land on the Salton Sea's north side. Image credit: Morgan R. Phillips based on US Bureau of Land Management data.

Indigenous, localized, state, federal, and multinational contexts. For example, drawing on a long history of working with environmental constraints rather than against them, TMDCI have been persistent in their efforts to incorporate traditional practices into contemporary dust mitigation efforts, which includes planting mesquite and other drought-tolerant plants at the sea's shore and elsewhere (Voyles 29–33, 35–37, 62–63). By working with the California Conservation Corps to plant mesquite and palo verde plants developed to be resistant to saline soils, the tribe continues to experiment in harmony with the landscape. "Getting back to the natural habitat speaks volumes" in terms of contemporary efforts, said tribal chairman Thomas Tortez Jr. (qtd. in Ulrich, "More"). The efforts also include observing what plants survive the harsh conditions over time, so those species and their seeds or cultivars can be used on other exposed playas to address the dust and other issues.

That environmental injustices disproportionately impact some bodies and patches more than others at the Salton Sea and elsewhere are plain, as are the power dynamics at work. As to the latter, settler-colonial attempts to control nature and water converge with racialized efforts to dominate, segregate, dispossess, and disenfranchise (Voyles 120–21). In the broader patch named California, it took a veritable stink bomb going off at the Salton Sea to generate action in the larger public sphere. Locals have been dealing with deteriorating environmental conditions at the sea for decades. Notably, an assemblage of Indigenous communities in the region have contended with intermittent patches of Colorado River flooding for millennia and have passed down how to navigate and flexibly adapt to wildly changing circumstances through oral histories and petroglyphs and within the patchy archive of the landscape itself (Voyles 21–53). The Salton Sea's breathy cacophony of stories mingle in the air and tell tales of life on "unruly edges" that constitute the "stuff of collaborative survival" in late-stage multivalent capitalism (Tsing 20, 70). How the land is artificially divided by the federal government is an adroit illustration of patchiness itself (see fig. 4), which I will elaborate upon in sections that focus on Indigenous-informed approaches to the Salton Sea's environmental issues (see the sections "Resilience, Relational Gifts, and Centering Reciprocity" and "Sniffing Out Patchy Successes and Indigenuity at the Sea"). Scent events also make patchy appearances and draw attention to a mosaic of overlapping environmental concerns and conditions unfolding at the sea. For example, in 1992 nearly 150,000 birds died, which resulted in olfactory and visual rhetoric that appeared in the mediated public sphere (McDonnell). Similar incidents occurred in 1995 and 1996. In 1999, 7.6 million fish died, and the reek once again drew attention to the sea and resulted in policy measures to address the issue (Salton Sea Authority). A 2021 scent event had a similar impact, and the "miasma of burnt garbage" spurred "movement on a couple of wetland projects" around the sea (A. Chen).

Emplaced Events, Causal Relations, and Redolent Ruptures of Sensation

Living lands, waters, peoples, and more are enmeshed in events of agitation, exchange, and double contingency. Agitation and exchange here reference anxiety or nervous excitement, vigorous stirring or disturbing of something, and raising concern about an issue and pressing for action upon it. Per social systems theorists Talcott Parsons and Niklas Luhmann, all socioenvironmental exchange involves double contingency, which refers to the fundamentally uncertain and contingent nature of interactions between two actors, agents, or systems. Double contingency describes the situation where behavior is contingent (dependent) on perception of another actor or agent's behavior, and vice versa. This creates a circular relationship of mutual contingency. One can never fully eliminate the underlying contingency enmeshed in an agitation event.

Scent events are agitating and prompt people to exchange ideas about how to address an environmental concern. Encapsulating the idea of double contingency, disparate groups (local, state, and federal) are concerned about deteriorating environmental conditions at the sea, and these dissimilar groups know that the environmental problems can be addressed in a variety of ways with myriad outcomes. Double contingency recognizes that life both responds to the socioenvironmental context in which it finds itself and actively contributes to how said contexts are shaped and maintained. The mutual influence between patchy geographies and life therein creates a continuous feedback loop, where actions and reactions are interconnected and recursive, highlighting the dynamic interplay and reciprocal relationships that exist between animated water, land, and life in patched landscapes.

Patchy agitations and cataclysms score the Southern California landscape. As illustration, in 1900, the California Development Company built a canal to connect the Alamo "barranca," a dry channel, and the Colorado River to irrigate the parched Imperial Valley and attract settler-colonial farmers, which was a successful colonialist enterprise (Kennan 21–24; Pollard). However, silt soon blocked the canal, and the same development company incompetently built a new canal from the Colorado River in Mexico in 1905 (Kennan 32). The construction crossed the United States/Mexico border and the approval permitting process with Mexican authorities was protracted, which delayed key floodgate efforts at the head of the new cut (37–39). As canal construction progressed, the Colorado River experienced a series of floods that overwhelmed the ungated canal route. The entirety of the Colorado River's flow poured into the once-dry Salton Sink, and the scouring effect of the flood moved four times the amount of dirt removed to create the Panama Canal (60). George Kennan witnessed the cataclysmic results firsthand and chronicled it as it occurred. He reports one geologist's observation: "Very rarely, if ever before, had it been possible to see a geologic agency effect in a few months a change which usually requires centuries" (Cory qtd. in Kennan 60). There was a rush of "360,000,000 cubic feet of water per hour" pouring "down a four-hundred-foot slope of easily eroded silt" into an area "big enough to hold Long Island Sound" (61). Images from the time show waterfalls more than 1,000 feet (305 meters) across (imagine the Empire State Building laid on its side) and up to eighty feet (twenty-five meters) high. The engineering mishaps contributed to a complete shift in the Colorado River's course, and the diamondback rattler's aqueous tail snuggled into its historical wallow in line with Cahuilla oral traditions and cosmology (Voyles 59–65). Downstream communities that relied on the Colorado River for sustenance, irrigation, or municipal water were agitated and left wanting because water that used to flow their way ceased altogether for several years.

Two years later, after railroad tycoon E. H. Harriman brought to bear enough rock and conscripted labor, the Colorado River stopped filling the enormous puddle and slithered into its former path (Forsman 371; Kennan 87). The emergent Salton Sea was more than twice the size of Lake Tahoe. Since the (re)born Salton Sea emerged in a desert environment, it was not expected to last for more than twenty years, thirty at the most (Stringfellow). In 1909, the US Department of the Interior, claiming that the water would evaporate quickly, reserved 10,000 submerged acres (4,047 hectares) for the TMCDI. Put differently, once flooding inundated the Salton Sink, the US government decided to give the now-flooded land back to the people from whom it was originally stolen. Submerged land cannot produce agricultural crops or provide places for human homes or communities. The land is still held in "trust" by the Bureau of Indian Affairs under the Department of the Interior, though the submerged acreage appears as patches that connect at points but fail to constitute a cohesive whole, like disconnected ceramic tiles in an incomplete mosaic (DeBuys and Myers; Voyles 198–201). On a map, the reservation land looks like a checkerboard (fig. 4).

By 1920, it was clear that profits gleaned from the Imperial Valley's agriculture needed a steady supply of water to keep lining the pockets of "a favored race" of white settlers who wanted to squeeze as much productivity out of dry land patches as possible (Voyles 121, 123; Wood). Established settlers were also worrying about an agitated Colorado slithering out of its usual path to strike yet again (Pearce, *When* 47–66; Voyles 123). Bigger dams and concrete canals were deemed an expedient fix to cage the diamondback. The damming move also features racialized and ethnic supremacies and what Black Marxist political theorist Cedric Robinson characterizes as "racial capitalism," a process that depends on racial hegemony and stratification by class, race, ethnicity, language, gender, and more that results in the most profit for the people at the top created on the backs of other groups who are less expensive to hire as laborers in capitalistic structures (Robinson et al.). In the US, this relationship is tied to white supremacy and settler-colonial systems. Harriman's railroad tycoonery is an apropos example of how racial capitalism works because it illustrates intersections among place, space, settler agro-industrial impetus, and a reliance on predominantly masculine Latine, Chinese, Indigenous, migrant, and working-class white labor at railroad, dam, and canal worksites, supported by feminized labor (cooking, entertainment, and so on) in camps and elsewhere.

In 1928, the US Congress authorized the construction of the Boulder Dam and the All-American Canal. Completion of both projects virtually eliminated flooding associated with the Colorado River (see the Salton Sea Authority's "Timeline" for additional details). Caging a diamondback has consequences, including eliminating cycles of flooding that refresh soil and human and non-human life on different patches of arid land through the influx of silt and waterborne species. As example, the Colorado and its tributaries transport fish, seeds, uprooted plants, and other wildlife to temporary patches where they thrive for a few years and die off in to-be-expected intermittent cycles that Indigenous peoples rely on as part of sustainable migratory relationships, plant propagations, and harvest patterns. These patterns have been wholly disrupted by an assortment of conflicting development agendas. Permanent human settlements and dams displaced the diamondback's ability to wallow around and refresh patches of the desert. Instead, the Salton Sea became a more permanent oasis of sorts.

In 1930, the Salton Sea Wildlife Refuge was established to protect avian species that had taken up residence or migrated to the area. By the early 1940s, commercial fisherpersons began to harvest mullet at the sea. In addition, the All-American and Coachella Canals became operational and began to deliver water to both the Imperial and Coachella Valleys for agricultural use. Excess runoff flowed to the Salton Sea and kept it hydrated.

Months prior to the US dropping nuclear bombs on Hiroshima and Nagasaki, Japan, in August 1945, B-29 bomber pilots and crews practiced the bombing runs by dropping hundreds of "dummy bombs" into the Salton Sea (Goolsby; Voyles 180–82, 185). Dummy bombs are filled with concrete and other ballast but are the same shape, size, and general weight (10,000 pounds, or 4,500 kilograms) as fully armed nuclear bombs. Many of the dummy bombs contained conventional triggering explosives and their affiliated chemicals, which wound up in the Salton Sea (Thomas and Witts; Voyles 180–81). A few detonations likely involved uranium, which was "less expensive than concrete and easier to use than lead" as ballast material (Voyles 185–87, 188). The Salton Sea is fairly close to the Wendover Airforce Base on the Nevada/Utah border. The remote location and sparse human population made it a convenient site for practice runs for those who only see certain lives as valuable. The US Navy also established the Salton Sea Naval Base to oversee the target range. The mission was secret and mostly unknown to the public (Goolsby; Voyles 178, 186–88). Keeping the bombing runs a secret would in effect prohibit environmental health concerns from emerging in the public sphere, as the US military could (and did) easily suppress or misdirect any media attempts to report on the situation based on wartime national security restrictions (Voyles

186–89). Rice argues that "public talk" matters in environmental discourse because "everyday talk is precisely where real activist work can be accomplished" (16–17). Framed through a RISE approach, public talk pertaining to what people sense in a community that merges into visceral publics often lends itself to policy changes. Hence, vernacular discourse about the dummy bombs' impacts would go no further than the dinner table or local bar at the time. That the military-industrial complex suppressed broader public knowledge about the practice runs is unsurprising, yet the damage deposit remains in sea sediment.

In the postwar era, the Salton Sea region witnessed an explosion of a different nature: capital investment and new development. A similar boom occurred in Austin, Texas, which Jenny Rice chronicled in *Distant Publics*. Despite the areas' differences in population density, they also share similarities worth noting. Like Austin, the Salton Sea region has been characterized as "weird," uncanny, and colorful, and it is known for harboring artistic "oddballs" who attract true believers and tourists alike (Metzler and Springer). Likewise, development has played a role in shaping how some people view the landscape. For instance, in the early 1950s, more fish species were introduced to the Salton Sea to encourage sport and commercial fishing. In the late '50s and early '60s, real estate developers began to develop resorts and residential subdivisions around the Salton Sea, including Salton City and the North Shore Beach and Yacht Club. The area subsequently became a hotspot for LA movie stars and other celebrities, which contributed to an influx of dollars, tourism, and property development more generally (Salton Sea Authority). However, by the end of the 1960s, the sea became increasingly saline due to evaporation, leading many celebrities and more affluent people to abandon the area. Penumbras of lost possibility, paved roads and cul-de-sacs are left as reminders of planned retirement communities and residential enclaves that were never built. Like Rice's Austin strip malls with "hopes that just never panned out," development at the Salton Sea is also a "living lesson in development gone wrong" (23). While Austin has experienced economic growth that coincides with gentrification and displacement of diversity, the Salton Sea's development is the opposite. Wealthy white people abandoned the area and more diverse human and nonhuman residents have taken up residence, though the situation is fraught with complexity and impending environmental justice disasters (Voyles).

As with the Sriracha sauce factory controversy, the Salton Sea case demonstrates injury claims and wound sites that Rice notes are common among people who protest new developments, although in the Salton Sea context it is less about development of a pristine wilderness area at this point and more about public "memory claims" related to actual development that happened in the past—the "heyday" of the Salton Sea development era during the '50s and '60s—and subsequent abandonment by both developers and illustrious seasonal residents who flew away to more habitable climes (103). Moreover, Rice writes that "memory claims create both possibilities for engagement, as well as spaces of exceptionality and nonparticipation" because "exceptional subjects" may not be involved in "deliberation" and yet retain a "public orientation" (103). This also extends to some TMCDI tribal members who take a longer view of the sea in its predevelopment stages as Lake Cahuilla. In 2021, tribal chairperson Thomas Tortez commented, "We no longer see it [the Salton Sea] as a form of life that the Creator allowed us to have every few hundred years . . . the kids don't have the chance to see it the way I once saw it, the way my grandfather saw it. They see it as a catastrophe, they see it as a toxic event" (qtd. in Baumann). As tribal chairperson, Tortez isn't an exceptional public subject, is involved in deliberation, and has a public orientation, yet the memory and injury claims clearly illustrate an ongoing wound site for the Indigenous peoples of the region.

In the '70s the Salton Sea was agitated by two major tropical storms, above-average rainfall, and more agricultural runoff and influx from the south and Mexico, which, when combined, destroyed key shoreline resort communities. The Salton Sea's salinity also continued to rise throughout the '80s, and by mid-decade, the state of California advised people that the fish had high rates of selenium that posed a threat to human health if they were eaten. In 1988, the Salton Sea Task Force was established by local and state government agencies to combat increasingly deteriorating conditions that continued in the early '90s with several enormous bird kills that drew national attention to the region. One in 1996 included a "four-month apocalypse" that included more than 10,000 brown pelican deaths (Simon). Pelicans are very large birds. They ate massive amounts of dead fish and contracted botulism. Workers had to cremate the dead birds' bodies around the clock for weeks on end to slow the spread of disease to other species and people, which added the smell of burning flesh and feathers to the region's smellscape in a fairly sustained scent event that impacted the region for months. The patchwork of problems kept the sea in the public eye and nostrils.

In 1997, California congressman Sonny Bono (a famous singer and Southern California native) became the Salton Sea's champion and initiated federal efforts to address regional environmental problems. After he died a year later in a skiing accident, Bono's partner, Mary Bono, was elected to the US Congress and took up the project, sponsoring a successful bill to address a patch of Salton Sea damage. Congress passed the Salton Sea Reclamation Act in

1998, which resulted in $327 million of funding to restore habitat within the designated wildlife refuge. The act fostered some nonhuman habitat patch restoration. Additional scientific feasibility studies ensued to better ascertain what could be done to redress other environmental issues at the sea, though none appear to include locals' perspectives. Then in 1999, nearly eight million fish died due to algae-driven oxygen depletion, which created a massive scent event that kept policymaking in the spotlight. Simon explains that the sea's "problems" associated with large fish die-offs that coincided with increasing salinity and dramatic temperature changes over time, though "disquieting," were accepted as "relatively tolerable occurrences" prior to the August 1999 scent event. Having millions of fish turn belly-up on a single day was an indication that the "Salton Sea had gone rogue" (Simon). Episodic scent events keep the pressure on to address the rogue sea, so rather than seeing recursive processes as failures, the events illustrate how material circumstances persuade.

In the early 2000s, a series of scientific reports using both air- and water-as-chemical-entity and resource models were designed to address the region's deteriorating water and air quality. An assortment of pilot restoration projects began, and more reports were written, though potential community partners and residents were often not consulted or dismissed altogether due to environmental racism (Newburger). Frank Ruiz, Audubon's Salton Sea program director and local resident, tells it succinctly: "If the sea was next to Los Angeles, it would have been fixed long ago. But it's next to poor [majority Latine] communities and they don't have the political leverage. I think things will change when the sea starts affecting wealthier [white] communities in Palm Springs" (qtd. in Newburger). Ruiz's point proved accurate. One pre-2012 report notes that without "extraordinary human intervention," the Salton Sea was likely to become a serious "ecological catastrophe," for once surplus irrigation water were to stop flowing into the sea (due to increasingly efficient irrigation and agreements to divert excess water to other users), it would evaporate at a predicted rate of more than twenty feet per decade (Forsman 387, 383). Unless the situation is adequately addressed, airborne contaminants will create a malignant dust bowl larger than the dry Owens Lake in California's Owens Valley—recently the largest sole source of "ultrafine" particulate matter in the United States (Calderón-Garcidueñas; Koehler et al.; Reheis; Thomson).

Unquestionably, airborne toxicity is in progress at the Salton Sea and has been for many years. Local schools fly red flags of warning outside to alert students and parents of dangerous air quality, which represents a response to ongoing air quality issues (Olalde). That is, local visceral publics report on the air quality issues and how this impacts asthma rates and so forth, and policy efforts include patchy efforts to evaluate air quality, though the efforts have not been holistically scaled around the sea's perimeter. Air that is tested in the Salton Sea region has failed to meet California's safety standards for over 150 days per year for the past five-plus years (Zelenko). Near the sea, childhood and adult rates of asthma and respiratory illness are three times the rate of other areas in California, and more than one in five children suffers from the effects (Farzan and Johnson; Lindberg; Pitzer; Zelenko). Now, the area's residents are primarily Latine farmworkers (85%), more than one-quarter live in poverty, and about one-third are "foreign born" (US Census Bureau, "Quick Facts Imperial" and "Supplemental").

The lack of effective mitigation and high levels of pollution exposure illustrate how environmental racism works across intersecting axes of oppression. As the water evaporates, the windswept playa areas (dusty, once submerged, beaches) kick up fine carcinogen- and pesticide-laden dust that coats everything. The dust is more like talcum powder than typical sandy silt, which is related to the sea's salinity (Reheis). The microscopic particles include organic and inorganic matter and noxious emissions that infiltrate noses, eyes, ears, and lungs. Like Ruiz, Miriam Juárez, a Salton City resident, veteran farmworker, and mother of two asthmatic children, who is recently asthmatic herself, points out that if the environmental "problem affected a wealthier, whiter area like Palm Springs, it would have been addressed already" (qtd. in Olalde). What Juárez observes are the a/effects of environmental racism inflicted upon her family and community. Nixon characterizes examples of environmental racism and classism like this as "discriminatory distribution of environmental visibility" regarding who is seen, who is not, and whose concerns are redressed and how and when, if at all, in slow violences (65). We might also ask why, how, and whether visibility trumps other sensibilities that attract our attention.

Olfactory Sensibility and the Toilet Assumption

People like Juárez who live adjacent to the sea have psychosomatic knowledge of the place through olfactory sensibility—the rotten smell of massive algae blooms fueled by excess fertilizer that result in massive fish and bird kills, the smell of toxin-laden dust, and other indeterminate airborne effluvia. Long-time resident and home day-care businessperson Noemí Vázquez worries based on embodied experience and makes an injury claim that characterizes the sea as an ongoing wound site. "Generations have been harmed and traumatized by the pollution," Vázquez reports, "and there's no escaping the noxious air" (qtd. in Singh). Rice notes that injury claims and woundings may keep "in place the same old structures, even as [they] rage against this system" (82). Vázquez, her daughter, and her grandchild all suffer from acute asthma. Vázquez has also witnessed her day-care charges go to the hospital for asthma attacks, and more than half carry "their own medical bags stocked with inhalers" and other crucial paraphernalia (Singh). Scent events and human intake of the experience are covalently bonded to environmental deterioration at work within and around the Salton Sea, and Vázquez's injury claims about the sea's conditions are literal, not figurative. As a stable wound site, the sea is both the "subject of injury" and an object of it (Rice 82). Vázquez and the sea illustrate localized trauma that can be addressed. Vázquez also shows how Latine residents are unwilling to suffer "private wound[s] without public remark" and how people push back against slow violences in the mediated public sphere (82). Feedback loops matter because they apply pressure to address environmental hazards. By feedback loops here, I refer to the ongoing work by folx like Vázquez and her neighbors and other community groups, who keep the pressure on local, state, and federal agencies and beyond to redress environmental hazards at the sea.

Because the sea is an inflow-only closed system—it does not contribute to other watersheds in a riverine feedback loop—Clean Water Act rules and regulations do *not* apply (Alida Cantor, "Public"; M. Cohen et al.; Rudy; Womach). Moreover, agricultural rules and regulations *do*, and those are laxer than factory-based effluvia regulations and monitoring, in part because the effluent is not single-point-source material like exterior building pipes present. Farmers flush their fields with extra water to prevent excess soil salinity and fertilizer buildup. This intentional "leaching process" is designed to prevent chemical "burns" on plants stemming from salt accumulations at the root zone (Hillel 435). The visible evidence of buildup looks like white crust on the soil surface. Imagine flaky table salt or kosher salt used for pickling or a light dusting of snow. The flushing process washes everything else away too, like biocide residue, fine topsoil, chemical- and organic-based fertilizers, rubbish, and so on. The excess water and detritus flows into the sea, where the flushed pollutants cannot be traced back to a singular source for mitigation or abatement (Polakovic). Philip Slater attributes phenomena like flushing the fields with excess water to remove visual evidence of salinity to people having an out-of-sight out-of-mind "toilet assumption" about what we see and smell or otherwise sense in our environment and not caring about what happens elsewhere as a result. The immediate problem appears to be solved, like when someone flushes scrap food or human waste down the toilet. The waste still goes somewhere, but "the notion[s] of unwanted matter, unwanted difficulties, unwanted complexities and obstacles [seem to] disappear if they're removed from our immediate field of vision" or smellscape, which means that once a problem is out of sight or other perceptual field, then people no longer care or pay attention, though the problem remains (P. Slater 19). The Salton Sea is not an open sewer, but the water is left untreated, and the chemicals and whatever else is suspended in the water migrates downstream and eventually sinks and merges with the sediment, where it becomes more concentrated over time due to accumulation.

Treating the Salton Sea—currently a key ecosystem in the Pacific Flyway—like a toilet has resulted in something that acts more like an open sewage lagoon with noxious sewer gas. The damage is visible, and it stinks on multiple levels. The Indigenous relationship to the geographical constraints of patchy inundation cycles were ignored, and now the region has permanent ecological damage that is toxic to many forms of life. It can be difficult to imagine how to address such a complex mess, though imagine we must, for to end the story solely with destruction is to give up on hope or get stuck in feedback loops of "promise and ruin, promise and ruin" across patchy geographies (Tsing 32). As Tsing corroborates, "We are stuck with the problem of living despite economic and ecological ruination. Neither tales of progress nor of ruin tell us how to think about collaborative survival" and what might emerge in damaged landscapes beyond industrial promise and ruin (32). The work of collaborative survival is relational and reciprocal because we are interdependently bound in multispecies, globally connected patchworks.

Resilience, Relational Gifts, and Centering Reciprocity

If, instead of viewing the Salton Sea as a toilet, we perceive the sea to be both a resilient relative and a provisional gift, then we can sense she needs some reciprocity, as do all our relations who rely on her gifts, like migrating birds, fish, insects, amphibians, reptiles, and people. In this section, I purposefully use the feminine gender pronoun to refer to the Salton Sea in alignment with ecofeminist principles that highlight how women and nature are subjected to exploitation within patriarchal systems, though this is not meant to dismiss nonbinary or gender-fluid ways of being or knowing. Moreover, the Cahuilla peoples of the region have Menily as a central gendered character in their cosmology, and she is a blend of both water and reflexive moonlight (Patencio). Menily attends to and/or is representative of water, childbirth, and teaching, specifically teaching girls (16–17). In English, the name translates roughly to "Moon Goddess" or "Mood Maiden." Menily animates Cahuilla discourse around teaching sustainable environmental habits to future generations through matrilineal approaches tied to specific traditions, which include gifts and abuses dished out by humans, deities, animals, and plants in the desert.

Resiliency emerges whenever and wherever water appears, though it can also bring destruction when people do not pay attention to her ebbs and flows.

At the Salton Sea, contemporary attempts at reciprocity pertain to privileging her survivance, since mutual interdependencies among humans and nonhumans are involved. Neglecting her survivance will also release tons of particulate toxins into the air-as-lifeblood, which can also be interpreted as a kind of environmental reciprocity tied to ill treatment. As a reminder from the introductory chapter, reciprocity is about living in balance with all our relations. In *Braiding Sweetgrass,* Robin Wall Kimmerer points out how a "grammar of animacy . . . could lead us to whole new ways of living in the world [with] other species [as] sovereign people[s] in the world with a democracy of species, not a tyranny of one," which is the very essence of reciprocal relationality (122). A being, entity, and place like the sea becomes a someone, not a some*thing*. The tilapia in the Salton Sea become Tilapia people worthy of more respect and reciprocity when we imagine them as beings worthy of care using a grammar of animacy. If their death at the Salton Sea were perceived as kind of genocide of a fellow group of people, would it be akin to a war crime to leave the environmental deterioration unaddressed? The Salton Sea under Kimmerer's counsel becomes/is animated, alive, breathes, gasps, nurtures life, experiences trauma, and is as lovable as Menily. A grammar of animacy shifts the view on environmental justice and extends it to include nonhuman peoples and encourages restorative action. At the Salton Sea, a grammar of animacy involves considering the sea herself as a lively being who is suffering and needs care. The grammar of animacy discloses our obligations within webbed relations. While it is true that we rely on other life-forms for sustenance, maintaining a grammar of animacy along with a reverence for those gifts results in a decolonial worldview—one in which we must give thanks for gifts bestowed, behave responsibly with those finite resources, and interrupt the promise–ruin feedback loop. It follows that myriad sensitivities to changes in environmental conditions are gifts that inform our and our relations' resiliency.

Resiliency is linked to survival but goes beyond that because it illustrates ways to resist harm. For example, part of Menily's story is tied to her abuse by Múkat (Patencio and Boynton 13–18).[5] To escape earthbound sorrow, Menily retreats to the sky and communicates as moonlight on the water's surface

---

5. Agua Caliente Cahuilla chief Francisco Patencio shared many Cahuilla stories that were published in the 1930s, republished in the mid-2000s, and most recently published in 2020. In the story Patencio tells about Menily, her abuse is not specifically indicated as rape, but the story as told indicates that Menily suffered from trauma I identify as rape or sexual abuse based upon my work with interviews and sexual assault reports. Menily disconnects from social interactions, becomes increasingly ill mentally and physically, and finds solace once removed from the site of trauma.

(16). Resiliency is about recovering from, redressing, or adjusting to adversity and change. At the sea, resiliency relies on human interventions just as her contemporary origin point did, and olfactory impacts inform contemporary efforts.

Human beings evolved an aversion to the smell of rotten *anything* as survival and resiliency mechanisms. Longtime Salton Sea researcher at the Pacific Institute Michael Cohen informs that the ecological activity at the sea is "eutrophic," meaning that the sea's productivity includes "algal blooms" and "cyanobacteria blooms and explosions of life forms that are toxic for people and [most] animals" (qtd. in A. Chen). The collateral damage of such vibrant matter includes an untimely death for other creatures. Now, imagine a crime show that involves a watery tomb for an unfortunate victim. Untethered bodies bob to the surface and then sink below. Consequently, the sea provides putrid plumes of volatile molecules that bombard the air along with submerged odor minefields that rest under the water's surface until they are agitated by atmospheric exchange and release a stink so rank it delivers a bodily hit. It may seem odd to think about smells being suspended in water, yet it informs how odorants travel across mediums (e.g., air, water, dirt) (Wolfe). Jude Stewart likens the process to a kind of "ghostly palimpsest" where what floats to the bottom of the sea drifts, gets agitated, and is taken up by other entities in air- and water-as-lifeblood exchange cycles (196). Storms, strong winds, geothermal activity, and temperature inversions agitate the water and reintroduce the reeking remnants back into the atmosphere. Generally, the smelly by-products (primarily trimethylamine) of decomposing foodstuffs like fish, birds, and produce and the odiferous results of different manufacturing or resource extractions (e.g., petroleum refining, uranium mining, coal production, paper pulping, oil drilling) are not meant to make their way into our mouths, eyes, ears, noses, or other orifices without doing damage in the process. Vultures, seagulls, flies, eagles, and other carrion eaters are made of more resilient stuff than their human cousins when it comes to eating or smelling rotten fish, but our nonhuman kin are as vulnerable as humans are to synthetic hazards. Measuring both synthetic and organic hazards involves air-as-chemical-entity, and technical expertise is key to the endeavor, though local residents need more accessible ways to evaluate the environmental hazards impacting them.

Environmental monitoring of the Salton Sea has existed in some form or another since its (re)inception in 1905. However, statewide concern for the sea's human and nonhuman eco- and socioeconomic systems evaporated as the well-to-do left and people who could not afford to relocate, or did not want to, or who needed to move to less-expensive places as an alternative to living in Southern California cities like Los Angeles or Palm Springs remained near the Salton Sea. Currently, at the Salton Sea, surrounding communities can only access available real-time air quality data through ArcGIS data that links to one monitoring station, which is near a wetland preserve in the Salton Sea State Park at the sea's south end (IQAir). Hence, residents must rely on their senses or highly localized air quality monitoring equipment placed near schools or other public property, if it is available. As Donnie Sackey notes, at sites where "environmental health data collection is needed the most . . . there are often not enough resources to monitor polluting industries" and associated impacts from cumulative nonpoint-source pollution that are also enmeshed in structural environmental injustices (33). The spotty monitoring makes it more difficult for residents to understand air quality index values, particularly when they fail to include real-time data from more isolated or ignored communities (South Coast Air Quality Monitoring Data; Salton Sea Air Quality Mitigation Program). Writing about how to develop "environmental sensing wearables" that would assist people placed most in harm's path to understand and evaluate the relative health and safety of their air quality, Sackey illustrates how incorporating residents into environmental monitoring efforts can help residents gain confidence and assert "more agency" when "communicat[ing] with experts" (43). By extension, residents could "be better equipped" to "effectively argue against plans to locate a factory" or other (re)development plans or industrial processes slated for their communities (43). Similarly, relatively inexpensive portable air quality monitoring devices like the technologies Sackey discusses, which work in tandem with human senses, could assist residents in identifying and evaluating initial events. Residents could then generate data designed to enhance their conversations in the mediated public sphere and better inform policy decisions that impact local conditions.

    Little attention has been paid to the data, perspectives, and embodied experiences of the people who reside near the Salton Sea. As a result, residents have raised many concerns and critiqued efforts to address the area's environmental health issues. The process is iterative and ongoing, which shares similarities with other majority-minoritized communities like Brunswick, Georgia, and Fresno, Texas, which I will address in the next chapter. At the sea, regional residents have critiqued the money spent on and results of the various reports generated by government agencies, as well as the lack of action that has resulted from those reports. In particular, one critique questions why more efforts have not been made to keep the lake bed damp, which is vital for minimizing the toxic dust (M. Cohen). As to the proposed mitigation efforts introduced in the early 2000s, Mary Belardo—then chairperson of the TMCDI nation—summed it up effectively: "Well, they've come up with five alternatives that basically suck, [and] just don't make any sense" because the alternatives fail to address either the patchiness or wholeness of the problem (qtd. in Nijhuis, par. 43; Rodriguez et al. "Conclusion"). In essence, Belardo critiques Western scientific attitudes toward complex socioenvironmental problems and their colonialist capitalist origins. Belardo also critiques a disconnected patchwork approach to what is now a wicked environmental problem. Tsing characterizes this Western approach to science as one that "stands ready to chop off excess parts and to hammer in those that remain into their proper places" without addressing connections among the parts (197). The effect is alienating to residents and fails to appropriately address the messiness of the situation.

Locals named proposed mitigation plans "Band-Aid solutions," which serve both as injury claims and as "wound sites" now manifest within the Salton Sea patch geography (Schall qtd. in Nijhuis, par. 44; Rice 82). According to Rice, "a wound site is a stable displacement for a more complex history of social wrong, yet it is [a] site of invention" because one can argue about the most effective approaches to heal it (82). Extending the metaphor to environmental report writing, a wound site invites researchers to investigate and report on their findings and propose potential solutions to redress environmental damage, yet if it is riddled with unacknowledged injustices or complexity, then it needs an equity poultice that includes local perspectives. Government reports related to the Salton Sea include documents from the US Fish and Wildlife Service, Geological Survey (Water, Biological, and Water Resources Divisions), Congress, Department of the Interior, Bureau of Reclamation, Army Corps of Engineers, EPA, and more. A quick search of my library database revealed at least 634 government documents. The cost involved for producing the research that went into those 634 documents is likely in the hundreds of millions of dollars, if not more.

I do not suggest that the reports were inaccurate, but the patchwork efforts to collect data did not result in a substantive change for residents in terms of their health outcomes or in terms of the overall environmental health in the region. Excluding residents' voices and concerns can both result in exceptional public subjects who feel voiceless and dismiss valuable local environmental knowledge when addressing problems. For example, Indigenous knowledge of the landscape's plants, animals, and conditions can support scientists' efforts to mitigate existing damage (Ulrich, "More"; Voyles 256–57). Acknowledging these kinds of oversights in 2021, Secretary Wade Crowfoot of the California Natural Resources Agency announced, "It's important for folks to actually see something happening at the sea" (qtd. in A. Chen). Addressing environmental health issues at the sea is "complicated," Crowfoot goes on to say, "but that doesn't mean we can't and shouldn't provide a very accessible way for local folks to share their input, so based on input, feedback that we received from the community we're actually expanding our public engagement effort" (qtd. in A. Chen).

Given the record of sluggish action on the Salton Sea's wicked environmental problems despite numerous studies, pilot projects, and so forth, it is no wonder that there is widespread skepticism among locals, and Crowfoot's conciliatory language admits as much. To give readers a better sense of why residents are skeptical, consider that between 2000 and 2003 there were at least ten separate (perhaps competing) studies conducted by different entities, and the results were not particularly effective. Kurt Schwabe, an environmental economics and policy professor at the University of California Riverside, explained the ineffectiveness of the early 2000s policy decisions as decisions based in engineering costs and little else. These kinds of decisions ignore the "massive costs to communities and ecosystems" (Rodriguez et al. "Environmental Policy"). Schwabe contends, "They [policymakers and technocrats] didn't necessarily look at the implication of their solutions in a systematic or quantifiable way on the communities," which led to inaction (qtd. in Rodriguez et al. "Environmental Policy"). In part, this is because the reports included research studies without direct calls to action and/or mitigation recommendations that were either underfunded or not funded at all (Singh; Voyles). The California Salton Sea Authority also expressed "frustration" with the US Department of the Interior because their promised feasibility study on dust mitigation and potential restoration efforts failed to appear (Salton Sea Authority, par. 90). Over the next few years, the Salton Sea Authority conducted some of its own localized studies and worked with Southern California water districts to try to develop a more effective environmental mitigation plan. Between 2003 and 2015, fifteen to twenty more studies were conducted, with similar results to the first ten. Patchy efforts and lack of coalitional coordination make it nearly impossible to fully address a wicked environmental problem successfully. However, there are examples of patchy mini successes associated with Indigenous-based coalitional efforts. In the next section, I will focus on Indigenous efforts, for a RISE approach attends "to diverse environmental histories" because that "narrative infrastructure" accounts for "future possibilities that are so much more interesting—and hopeful—than decline" (Voyles 269).

Sniffing Out Patchy Successes and Indigenuity at the Sea

As with most wicked environmental problems, successful mitigation efforts are often patchy and necessarily include recursive community-inclusive efforts. No one-and-done effort exists where wicked problems lie. Consequences collected at the Salton Sea for more than a century have no easy solutions. Collective will to "fix" the sea requires the "public to understand [what] is likely to happen more often as time goes on" and is crucial "to find a way to finance and pay for this thing," as Schlange notes ("Salton Sea"). I reiterate the quote here from the introductory paragraph of this chapter because it bears repeating. Clearly, sea scent events trigger public will, though persistent follow-though is patchy and expensive. Though people can be triggered out of their stupor by a jarring odor, exceptional public subjects contribute to the lack of united will to holistically address the sea's wicked problems. There are at least two reasons for this. First, as Crowfoot notes previously and Voyles addresses throughout *The Settler Sea*, there are perhaps dozens of overlapping issues to address: evaporation, eutrophic conditions, exacerbating impacts of global heating, decades of soil and water contamination, earthquake zone complexities, environmental injustice, the impact of colonialism and capitalism, and their cumulative effects. To address any one problem well is likely to reveal another emergent problem. For example, in discussing the "bomb-centric" era of the sea (1930s–1950s), Voyles explains how "material and ideological consequences flowed back from the sea to far flung places, just as they affected local communities" (179). That legacy still applies. To illustrate, one dust mitigation effort is tied to disrupting soil along parts of the sea's expanding playa zone by furrowing rows of soil (Anderson). Akin to an emery board scratching on the surface of a fingernail, the playa's surface is roughed up, which is aimed at keeping the finest particulate matter from becoming airborne because the flaky top layer is rolled underneath. Inherent risks in this endeavor include potentially uncovering radioactive sediment further down in the soil substrate or perhaps unexploded ammunition (Voyles 177–202). Experiments always have risks and potential rewards. Figuring out what works and why hails what Daniel Wildcat names "indigenuity" (48). "Indigenuity" expresses an "ability to solve pressing life issues facing humankind now by situating our solutions in Earth-based local indigenous deep spatial knowledges" that emerge from "tribal peoples," which constitute "a practical merger of knowing with doing" (48). Indigenous "lifeways" are "not at all simplistic or easy"; rather, they illustrate "an ability to work with what they have available and the wisdom to ensure . . . that they can continue doing it" (48). Wildcat's lesson is one of localized resilience.

Scent events spur public action and funding. However, localized work to mitigate wicked environmental problems often emerges in patches, resulting in a messy assemblage that makes holistic success difficult to define. Failure is easier to pinpoint due to its totality—problem patches merge. One example I noted earlier in this chapter is the Owens Dry Lake, where mitigation efforts were patchy at best and simply ignored for too long. Failures at Owens inform efforts at the sea because both are in arid regions impacted by the Colorado River's rattling tail and subject to tumultuous weather patterns stirred up by global heating (Thomson). Ultimately, drawing upon Indigenuity assists us to "understand the stakes and possibilities in questions about how stories about the past shape the future," for "stories of decline" leave "little hope or a sense of future possibilities" that Indigenuity can resuscitate (Voyles 268–69). In the next section, I focus on Indigenuity from the Torres Martinez Cahuilla who have navigated the diamondback sea for eons.

Torres Martinez Salton Sea Initiatives

In 2012—the date of the major scent event that opens this chapter—the state of California set aside about $3 million to create or restore wildlife habitat. Out of this, $1 million went to the TMCDI for tribal wetland mitigation efforts, which have been more successful than other efforts because the tribe addresses very specific patches of the sea effectively while considering the larger ecosystem and economic concerns of the people reliant upon it (Rodriguez et al. "Tribal Policy"). The tribe planned the wetland restoration project on the north end of the sea next to the reservation's dry land. Otoniel Quiroz, the current head of the tribally controlled branch of the Department of Natural Resources at the reservation, explains wetland restoration has been a priority within the tribal lands above and below the sea's water due to their kincentric perspective and long-term webs of relation (Nijhuis, par. 43; Rodriguez et al. "Tribal Policy"; "Desert"). Moreover, Quiroz explains that tribal elders wanted to "create a sustainable project," as they developed "an independent sovereign project for the tribe that it can manage and enjoy for generations" in collaboration with federal, state, and other local initiatives (qtd. in Rodriguez et al. "Tribal Policy" par. 10). The Torres Martinez nation remains sensitive to the grammar of animacy and open to addressing difficult truths as they advance socioenvironmental justice efforts. Their restoration patch is doing better than other places at the sea because it incorporates nuanced understanding of the landscape. The difference between this project and prior efforts at the sea dominated by nonlocal actors and agents illustrates how mitigation efforts include local knowledges and needs in a way that fully includes people who value the place as home.

Part of the TMCDIs' post-2012 scent event initiatives included a pilot project that incorporated solar power and created deeper ponds within tribally managed wetlands. Strategically channeling water so that some places are deeper than others allows fish to continue to thrive in those locations and by extension produces more places for fish and birds overall. Quiroz specified, "The first phase of the project was to really try to repurpose the wetlands" near the sea's north shoreline to include differentiated habitat. About eighty-five acres (thirty-five hectares) of wetland habitat were converted to a patchwork of seven one-acre "cells" (one-half a hectare) and four deeper ponds, which created an "eco-tourist attraction," a "recreational area," and "a sustainable food source for tribal members in case of emergencies" (Quiroz qtd. in Rodriguez et al. "Tribal Policy"; "Desert"). The Indigenuity aligns with traditional Cahuilla practices that include fish traps when the diamondback's floodwaters recede. Evidence of ancient fish traps was visible in different places around the Salton Sink before it flooded at the turn of the twentieth century and before US bombing experiments destroyed many (Voyles 24). Cahuilla consider associated petroglyphs at old fish-trap locations to be their "national treasures" and key to their "sacred past" (Voyles 24). The lessons yet rendered in stone inform contemporary efforts. Quiroz explains that the tribe has developed a sustainable project designed for "an independent sovereign" nation's future. The TMCDI recognize that the sea needs coalitional investments too. Quiroz remarks, "This is a collaborative effort, and if we have any kind of division within the group of stakeholders [tribal, regional, federal], I don't see us getting very far" (qtd. in Rodriguez et al. "Tribal Policy"). Hence, a visceral public's mediated efforts included exchanging information with policymakers in other agencies (state and federal) in grant applications and negotiations for other resources.

In 2020, amid a global pandemic, Torres Martinez elders and the tribal council introduced and collaboratively sponsored an annual poster project and youth internship program designed to honor the sea and the role the shifting landscape plays in Cahuilla life (Voyles 261). Art enters the scene here, both disrupting and complementing scientific and technocratic approaches designed to redress Salton Sea woes. Enrolled TMCDI residents are working with Swiss American land artist Hans Baumann to bring the poster project and a much longer art project to fruition (Ulrich, "Torres"; Baumann; California Institute of Contemporary Art). The project focuses on life, not ruin, which differs markedly from other artistic endeavors associated with the sea (see Metzler and Springer's documentary film *Plagues and Pleasures* for a focus on ruination). The TMCDI-inspired coalitional project will continue until 2030, which is unusually long for a grant-funded project, as they usually last three to five years maximum (Baumann).

In part, increased frequency of patchy scent events since the massive 2012 plume has fostered collaborative federal, state, and local efforts, which subsequently ushered in a "multi-phase restoration" project that was signed by California governor Jerry Brown in 2017. Part of the funding has gone to the Torres Martinez nation to continue and expand what they started independently ("Desert"). The expansive project broke ground early in 2021 and was intentionally designed with community involvement that included "subjective evaluations of possible outcomes" and equity, which contrasts with policy that relies primarily on "cost-benefit analysis," as was the case with the policy planning that occurred at the turn of the twenty-first century at the Salton Sea when scent events were less frequent (Rodriguez et al. "Environmental Policy" par. 1; Bardach and Patashnik). Olfactory rhetoric in this case has had a predominantly positive persuasive impact on policymakers, and the Salton Sea may serve as an example of how to engage in reciprocal relations to mitigate a wicked environmental problem that has multifaceted origins and a meshwork of complexity. It may also serve as an example for freshly equivocal governing bodies facing the Augean challenges of global heating and the "weird" affects it imposes. Climate scientist Katharine Hayhoe, also known for accessible science communication work, replaces the term *global warming* with "global weirding" to reflect the inadequacy of the word *warming* to encompass the effects of intensifying extreme weather on Earth. Global weirding reflects how disruptions to the jet stream, ocean currents, and water cycle result in increasingly unpredictable storms, droughts, floods, and temperature fluctuations that threaten food production and so much more. Such indeterminacy is the stuff of science fact, not fiction.

Conclusion: Zones of Indetermination and Variegated Materialism in the Salton Sea

Returning to the Salton Sea, in 2012 it became a body of water whose bodies of matter released odor molecules that traveled for over 150 miles on airwaves to be inhaled by many forms of human and nonhuman life. While my interpretation of odor molecules as bioinformation technology or as a rhetorical rupture may feel abstract, the real abstraction is everyday life that enables one to filter out the smell of environmental distress for which humans must accept healthy blame and accountability. The Sriracha sauce factory emissions also alarmed human attention, though the source of the odor was point-source specific, adjacent to the impacted community, and human-induced, which made accountable remediation and appropriate blame more straightforward. At the sea, remediation is complicated and blame distributable. The Indigenuity of the TMCDI includes leaning into patchiness and addressing bits and pieces while keeping the whole pattern in mind. Extending the example to a quilt, one can design the whole quilt and have a unified idea of what the entire pattern will look like when it is complete, yet one must create each patch separately before putting the pieces together. A key takeaway for readers: To contend with wicked environmental problems like those the sea represents appears to require a combination of hyperlocalized responses to problems in combination with having a holistic vision for potential long-term impacts intersecting (non)human life-sustaining needs. Short-term profit models make the latter more difficult to do.

A RISE approach considers a web of relation and encourages us to practice responsive accountability as we acknowledge the material agency of "thing-power" to move human consciousness toward action that redresses "emergent causalities" as we sense them (Bennett xvi, 32–34).[6] The startling nature of the 2012 Salton Sea scent event represents one such emergent causality or sensational rupture that inspired human action and policymaking, for as Stewart rightly asserts, "Smells underscore reality with a kind of inarguable force . . . [that] snaps people to attention" (245). Describing and acting on what that feels like has affects.

In the next chapter, using the SCENT heuristic, I turn to a different location in which smell-forward circumstances inspired human action to address a poorly managed landfill in two adjacent majority-minoritized communities, Fresno and Pearland, Texas.

---

6. Bennett's definition of "thing-power gestures toward the strange ability of ordinary, man-made items to exceed their status as objects and to manifest traces of independence or aliveness, constituting the outside of our own experience" (xvi). The Salton Sea is a man-made object in many ways. Bennett elaborates on "thing-power" in her second chapter, writing that it "has the rhetorical advantage of calling to mind a child's sense of the world as filled with all sorts of animate beings, some human, some not, some organic, some not . . . drawing attention to the efficacy of objects in excess of human meaning," though important to human meaning-making (20).

CHAPTER 4

Nasal Rangers at the Blue Ridge Landfill

> Law, through its conventional association with reason, has been seen as opposed to, or at least situated outside, the realm of the senses—although very much involved in its regulation.
>
> —David Howes and Constance Classen, *Ways of Sensing*

The Texas Commission on Environmental Quality (TCEQ) characterized the odor as "a putrid garbage stink, with notes of sulfur, garlic, [and] decaying onions," featuring notes of "a honeysuckle deodorizer" designed to "mask the scent" (Kadifa). Beginning in 2015, a stench intermittently wafted over the Shadow Creek Ranch neighborhood in Pearland, Texas, a community located on the southern front of the Greater Houston metroplex. Across Highway FM 521 (see fig. 5), people in Fresno, Texas, also contended with the stench, and the prevailing wind direction more consistently blew it their way. Fresno and Pearland residents' efforts to address environmental injustices across the two majority-minoritized communities offer lessons of persistence, coalition, and time. Scent events in this chapter are connected to the Blue Ridge Landfill in Fresno. The chapter's focus pertains to Pearland's process that resulted in coalitional action and policymaking to address the odor problem, though the problem will likely recur due to entropy and other intermittent environmental factors like hurricanes and flooding, for contemporary landfills invoke a sense of both kairotic (immediate) and chronotopic (long-term) time. The applied SCENT heuristic in this case study illustrates how two communities' narratives and tactics transformed public and political responses to poor air quality.

Kairos appeals to a fixed sense of time and the need for immediate response lest the timely, frenetic moment pass one by. Chronotopic time

FIGURE 5. Map of the Blue Ridge Landfill location and adjacent communities. The base map is from Google Earth, with modification by the author. Image credit: Lisa L. Phillips.

involves a different sort of investment, one of future imaginings and "critical horology" (Bastian, "Liberating"). Critical horology involves a critique of timekeeping practices and how political decisions behind timekeeping practices are shaped by power structures that have implications for a shared future (Bastian, "Liberating," and "Retelling"; Wajcman). Critical horology provides a rhetorical and temporal framework to interrogate waste disposal as an enterprise that affects BIPOC and other global communities' health outcomes. Critical horology retells time and timekeeping practices, which lends itself to long-term impacts of landfills to illustrate time-based contemplations of such environmental behemoths as social determinations of time that have cumulative consequences.

A surreal Daliesque sense of time that simply melts away is apropos for landfill time in which all sorts of toxins are temporarily confined, capped, and captured and doomed to entropy-forward leakage and seepages. Meltdowns are simply a matter of and for time. Michelle Bastian's sense of "slow time" and "retelling time" to encourage "long-term thinking" and a "clock of the long now" rhetorically reorient us to the long reach landfill mismanagement imposes on communities like Pearland and Fresno, Texas ("Retelling" 40, 43–44, 49).

Narrative and Context

Landfills stink, and, as one Pearland resident put it, "they are everywhere" (Kadifa). Poorly managed landfills positively reek. The effects on downwind human casualties are akin to tear gas, producing nausea, retching, coughing, and burning eyes and noses. People in the United States and elsewhere who have routine, effective garbage collection pay neither landfills nor trash volume much heed, though such elemental forces wreak glocalized havoc on the planetary lungscape. People seldom pay much attention to where their garbage goes once it is removed from their house or workplace either, unless there is a municipal strike, disaster, or other global or local interference that forces trash bags into the smellscape or on the sidewalk.

Mute scent events in both Fresno and Pearland have resulted in vernacular discourse and visceral publics multiple times. Stage 3 and 4 application of the SCENT heuristic in this chapter reveals how visceral publics have gained significant traction in the mediated public sphere, leading to direct action and policy efforts, though the success has been incremental and more successful in Pearland than in Fresno, which is tied to differences in local governance structures and in educational and economic resources informed by intersectional axes of oppression that manifest differently in each community. Both communities meet the RISE criteria as BIPOC-majority communities.

In coalition with city planners and the TCEQ, residents of the Shadow Creek Ranch neighborhood in Pearland established an "Odor Task Force" designed to identify, catalog, and pinpoint the source of noxious odors. This is an example of T in the heuristic, as it illustrates both tactics and transformation. The Odor Task Force included TCEQ training for residents on how to consistently collect and record smell-data over time. Lived experience of nuisance morphed from anecdotal evidence into identifiable patterns and point-source evidence, which were then used to establish legal interventions to address the Blue Ridge Landfill emissions issue in Fresno.

A recurrent theme throughout this book's case studies is the interplay between scientific, technical, and legal ways of knowing versus public, sensory, and embodied ways of knowing. In *Rethinking Expertise,* sociologists Harry Collins and Robert Evans outline how public distrust of science and expertise came about as the positivist tower of technocratic science toppled under scrutiny, yet the authors caution against "an age of technological populism" in which "ordinary people are said to have a more profound grasp of technology than do scientists" (2, 8). For instance, think of how some people claim to be an expert on something after viewing a short YouTube or TikTok video. Quick information uptake does not expertise make. Concurrently, Collins and

Evans suggest that we need ways to understand science and technology along with its affordances and limitations, as we evaluate the "meaning of expertise upon which the practice of science and technology rests" (2). For Collins and Evans, acquisition of expertise is a social process and there are "different ways of being an expert" (3–4). As a reminder from the introductory chapter, separating scientific or technical expertise from nonscientific publics has been characterized as a deficit model, and it assumes that nosewitnessing publics are ignorant and must be educated by scientific and technical experts (Walwema 246–47). Critics of this model point out that it disregards legible and legitimate forms of embodied environmental experience, and they also point out that nosesay publics are not interchangeable with ignorant publics (Simmons). One form of embodied expertise that manifests in this case study is through residents' encounters with changes in their smellscape—the *E* aspects of the heuristic—how they record those experiences, and how they share that information with TCEQ investigators and other public officials as they seek relief from noxious landfill off-gassing.

Nonetheless, there remains an unresolvable tension between what expertise involves, how it is defined and by whom, and for what intents and purposes it is defined (Graham et al. 72–73; DeVasto et al. 134–35). Internalized tacit knowledge built through embodied experience and social connection matters, for it leads to mediated visceral publics who act. However, Collins and Evans caution against "folk wisdom" that dilutes a depth of knowledge with surficial claims, as in the YouTube/TikTok example (Collins and Evans 6–7). In other words, someone can spout an observation without much practical wisdom on the matter, which can lead to poor outcomes. To illustrate, during the height of the COVID-19 pandemic, then president Donald Trump suggested people use ultraviolet light or ingest disinfectant to address the virus, which some people believed, to their peril (Jarvis). It is a cautionary tale that Collins and Evans tell and one in which "the speed of politics" outpaces scientific consensus (1, 8). When it comes to policymaking, Collins and Evans note how the rigidity of scientific expertise is often too "fragile" when taken on its own to handle the political landscape and policymaking (9). Because science is like "glass," which is hard, rigid, and prone to breakage when pressed by an outside force, be it rocks tossed its way in the form of new discoveries or the cudgels of political (dis)investment, it is not malleable, and policymaking requires elasticity—something that bends a bit to address more than one audience (Collins and Evans 9; DeVasto et al. 135). Instead, we need a timely mix of "expertise mixed with experience" across publics (Collins and Evans 9).

Nosewitnessing efforts by local residents in Pearland and Fresno contribute to that mix in this case study. Human noses constitute affordable equipment, and recording composite sensations across a range of noses provides qualitative evidence that can be documented over time in the mediated public sphere, which is what Pearland and Fresno residents have accomplished. By now, readers of this book will also know that it is difficult and requires money to gather quantifiable scientific and technological proof of direct malfeasance when odors are involved. Economic issues are baked into the "hard rigidity" of science and technology, making it more difficult to inform equitable policymaking. Although science and technological interventions are privileged in legal discourse, ordinary people and small municipalities usually have financial constraints that do not lend themselves well to an air-as-chemical-entity model. As with the Salton Sea case, it is also difficult to determine a point source for pollution when there are multiple contributors in a given region. While the landfill is the most obvious source due to its enormity, there are other potential air and water pollution sources in Fresno, like Champion Technologies, which is affiliated with the oil industry, and ten other industrial facilities, like a now-shuttered paint solvent recycling plant that is a Superfund site (D. King et al., "Residential" 52). Though unjustified, landfill operators and their legal team initially deflected blame for the odiferous emissions problem. This chapter's case provides insight into how communities develop protocols and procedures centered upon human olfactory experience to advocate for better pollution mitigation efforts, even with multiple pollution sources present (TCEQ, "Odor").

United States legal doctrine is built on ideological assumptions that privilege certain forms of inequality, though "inequality mocks [legal] discourse" (Sherwin 730). That is, a legal system predicated on the very idea of justice is one that ought to eradicate inequalities rather than reify them. Specifically addressing rhetoric used in legal domains, legal scholar Richard Sherwin asserts that "in [US] law, the distribution of power proceeds from authorized modes of discourse" (e.g., scientific and technological expertise) and "crime control" developed by way of "Scientific Policymaking" instead of "Prudent Interpretation" (731, 733–34). Scientific policymaking, in Sherwin's assessment, privileges a cost-benefit framework before all else—glasslike rigidity. Scientific policymaking is based on utilitarian principles that privilege the greatest good for the greatest number. In contrast, prudent interpretation involves phronesis, introspection, equity, and intralegal dialogue that considers how people from diverse backgrounds ought to be treated in the justice (and political) system—relational elasticity. Prudent interpretation is tied to virtue ethics and concerns about inequitable treatment, which aligns more with a RISE approach. Virtue ethics informed by intersectionality are also tied to just practices, including attending to inequity. Moreover, the stories that lawyers and judges tell, along with the judgments those stories allow, shape the types of facts that "make more sense" and are thus rendered more "relevant" based upon the values, beliefs, and assumptions a "decisionmaker" holds (731). Those values, beliefs, and assumptions are rooted in ideological notions of "human nature," how "social institutions function," and who is "authorized to speak" with authority on a given topic and informed by "pervasive cost/benefit analysis" (731–32). Hence, legal rhetoric shaped within scientific policymaking can be used to "mask particular" interpretations of texts or situations and the choice of approach is subject to critique (732).

Further, across all three case studies in this book, legal rhetoric plays a role in how visceral publics' mediated messages are valued or downplayed in both legal and policymaking domains. Legal rhetoric also influences how vernacular discourse unfolds and how people interpret the validity of their own sense experiences when considering how to contend with intense odor nuisances that impact their well-being. In illustration, when considering composite sensations before moving toward a visceral public, people discuss whether they think their cause of complaint will have legal grounds. In the Brunswick, Georgia, example in chapter 1, one resident noted in an online post that people would need to file a "health complaint" rather than an odor complaint based in nosesay because the resident felt an odor nuisance report would not be taken seriously by local authorities. Nosesay is more effective when combined with health implications. In the Sriracha sauce case, the stories used in court privileged technocratic approaches to residents' smellscape health concerns, and e-nose technologies were used to corroborate what residents specified in their nosewitnessing about environmental conditions. Judge O'Brien used hedging language when referring to residents' reports, and the defense attorney attempted to render the nosesay irrelevant in his argumentation strategy, though it drove the case's story. In the Salton Sea case study, scent events had a direct impact on policymaking and mitigation efforts. Likewise, scientific consideration of the health impacts required corroborating evidence from e-nose technologies and from technical experts (e.g., air-as-chemical-entity). In the Pearland/Fresno case, the landfill-inspired scent events residents reported also required technical expertise and e-nose technologies to lend credibility to residents' reports used in court. However, in Pearland, residents worked alongside technical experts and incorporated human-augmented digital sniffing technologies into their injury claims. I address both in more detail later in the chapter.

First, I will explain the regional context and disparate histories of environmental injustice associated with the case study settings in both Pearland and Fresno. Informed by Julie Collins Bates's environmental justice work, I then evaluate the role of amplifiers and attenuators at work in the respective communities' sensory rhetorical ecologies. Amplifiers and attenuators draw attention to or detract from environmental problems for specific reasons (e.g., public health risk, economic impact, quality of life, lawsuits) (Bates, *Toward* 11–13). Next, I address intersectional affluence that shifted perceptions and actions taken in Pearland and Fresno, respectively. Afterward, I characterize the Blue Ridge Landfill odor concerns and how they were addressed. I then analyze Pearland's Odor Task Force and Texas's nuisance law enforcement policies used to address the source of the stench. The chapter addresses how a combination of human and digital sniffers were calibrated to work to the residents' advantage, combining technology with embodied experiences to enhance legal uptake of the nuisance problem. The results informed Pearland's class action lawsuit against the Blue Ridge Landfill and Republic Services. I juxtapose Pearland's efforts with those of their neighbors to the west in Fresno, as the unincorporated community has met with less success when addressing environmental hazards. I speculate how incorporating inexpensive environmental-monitoring wearables could enhance a visceral public's ability to shape public policy efforts. To conclude the chapter, I reconnect the case study to the Sriracha sauce and Salton Sea case studies, providing readers a synopsis of key takeaways before proceeding to the book's concluding chapter.

Regional Context

Pearland

Pearland, Texas, is a newer suburb of Houston located near the edge of urban development on the greater metropolitan area's southern front. Roughly situated between Texas Highways 288 and 35, Pearland is a planned community. Planned communities are typically built on previously un- or underdeveloped land and have a residential focus. Recreational amenities, schools, shopping centers, and so forth are usually placed at the edges of planned communities along major thoroughfares to provide a buffer between outside development and family homes. This differs from typical urban subdivisions, which are more ad hoc in appearance and organization. Planned communities tend to be more common in Florida and Texas than they are elsewhere in the United States, though the trend is growing across the nation at a rapid rate (Nishimi et al.; Foundation for Community Research). Residents of these communities tend to be more affluent and often exclusionary, either by design or default (Kinney 252; Rice; Zenou and Boccard).

The Blue Ridge Landfill is to the west of Pearland's Shadow Creek Ranch neighborhood across Highway FM 521 in Fresno, Texas, which is beyond the planned community's boundaries. Republic Services currently operates the landfill, and the company is the second-largest provider of nonhazardous waste disposal services in the US. The Blue Ridge Landfill has been slowly rising and is currently permitted to reach a maximum of 130 feet tall (40 meters), which is as tall as the Arc de Triomphe in Paris, France. It will also be permitted to cover about 784 acres (317 hectares) with trash at that height level (Evans). Landfills can be framed as "irreparable injury" or "wound sites" in that once they exist, they make an irreparable mark on the landscapes they occupy, and as wound sites, they ooze (Rice 79, 82). They also have "the ability to generate multiple, and even conflicting, discourses" because US consumption patterns require their existence, yet few want to live next to one, nor do most try to limit their contributions to the pile (79). Circa 1960, people in the United States produced about 2.7 pounds (1.2 kilograms) of garbage per person daily, and by 2018, it nearly doubled to about 4.9 pounds (2.2 kilograms) per person (US EPA, "National"). While recycling and composting initiatives in communities with those options keep some material out of landfills, this does not offset population growth or increases in postconsumer waste. Wound sites are bound to social conditions and interlocking axes of oppression that foster their development and distribution in space and time. This extends to the contemporary placement and expansion of landfills in majority-minoritized communities.

Midden piles—the landfills of yore—reveal what people tossed aside and disclose details about the everyday life of the people who contributed to them. Historically, midden piles occurred on the margins of human settlement, not amidst them. Archaeologists excavate them to understand changes in human beings' ways of life, diets, cultures, and more over time (Rathje and Murphy). The enormous scale of contemporary "midden" piles combined with proximity to residential communities poses myriad health threats to nearby human and nonhuman residents. Middens of the past did not contain "forever chemicals," like polyfluoroalkyl substances used in waterproofing, nonstick pans, and fire suppression agents, or petrochemicals, like benzene, toluene, ethylene, and propylene (Kempisty and Racz). An enormous pile of garbage is prone to seepage—known as leachate—and stinkage no matter how conscientious the risk-preventive efforts may be. Given the atmospheric volatility inherent with global heating, we can also understand that heavy rainfall and associated flood scenarios in places like Houston (e.g., Hurricane Harvey) also have the potential to destabilize landfills and to increase water contamination in both municipal and natural settings. Entropy also plays a role because even the most well-designed landfill will eventually leak into the soil substrate or off-gas into the air. Entropy matters in terms of placement and is tied to environmental racism and long histories of placing hazardous materials in BIPOC and poor communities.

The Blue Ridge Landfill facility opened for business in Fresno in 1992, when there were fewer residential neighborhoods in the vicinity—like midden piles of the past but with a decidedly inorganic twist. Facility owners proposed a massive expansion plan in 2006, which residents successfully restricted in size and scope. To limit the size and scope of the expansion, Black and Latine women residents like Donna Thomas drove community activism by circulating petitions and knocking on other residents' doors, citing increased concerns about the landfill's impacts on their families' health (Zheng, "Residents" and "State"). Since 1992, the Houston metro area has experienced record growth, and regional landfills have had to petition to purchase more land, build upward, recycle more, incinerate, and so forth to accommodate the trash influx. Midden piles are now in the middle of suburbia as urban sprawl dictates and developers develop. Rice writes that "urban development is an unavoidable fact of life in most U.S. cities," and one that is "a hard thing to embrace," as it "chips away at people's lives in small ways" (5). In the Houston metroplex, development includes displacement of natural ecosystems and additional encroachment into historically Black and Latine communities to place garbage or other industrial wastes. Mary Ross, president of a Fresno neighborhood association in the expansion impact zone, stated at a public meeting: "I want to bring up the issue of parity. This area has been historically underserved. Why can't a landfill be put in the [Fort Bend] county's far [west] end or in a more affluent area where there's plenty of land?" (qtd. in Zheng, "Residents"). Ross's argument about parity is an injury claim grounded in a wound site, which is the legacy of redlining and environmental racism throughout the Greater Houston metroplex as well as class-based discrimination. Ross's question likewise foregrounds why minoritized neighborhoods should not bear additional garbage produced by wealthier communities. At the same meeting, Dora Olivo, a Democratic state representative from a neighboring community, stated that plans for the landfill would be unjust "in a densely populated high minority area" (qtd. in Zheng, "Residents"). After the landfill was constructed, changes in the Pearland and Fresno smellscape cultivated a different kind of public subjectivity and talk tied to a smellscape crisis that could not be ignored. "Chronic stench" inspired people to up their protests when they caught wind of the expansion plans (Zheng, "Residents").

It should be easy to imagine how malodorous an uncovered trash pile might be on a steamy 95°F (35°C) day in Houston. The TCEQ requires a nightly top cap of soil that is at least six inches thick for some kinds of garbage but none for other types, though they may still emit odors or off-gas other harmful particulate matter (e.g., some Class 1 nonhazardous materials like medical waste solids or construction debris can emit both) (Evans, par. 9). Between 2007 and 2009, the city of Pearland spent $70,000 in attorneys' fees to negotiate with Republic Services, Inc. in their expansion efforts for the Blue Ridge Landfill (Evans, par. 4). The negotiations resulted in a more modest expansion plan, reduction in medical wastes, and a requirement for a clay or soil top cap on all garbage types to mitigate potential odor issues. As executed, capping efforts were insufficient, however. Residents in Pearland began filing odor complaints in 2014. Complaints escalated late in 2016 and evolved into a lawsuit to attempt to staunch the stench.

Pearland residents leveraged community and Texas nuisance rules put into place by city planners and state regulatory agencies and used their expertise and relative affluence to create Pearland's Odor Task Force to confront the issue. In part, residents deployed citizen science to convince both Republic Services and the TCEQ that there was a persistent problem and to force the landfill operators to address the problem, and they did so with city and state government support. In *Participation and Power,* Michele Simmons explains that creating more effective approaches to environmental mitigation and policy efforts requires that the public "be seen as capable of contributing knowledge to the process and brought in early enough in the design phase to actually [affect] policy" and inform mitigation efforts (14). The collaboration at Pearland is atypical for government entities. Simmons explains that government officials "often view citizens as both hostile and devoid of knowledge that could inform a scientifically sound policy" and "argue that more significant involvement with 'lay' citizens would only delay [an] already long and tedious policy process" and mitigation efforts (12). Put differently, residents are routinely excluded from decision-making processes because it is a hassle to involve them, and many government officials do not think ordinary residents can contribute to the empirical research efforts. However, nosewitnessing is an important form of localized expertise because it can disclose composite sensations that emerge in vernacular discourse that leads to a visceral public and ideally to policy measures or other direct action to address environmental hazards. Nosesay can and should inform scientific and technical expertise, and in this case study, it does.

I also want to make a distinction between citizen and resident because I do not assume all members of a given community are US citizens. Nonetheless, I will use the term *citizen science* because it is a more well-established term, and *resident scientist* has a different academic implication. Central to the concept of citizen science is public engagement and participation, which a RISE approach values. In assessing an environmental issue or risk, a citizen scientist must decide why and how to be involved and what role to play in assessing or addressing a risk. Citizen scientists must also ascertain what sorts of support or deflection they will have from government or industry entities in a given community. The goal of citizen science has been described by the European Commission as

> public engagement in scientific research activities when citizens actively contribute to science either with their intellectual efforts or surrounding knowledge or with their tools and resources. Participants provide experimental data . . . raise new questions and co-create a new scientific culture, . . . [and] acquire new learning and skills, and deeper understandings of scientific work. (Serrano et al. 8–10)

Characteristics of citizen science inform how and why Pearland city officials and the TCEQ took positive advantage of residents' expertise and willingness to contribute to efforts to grapple with the Blue Ridge Landfill's nuisance issues. City and state officials recognized that residents could do citizen science, helping to pinpoint where and when odor nuisance problems occur and uncovering patterns to scent events in their community.

Parallels between Pearland and the Sriracha sauce factory controversy revolve around money, local influence, olfaction, and regulation enforcement. What differs in the Pearland case is the type of effluent, population density vis-à-vis industry, relative affluence of residents, and how residents of Pearland perceived and communicated their perceptions of risk. The Pearland example provides readers insight into how communities successfully deploy olfactory rhetoric in attempts to fight environmental hazards in their midst by using science and their embodied experiences in collaboration with city and state officials. I will also contrast how the neighboring community of Fresno has contended with the landfill problem.

Fresno

Fresno is within the northeastern portion of Fort Bend County, Texas. In contrast, Pearland spans parts of three counties in Texas—Fort Bend, Brazoria, and Harris—which gives the community broader access to regional policymakers and political representation. Fresno residents' socioeconomic status, health care access, and educational opportunities differ from those of their neighbors across the highway in Pearland. Fresno, a Census-designated place, is an unincorporated/unplanned community that predates Pearland's founding and the Blue Ridge Landfill's existence. Beyond the Blue Ridge Landfill concern, Fresno has two Superfund sites, a couple of chemical companies, and other industrial facilities that impact residents' air, water, and soil quality. Fresno residents have "voiced concerns about long-standing undocumented environmental hazards" for far longer than Pearland residents (D. King et al., "Initial" 22). Fresno has a higher percentage of Black and Latine residents when compared to neighboring communities (US Census Bureau, "Fresno"). Thus, overlapping intersectional concerns are always already present in Fresno. It is like the Brunswick, Georgia, example from chapter 1 in that residents have faced environmental issues for decades, though the Fresno community does not appear to have had as much success in leveraging tactical community organizing to shape policy. I would define Fresno's efforts as limited in success due to structural racism combined with lack of city governance, which limits residents' abilities to force compliance or establish policies to address issues (Feldman and Hanson). As with the Sriracha sauce case and Irwindale residents, Fresno residents also leverage injury claims, though to varying degrees of success. For example, some Fresno residents situated themselves as victims of landfill developers and used injury claims to advocate for municipal sewer and water supply lines. However, the distribution of water and sewer lines was haphazard and limited in range, leaving some residents yet unserved or underserved (D. King et al., "Initial"). They also successfully limited the size and scope of a 2006 landfill expansion plan, which included restricting the type of waste disposed at the facility and the total height and acreage of the expansion. A mediated visceral public included television and other audio/visual media outlets concerned that the landfill's proposed height would interfere with radio and cellular tower transmissions. Thus, the injury claims of impacted residents were amplified by media outlets claiming future economic injuries. While it is difficult to know if this was intentional coalitional effort, the combined result had a positive, if not ideal, effect—limiting wholesale landfill expansion in the BIPOC community. The ideal effect would have been to prevent *any* landfill expansion within the community. Instead, Fresno will continue to have trash influx from external communities like Katy, Texas, which is a majority-white suburb on the northernmost edge of the Houston metroplex (Jones; US Census Bureau, "Quick Facts Katy").

Environmental justice researchers Maricarmen Hernandez, Timothy Collins, and Sara Grineski note that environmental justice analysts have routinely "failed to clarify how race and ethnicity intersect with other axes of social inequality in contributing to unequal risks" (84). The researchers conducted a qualitative study of "residential decision-making processes among Hispanic groups" living at "relatively high and low risk to Hazardous Air Pollutants" in the Greater Houston area, which includes Fresno (83). Quantitative research in the study clearly shows much higher hazardous air pollutant exposure in marginalized Black and Latine communities within the Houston metroplex, which includes Fresno (Chakraborty et al.; Grineski et al.; Liévanos; Linder et al.; Sexton et al.).

A second study by D. King and colleagues conducted in Fresno in 2006 specifically addressed "key informants' perceptions of environmental health in Fresno" ("Initial" 23). The qualitative study featured interviews with Black and Latine low-income residents and Fort Bend County officials. Because Fresno is an unincorporated community, the community did not have a mayor or other city officials for the researchers to interview. County officials were the closest equivalent. This matters because Fresno residents lacked the support structure that Pearland residents used as part of their coalitional efforts to address the landfill nuisance. It also matters because the lack of locally elected representatives made it easier for Allied Waste to push through landfill construction in 1992 despite residents' vocal opposition and concern about potential water, air, and other environmental pollution problems that they correctly feared would arise along with the rising trash. For context, Allied Waste proposed and managed the Blue Ridge Landfill before Allied Waste was acquired by Republic Services in 2007. Unlike Irwindale, California's, more restrictive building permit process in the Sriracha sauce case, the lax permitting process in Fresno illustrates how creation of a "permanent nuisance" could slip under the radar of Fresno residents because no local government representatives (e.g., a mayor or city attorney) would have reviewed the permitting process. Only county officials would have done that, and if those officials did not live in Fresno, they might not have considered, or cared about, the nuisance implications for locals.

In addition, the D. King et al. 2006 study addressed environmental injustices tied to racism, and the researchers' goals included understanding how people in the community perceived "environmental hazards [that] could be affecting their health and [identifying] what community resources were available to hear [and to address] their concerns" ("Initial" 22). Residents' injury claims also included "inadequate public water supply," "water contamination," faulty septic systems, "lack of access to healthcare," and lack of community organizations among their major concerns (22–24). They also pointed out the proximity of the landfill to their wells and expressed concerns about their water due to landfill leachate along with the sewage issues from poorly maintained decentralized septic systems (25). The long history of environmental problems in Fresno related to other industries like the paint solvent recycling center—a Superfund site—informed residents' concerns about the introduction of new contaminants from the landfill (D. King et al., "Initial").

Just after D. King et al.'s 2006 study, fourteen years after the original landfill was emplaced in 1992, Allied Waste wanted to expand the landfill prior to its merger with Republic Services. East-side Fresno residents cited "chronic stench" and "concerns about [the proposed] expansion plan" (Zheng, "Residents" par. 8). East-side resident Donna Thomas used the following olfactory rhetoric to characterize her community's lived reality: "We smell it day and night. We wake up with it. We are very opposed to the expansion" (Zheng, "Residents" par. 9). Thomas also presented a petition she had circulated among residents that was signed by at least seventy homeowners who vehemently opposed the expansion plans due to health and property impact concerns (Zheng, par. 10).

The proposed Allied Waste expansion was not the first time lack of representation negatively impacted Fresno residents. In 1991, just prior to the landfill's construction and tied to the permitting process, Allied Waste dangled a carrot in front of residents' and Fort Bend County officials' noses. Allied Waste representatives promised a "tipping fee" that would go to Fort Bend County and would contribute to a proposed new centralized public water and sewer system for Fresno. The tipping fee was a "Host Community Fee" tacked on to garbage deposited at the landfill that started as $0.125 in 1992 and in 2005 went up to $0.30 "for each cubic yard of waste disposed at the landfill" (Franks). In 1992, residents were skeptical that Fort Bend County officials would use the funds as promised to build a functional public water and sewer system. Again, lack of local representation mattered. Residents' concerns were merited. The new system's proposed cost was about $40 million, and the fee collected from the landfill operations only generated $3 million over a ten-year period (Zheng, "Residents" pars. 21–22). The Houston metroplex is in the top three for worst drinking water in the country, and it is worst in majority-minority communities (Sansom et al.). It is unclear to this author, despite poring over fresh water supply district maps near the east side of Fresno, that a public waterworks and sewer system was ever broadly implemented.

Both Fresno and Pearland residents are impacted by Blue Ridge Landfill effluents. Fresno residents have a longer history with the landfill and other preexisting environmental hazards, like two Superfund sites and potentially contaminated groundwater concerns for residents who must rely on private wells or septic systems, yet Pearland residents' efforts appear to be more effective due to their economic and infrastructural advantages along with greater access to health care services and educational opportunities (D. King et al., "Initial" 24).

Amplifiers and Attenuators at Work in a Public's Sensory Ecology

Pearland community members who raised the alarm about deteriorating environmental conditions acted as "amplifiers," which environmental risk communication scholar Craig Trumbo distinguishes from "attenuators" who wish to minimize or eliminate the concerns raised by those who amplify risks associated with an environmental issue (200–204). Attenuators strive "to reduce a risk issue's intensity on the public agenda or [try] to keep it off the agenda entirely" (201). Amplifiers and attenuators tend to polarize issues, with the former raising alarm and the latter dismissing it. Pearland has amplifiers among its residents, among Pearland city officials, and within TCEQ domains. The three distinct entities assembled to sort out environmental damage in a manner that was collaborative and coordinated and by extension created a different sort of public beyond a visceral one. Gerard Hauser describes a "public" as "interdependent members of society who hold different opinions about a mutual problem" but choose to work together to combat it more effectively (32). Pearland's mediated visceral public morphed into a coalitional public, one in which residents and policymakers worked together to improve living conditions. While the Blue Ridge Landfill operators hoped to be attenuators, coalitional public outcry (amplification) about the situation forced a response that made the landfill operators become unwitting amplifiers versus the attenuator role they might be expected to play. They became unwitting amplifiers because they had to attend to the situation in writing and deed, which resulted in a formal, actionable plan that had to be circulated and implemented to meet TCEQ constraints within a legally binding enforcement decree. I elaborate on the enforcement degree more in the "Odor Task Force and Texas Nuisance Law Enforcement" section in this chapter. However, part of the decree includes the embodied impacts of the stench on TCEQ investigators who conducted Blue Ridge Landfill inspections between May and November of 2016. "Highly offensive landfill gas" that came from the site resulted in "nausea" for TCEQ staff and certainly for residents working in coalition with TCEQ staff (TCEQ, "In the Matter" 2). The decree lays out the violations, how landfill operators must address the violations, how much the company must pay as a penalty for violating health and safety codes, and a reduction in economic penalties if the violations are addressed swiftly and effectively.

The Pearland coalitional public also constitutes a "local public," which Elenore Long describes as "constructs enacted in time and space around shared exigencies" (15). Coalitional local publics are "at once discursive and physical entities" that pivot around "distinct rhetorical agendas" at circulation within a community setting, which can be either geophysical or more abstract (e.g., an online community or a community of scholars or activists) (15). For example, we can safely assume that Pearland (and Fresno) residents had a different agenda than TCEQ officials, that TCEQ officials had a different agenda than Pearland city council members, and so on, yet the myriad agendas did not devolve into inaction regarding the odor problem. Rhetorical scholars Hauser, Long, and Warner each assert that to be considered a local public requires circulating discourse like that at work in a mediated visceral public. Put another way, for Hauser, Long, and Warner, respectively, there must be open talk and materials (like texts or images) moving among different audiences in a rhetorical ecology for a group to be considered a local public. This extends to vernacular discourse around composite sensations and mediated visceral publics. I expand that argument to include materials that circulate in a sensory ecology. As a reminder from the Salton Sea case study, a sensory ecology relates to how we and other entities gather and use environmental information, considers the role of ecological enmeshment and interdependency, accounts for "the form and function of sensory systems," and interrogates how sensory information processing and interpretation work (Stevens 4). That is, rhetoric circulates in a sensory ecology that informs how we make sense of our surround from nondiscursive "texts" like smells that exert suasive force, causing people to act as a quasi-unified public to redress environmental harms. Things (noisome odors, eyesores, loud noises, etc.) complicate Hauser's, Long's, and Warner's respective conceptions of what legible "texts" circulate among local publics. Put differently, people were accurately reading environmental distress signals emanating from the landfill and interpreting the indexical signals as signifiers of health risks that needed to be confronted.

Diane Davis's layered exhortation to "accept that life weaves 'itself' as a tissue of traces, a delinguistified text-ile whose inextricable 'meaning' remains 'this side of or beyond all signification'" informs my analysis of what circulates in Pearland and Fresno's local publics (Nancy qtd. in D. Davis, "Rhetoricity" 433). Put plainly, what constitutes a "text" is also inscribed upon and within us—the nondiscursive stuff leaves a trace that we can sense in local publics and in private or both simultaneously. This is certainly the case with the emergent and energetic traces of methane and off-gassing effluent ejected by the weeping landfill's anaerobic processes. I assert that the landfill's noxious odor constitutes a sensible text people read with their bodies and that rhetoric studies is more prepared to be open to this sort of possibility than it was in response to George Kennedy's "Hoot in the Dark" in 1992. A snoot in broad daylight or in the dark informs a body politic or a body particular. Controversially at the time, Kennedy suggested that rhetoric goes beyond words and that it has a kind of "substance," an "energy" found in "nature that either resembles rhetoric or possibly constitutes the starting point from which it has culturally evolved" (1). Put another way, Kennedy's rhetorical energy flows between people and nonhumans, "exceeds verbal language," and "brings forth a decidedly sensuous, lively, and kinetic" approach to rhetorical inquiry and action (Hawhee, *Rhetoric* 3). Moreover, and rewinding to chapter 1 highlights on embodiment, Diane Davis proposes that there is a

> profound urgency underscoring this radicalization of the rhetorical text, since what's left of the world is at stake in it, as is the survival of a habitable planet. . . . [There is a] world opened each time . . . whenever some singularity—human or not, carbon based or not—manages to address some other by leaving a trace of "itself" . . . in the fragility of an appeal [that constitutes] . . . the only hope for the biosphere and its extant life-forms, "us" included. ("Rhetoricity" 433–34)

Davis draws our attention to the interdependent entanglement of bodies in motion, tracing how enmeshment amplifies material environmental conditions, denies the centrality of language, critiques quantitative instrumentation used to identify environmental problems, and complicates our notion of symbolic argumentation as a distancing metric. Paying attention to what circulates in a sensory ecology or, more accurately, a sensory rhetorical ecology, explains why and how people and/or nonhumans may react to changes in environmental conditions that threaten public health. How attention is directed by sensational events and how that response is communicated is also imbricated in systems of power that can either limit effective response to an environmental hazard or enhance it, depending on who wields that power and to what ends. Powerful attenuators can suppress both the hazard and how to curb it.

Pearland residents have more money than the average US resident, and the community ranks as the nation's seventh most prosperous (Dulin, "Pearland"). I surmise that prosperity enhanced the community's ability to amplify the environmental problem. However, Republic Services' estimated net worth as of March 2022 is $41.2 billion ("Republic"). Net income in 2021 topped $325.5 million, which was the "best year of financial performance in company history" (Ark qtd. in Kamczyc). This Big Waste company earned more than

$3 billion before taxes and other expenses. Pearland and Fresno residents can amplify but cannot outspend.

Intersectional Affluence Shifts Perceptions and Actions Taken

United States Census Bureau data indicate that Pearland represents an ethnically, racially, and linguistically diverse community of about 125,000 people. Of these, 42% are white, 18% are Black, 14% are Asian, 23% identify as Latino or Hispanic, and the remaining 3% either identify as American Indian or Alaskan Native or list two or more racial/ethnic affiliations. Thirty percent of households speak a language other than English. The community has a median household income of approximately $105,000 for a four-person household and $42,000 per capita income for those over sixteen. For comparison, the median household income in the United States is $67,000. Fewer than 3% of people in Pearland live in poverty. US poverty rates are in the double digits in other communities and typically much higher in majority-minoritized communities. Most residents live in owner-occupied housing, and the average house is worth upward of $245,000. In the Shadow Creek Ranch neighborhood of Pearland, the average house is worth approximately $350,000. Pearland residents have also attained higher levels of education than the US average. Ninety-four percent have a high school diploma and almost half of residents twenty-five years or older have at least a bachelor's degree or higher. Very few identify as disabled, and more than 91% have health insurance. Finally, almost all have broadband internet and household computers ("Quick Facts Pearland").

More than half of current Fresno residents identify as African American or Black, 35% as Latine, about 19% as white, and 9% with two or more categories. Nearly 20% of all Fresno residents claim immigrant status today (US Census Bureau, "Fresno"). According to a 2006 to 2007 study, about 15% of Fresno residents lived below the US poverty level (D. King et al., "Residential" 49). Subsequent population demographics have shifted from Latine to Black in Fresno. In 2006, half of Fresno residents were Latine, and African Americans equaled about a quarter of the populace (49). As the population demographics have shifted, environmental hazards like the landfill have expanded.

Unlike Fresno, Irwindale, or Salton Sea communities, Pearland residents have greater access to communication resources, educational resources, homeownership, and wealth, which theoretically makes it easier to address environmental harms and to participate in citizen science. Pearland residents appear to understand and exercise their civil rights and intervene when public health is threatened through environmental contamination and/or industrial negligence. Environmental rhetoric scholars invested in redressing environmental injustices can learn from what happened in Pearland and Fresno, apply some of the lessons learned to consider other places and spaces, and interrogate how communities that have more limited access to wealth and education collaborate to address deteriorating environmental conditions before a situation becomes untenable.

Many of the problems associated with the Blue Ridge Landfill stem from lax regulations and oversight and from choices corporate entities make based upon the bottom line, irrespective of evidence of environmental damages inflicted upon local publics, acknowledging that some publics are more deeply impacted than others due to power imbalances and systemic axes of oppression. Moreover, restrictive constructions of what constitutes evidence and constraints on who is viewed as qualified to collect it coincide with the emergence of impromptu activists, which are the opposite of exceptional public subjects characterized by Rice because they feel compelled to act on their concerns. People forced to adopt an activist stance in local publics do so because they feel they have no other choice in order to make their voices heard and to have their concerns addressed. Visceral publics form as a result, and collaborative efforts can move forward from there to address localized environmental problems. The tactics they take up are important to study because they can offer success stories of how communities contend with localized environmental issues, though those issues have a larger consequence or at least stem from larger consequences. The tactics also suggest how different communities may build coalitional publics designed to intervene in environmental risk.

Blue Ridge Landfill Odor Concerns

Circa 2015, residents of the Shadow Creek Ranch neighborhood raised complaints about a stench that seemed to be the most oppressive late in the afternoon and throughout the night, which coincides with traditional nonwork hours when more people are home. Deploying injury and memory claims, reviews of the Blue Ridge Landfill posted to the Google Maps site interface and public comment sections illustrate olfactory rhetoric Shadow Creek Ranch residents used to draw attention to a public nuisance.[1] Public commen-

---

1. In line with Sugiura et al.'s 2017 article "Ethical Challenges in Online Research: Public/Private Perceptions" in *Research Ethics*, I have removed or anonymized names and direct links to online comments connected with residents' addresses.

tary shared online provides collective remembering and sharing of sensory experiences tied to landfill effluvia. Rice situates public memory of spaces and places lost to development as "a powerful force" that can "circulate a narrative of loss, displacement, and harmful development in a city" (1010). "Memory narrative" may not be "unified" across a group of people, but it can nevertheless illustrate a "shared narrative of loss and public memory" that can be "palpably real" throughout a given scentscape. The relationship between olfaction as a memory trigger and disgust as an injury claim appears in public commentary related to the landfill. In the comments, people express both memory narrative and injury claims steeped in embodiment, not nostalgia for a place lost to development. Landfills may result from development, however.

Central to olfactory rhetoric, as illustrated via the quoted material below, is how ordinary people use it both to bring awareness to an issue and to hail other people who may share a similar perspective. Likewise, olfactory rhetoric is used to indicate needed action or mitigation by the perpetrators and/or regulatory agencies or government entities who possess the authority to redress the harm. In the Blue Ridge Landfill context, residents impacted by the stench decided how and where to express their embodied realities and injury claims associated with the landfill's poor odor controls. Nausea, vomiting, social implications, financial costs, and more bubbled up to the surface like the noxious gases emanating from the landfill. One commenter elaborates:

> The toxic smell from [the Blue Ridge Landfill] reduces the quality of life of the people in West Pearland. I can't run outside anymore without fear that I'm inhaling toxic fumes. Several times I've had guests over who don't want to stay because the toxic trash and garbage fumes fill the home. I can no longer enjoy my back patio due to the sickening smell. Even a drive home on a nice day is ruined because of the fumes seeping into your car and making you feel like you will vomit all over your car. You [must] hold your breath as you [drive] home when the god-awful smell hits you. Blue Ridge needs to fix the issues quickly or be shut down. People in the SCR [Shadow Creek Ranch] community are ready to picket and fight this until it stops.

Informed by what circulated in their sensory rhetorical ecology, residents' comments regarding the landfill illustrate how they leveraged affective response and injury claims to drive home the message that something was wrong with the landfill operations, pinpointing the issues and building webs of relation among residents impacted by the problem and highlighting the need for relief. Public commentary like the example above establishes how olfactory rhetoric worked in the public sphere in this case study to address nuisance situations that people might otherwise gloss over since our sense of smell is not viewed as an important sense perception affecting our overall health and well-being. A second commenter shares a similar refrain rife with irony:

> Dear Blue Ridge Landfill, I would like to thank you for the other morning when my 10-year-old daughter was dry heaving in the car on the way to school because of the noxious gas odor coming from your landfill. Nothing like the smell of diarrhea and gas to wake you up in the morning. I think I speak for all of Shadow Creek when I say that we have had enough. Enough of walking outside and having an [odor] so offensive that [it] sends you back into your house. Enough of lying in bed at night and wondering if you have a gas leak in your house and then realizing it's just the [odor] from the landfill seeping into your bedroom. Enough of not being able to walk my dog or take my children to the playground because the outside smells so bad. Shame on you for not fixing this problem long before it's made people physically ill.

Another resident suggests that "money talks," and describes:

> This place is in constant violation of code. At least once a week we can smell it. Blue Ridge is happy because local and state governments do not enforce the terms of their contract to operate. Make your voices heard by filing a complaint with the tceq and contesting your property taxes. I had the county cut 40K off the value of my house. Took less than an hour.

Aspects of olfactory rhetoric included in the above comments inform how Pearland community members enact or express the embodied realities of living near a poorly managed landfill. As I think about the shifting demands olfactory rhetoric implies of industrial facilities management, environmental risk, and city, state, and national environmental protection protocols in densely populated neighborhoods, I have come to realize that concern for a healthy environment and olfactory rhetoric can orient readers to two key tensions. First, targeting olfactory rhetoric helps to both identify and document people's perceived challenges in dealing with environmental risks, regardless of urban or rural contexts. Second, olfactory rhetoric illustrates tensions associated with sustaining momentum to resolve an intermittent environmental problem that is nuisance-based rather than threshold-based. That is, while the landfill's odor is a bona fide nuisance, it has not been determined to be a significant health threat in terms of the amount of volatile organic compounds emitted into either the air or the water (TCEQ, "Fact Sheet"). What is obvious in the public reviews people posted about the landfill is how the odor affected people in adjacent settings. Importantly, residents took the initiative to register official complaints with TCEQ. Residents have filed almost 7,200 complaints as of November 2021, and TCEQ has conducted 300-plus investigations to date.

Odor Task Force and Texas Nuisance Law Enforcement

In April 2016, the city of Pearland created an Odor Task Force in collaboration with residents. As described in the April 27, 2016, meeting minutes, the purpose of the task force was to establish a communication channel that allowed the city of Pearland and the TCEQ to inform and confer with residents on what both entities were doing to address the odor nuisance issues. Part of the communication plan included an opt-in web page where residents could register to receive updates and attain "factual information about a variety of issues related to the odor issue" (Odor Task Force Minutes, April 27, 2016). The opt-in web page was to include a section for frequently asked questions. The new Odor Task Force planned to meet biweekly until the odor issue was resolved. In the "Open Discussion" section of the meeting minutes, which included residents' input, a discussion of training for residents included teaching people how to "differentiate between and describe different categories of smells" in a collaborative effort to identify the problem in a more deliberate fashion. The nine Odor Task Force members included residents and city officials. One resident, Lucian Hill, was an environmental engineer with subject matter expertise (J. Ahmed).

The task force would teach residents to describe and identify odors and later introduce an augmented human/digital sniffer apparatus and potentially train resident volunteers to use the sniffer technology. The goal was to collect quantifiable data to pinpoint the source of odiferous emissions to fully corroborate nosesay. Readers may recall from the last chapter that to have a specific point source supports efforts to hold guilty parties legally and financially accountable for nuisance and pollution violations. It is also important to note that the digital sniffing technologies work as a kind of translation tool in line with legal rhetorics that require conversions of qualitative human experiences—something deemed semi-unreliable or sometimes described as "nonsense" in court—to something measurable in the privileged air-as-chemical-entity model.

It costs time, and therefore money, to train people (professionals and laypeople) to use digital sniffing technology. Attributable to time constraints involved in learning how to use the equipment, residents opted not to be trained to use digital sniffer technology, though they did have access to and used how-to protocols to define odor nuisances circulating in their sensory rhetorical ecology more accurately. The TCEQ liaisons explained how and why to record nuisance reports online, as evidence helped target the source, duration, intensity, and impact of odors. Residents lodged thousands of complaints, which was sufficient evidence for the TCEQ to file an "enforcement action" or enforcement decree and fine the landfill operator $43,712 (TCEQ, "In the Matter" 1). Moreover, the Pearland resident with environmental engineering expertise, Lucian Hill, created odor nuisance modeling that supported TCEQ's efforts, and the dates listed on the enforcement action—May 4, 2016, to August 16, 2016—correlate with Hill's comments in the Odor Task Force meeting minutes for August 17, 2016, wherein he offered to do more extensive odor modeling as needed (Odor Task Force Minutes, August 17, 2016, 2). A citizen scientist made a significant contribution to enforcement action and mitigation efforts as part of a coalitional public designed to address the problem. Granted, it is difficult to ascertain how many communities have access to what is, in effect, a pro bono environmental engineer. Nevertheless, it harkens back to Simmons's missive that we ought not dismiss the public as uninformed in matters that concern the health and well-being of their communities. Because Pearland city officials asked for residents' input, they solidified their case against the landfill owners, created resident buy-in among community members, and avoided hostility for inaction or lack of immediate resolution to the odor problem. The results are also clear in the uptick of odor nuisance reporting by residents. While this could be simply an effect of increasingly noxious air, it also stands to reason that the coalitional efforts of local and state government and citizen scientists generated a tipping point that forced the landfill operators to address both the odor issue and other harmful environmental impacts targeted by TCEQ, which also included water quality and leachate concerns.

While TCEQ enforcement action differs from judicial action in a court of law, the enforcement action result is more serious than a TCEQ "notice of violation" warning, which requires no direct action and planning on behalf of the violator to correct the problem. The latter acts primarily as a shot across the bow. An enforcement action bullets specifically what action must be taken and often fines the perpetrator for prior inaction. The docket for the enforcement action includes sections that explicate the jurisdiction and legal stipulations, allegations, denials, direct orders, and signature and order affirmation page. Blue Ridge operators denied most of the allegations, as Big Waste is wont to do, but the Pearland city officials, TCEQ, and residents pushed back against

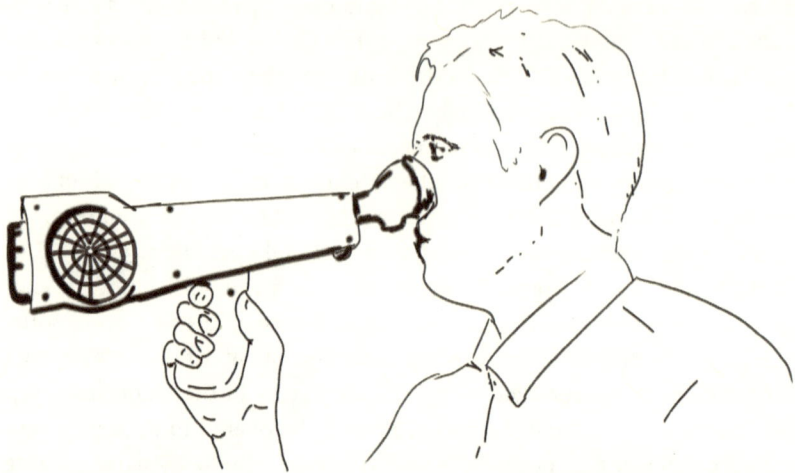

FIGURE 6. The Nasal Ranger Field Olfactometer. The image is loosely based on photographs of existing equipment used in the field. Image credit: Lisa L. Phillips.

such nonsense by continuing to document impacts and enforcing remediation efforts.

Hence, the enforcement action required the Blue Ridge Landfill to both mitigate the odor problem and pay a fine. The landfill operators arranged to offset $17,485 of the fine by creating a "supplemental environmental project" plan wherein the operators describe how they planned to mitigate the odor problem. The plan describes the project, includes environmental "benefits" to be addressed, estimates a cost, proposes a timeline, establishes documentation, explains consequences for failure, and accounts for publicity management (TCEQ, "In the Matter," "Attachment A" 1–4). Ergo, the supplemental environmental project action plan turned the landfill operators into unwitting amplifiers because they were forced to acknowledge and address the environmental impact circulating in the Pearland residents' sensory rhetorical ecology.

The Blue Ridge Landfill plan included "Nasal Ranger" technology and training for site employees to use the technology to monitor and track changes in odor conditions (see fig. 6). Thus, the cost to residents and Pearland was passed on to the landfill operators, though this implies a fox-watching-the-henhouse scenario if one were skeptical. Conversely, it shifts both the accountability and the responsibility for the odor nuisance squarely onto the noses of the landfill operators. In the next section, I explain what Nasal Ranger technology is and what it does after I explain how Pearland residents were informed how to contextualize their nonaugmented olfactory experiences and the role that wearable e-nose technologies could have played in that contextualization.

Calibrating Human and Digital Sniffers

Prior to Pearland's Odor Task Force creation, the Texas Commission on Environmental Quality developed a "Nuisance Odor Protocol" designed to assist people in providing "consistent nuisance determination" and describing the associated odors (TCEQ, "Odor"). The protocol includes a chart that helps people to log the "frequency, intensity, duration and offensiveness" (FIDO) of an odor. There are four tables on the chart. Each table characterizes the level of offensiveness of the odors: highly offensive, offensive, unpleasant, and not unpleasant. Charts also include intensity values for odors, which include very strong, strong, moderate, light, and very light. Frequency is also tallied along with duration.

Trained investigators who conduct complaint investigations on behalf of the TCEQ use the official protocol. Members of the public use the TCEQ website, "Odor Log," to register complaints and can use the FIDO charts to support their descriptive efforts to better characterize odor complaints and to be more consistent in describing nuisance odors. The protocol includes characterization of the highly offensive, offensive, unpleasant, and not unpleasant categories. Olfactory rhetoric ranges from highly offensive things like landfill gas to not unpleasant things like the smell of coffee brewing. The last page of the document includes examples of chemical odor descriptions, which the TCEQ warns "should only be used as a guide, based on the investigator's experience and training" (TCEQ, "Odor" 13). The city of Pearland "provide[d] odor identification training [materials] to the public to help identify 'categories of smells' during an odor event," though they stopped short of training that involved digital sniffers (Odor Task Force Minutes, May 25, 2016).

In addition to the FIDO odor surveys, the task force in conjunction with the TCEQ used toxic vapor analyzers and a handheld hydrogen sulfide analyzer known as a "Jerome J605" commonly used by the EPA and other entities to inform cleanup applications. The price of toxic vapor analyzers ranges from a couple hundred dollars to a few thousand. The Jerome J605 costs $20,000 and would not be a routine part of citizen science, yet having a baseline understanding of residents' embodied experiences informs when the equipment is used by government environmental response agencies to provide evidence designed to persuade in a court of law or regulatory body. Inherent in an air-as-chemical-entity model, toxic vapor analyzers also require significant technical expertise to understand the data collected. Had the TCEQ embedded environmental justice principles into their research design processes in the majority-minoritized community and made those "principles visible to a variety of stakeholders" using an air-as-lifeblood model, then providing inexpensive "environmental health-oriented wearables" to affected residents and instructing them how to use them could have recorded their everyday exposure to air pollution (Sackey 33–34). The associated effort would have done more to "transform users into participants rather than passive data collectors" (34). Residents' use of air-monitoring wearables could be a valuable addition when future problems arise, as it would gather residents' experiences using e-nose "wearables as technologies [to] assist public policy deliberation" and to capture "personalized environmental data" (Sackey 33–34, 35). Current wearable technologies can track common volatile organic compounds. They cannot yet capture nauseating experiences associated with noxious odors that make people ill. However, residents could use an associated software application to correlate their qualitative experiences with the quantitative data, which could include pulse rate and blood pressure changes and so on. Put another way, when something stinks, it may not be considered "dangerous" to one's long-term health within an air-as-chemical-entity model, yet it is dangerous in terms of repeated exposures and the associated stress that impacts the entire body over time, leading to increased risk for chronic illness.

Nasal Ranger technologies allow technicians proficient in their use to log qualitative experiences and capture volatile organic compounds. A Nasal Ranger is a piece of equipment used with the human nose in "field olfactometry," which means measuring the odors in a specific setting so that one can "confidently [measure] and [quantify] odor strength in the ambient air" (St. Croix; Delbert). The portable devices help people to determine "ambient odor Dilution-to-Threshold (D/T) concentration objectively with [one's] trained nose," which means that stinky air is trapped in the device and then diluted with odorless purified air (St. Croix). Field technicians can then indicate the odor's relative intensity systematically and collect the volatile organic compounds in the filter mechanism. The fourteen-inch-long, handheld smell-measuring device looks like a police radar gun that measures a passing vehicle's speed (see fig. 6). It has a nasal mask that goes over the human nose and creates an airtight seal, a set of odor-filter cartridges on either side of the tube that extends from the nose, and an associated app, the "Odor Track'r" that allows field investigators to log data results online. The device is the brainchild of Chuck McGinley, who is a chemical engineer and former inspector for the Minnesota Pollution Control Agency, which informed his career path and later air quality assessment business (Choi-Schagrin). The devices cost about $2,000, and certification and training to use the device accurately is around $300. As part of the odor nuisance enforcement efforts, Blue Ridge Landfill operators included the use of Nasal Ranger equipment in their air quality monitoring efforts starting in 2018 (Blue Ridge Landfill and Republic Services 8).

Pearland's Class Action Lawsuit against the Blue Ridge Landfill and Republic Services

Given that thousands of odor nuisance complaints have been filed with the city of Pearland and the Texas Commission on Environmental Quality, it is unsurprising that court cases have ensued. I will focus on one at the Travis County court level that reached the Fifth Circuit of the United States Court of Appeals in 2018–19. The lawsuit failed to immediately resolve the odor nuisance problems, though the initial case and its appeal made positive impacts on residents' quality of life in an improved smellscape because the case acted as an amplifier for community concerns. It also involved a negative public relations mess for landfill operators. For readers still wondering about the relative success or failure of olfactory rhetoric to resolve environmental issues, it is fair to say that olfactory rhetoric makes a difference, but it is not a cure-all. Olfactory rhetoric requires community persistence in the face of large-scale problems posed by landfills that will always leak no matter how well designed or managed they are. Persistence takes time, energy, and money, which are in short supply in communities like Fresno where access to health care, jobs, and the like are inequitable due to intersecting axes of oppression. The Travis County court lawsuit was a million-dollar class action lawsuit filed by residents and the city of Pearland in 2019, which was dismissed in part because the landfill is in an adjacent community and as such is primarily responsible to the Fresno community regarding nuisance laws and legal standing (see US Courts of Appeals, Case No. 19-40062). Though odors easily drift across highways, legal jurisdiction and standing can be extremely localized. Pearland residents lacked standing because the landfill is technically outside of Pearland city limits. As Matt Dulin reports, "The [Fifth Circuit appellate court] determined that the jurisdiction for this type of lawsuit is determined by the location where the odor is initially emitted, not an adjacent jurisdiction where an odor has a negative impact" (Coker qtd. in Dulin, "Travis").

Recall my description of the hog factory and our failure to resist that development. Only residents who lived less than a mile from the proposed facility were deemed to have legal standing to oppose the facility due to proximity, yet noxious odors and their impacts on bodies can drift for miles, as the 2012 Salton Sea scent event confirms in the extreme. As a condition of limited partnership under US law, Blue Ridge Landfill is also considered "a citizen of the State where it has its principal place of business and the State under whose laws it is organized" (28 U.S.C. § 1332(d)(10) qtd. in US Court of Appeals, Case No. 19-40062, 3). In other words, because the corporate headquarters of Republic Services are in Delaware and Arizona, the Fifth Circuit court could decide the appeals case related to the Travis County court decision and could have tossed out earlier verdicts that went in favor of the defendants—Blue Ridge Landfill and Republic Services. The appellate court opted not to rule in favor of residents. Odor drift was not deemed a responsibility of the landfill per Texas law in the appellate court opinion, yet prudence interprets otherwise. Moreover, because the landfill's original permit was filed in 1992 and predates most of the residential buildings in Pearland, the landfill is grandpersoned in as a bad neighbor and potentially known risk, placing blame on unwitting victims. The permitting process builds in the permanent nuisance aspect before a dump like this is constructed. Therefore, the landfill was construed by the appellate court as a "permanent nuisance," and the plaintiffs' claims were "barred by the statute of limitations" on nuisance injuries, which time out after two years (3–4). To explain, the statute of limitations is a doctrine that indicates the time frame in which one must bring a complaint to court. The statutes of limitations vary for different types of cases. For example, in many states there is no statute of limitations on murder. However, "two years is a standard amount of time to hear a case, any case" (Christofides, Email).[2] The legal moves in this example illustrate Sherwin's observation about the types of "inequalities" baked into US legal doctrine that rely on scientific policy's glasslike rigidity and not relationally elastic prudent interpretations built upon phronesis, intersectional ethics, intralegal dialog, and socioenvironmental justice.

The original landfill-permitting process favored the landfill owners and not the residents of either Fresno or (later) Pearland, though their use of olfactory rhetoric did have positive community impacts in moving policymakers to act and to enforce TCEQ mandates when odors emerged. However, the appellate court determined that since the landfill was a permanent nuisance and because the residents in the area have complained about the landfill for more than a decade, that fact alone meant that the statute of limitations had run out. Put another way, the judges determined that the residents of the area simply waited too long to bring this to the court's attention beginning in 2014, as the landfill was operating in 1992. Prudent interpretation is subsumed by scientific policymaking that privileges short-term economic outcomes and neglects long-term impacts that prudent interpretation calls for. Further, Pearland was not established until 2002, and that is when residents first moved there. The survey the plaintiff's lawyer filed on behalf of Pearland confirmed that residents have experienced the odors upon moving to their homes in 2002. The

---

2. I consulted Chris Christofides, JD, PhD, about the legal language used in the Pearland lawsuit to better understand the appellate court decision and the permanent nuisance considerations at work in the case (Christofides, Conversation).

plaintiffs filed their first complaint in 2014, so twelve years had elapsed, and the claim was barred by the two-year statute of limitations.

Thus, while Pearland residents, city of Pearland officials, and the TCEQ did everything "right" and did make improvements to the smellscape, the legal outcome favored Blue Ridge Landfill operators and Republic Services. Moreover, because Republic Services is a multi-billion-dollar business, the cost to retain lawyers and pay for other legal and administrative services was an inconsequential barrier for the company and preferable to having a legal precedent set that could impact future claims and lawsuits. However, by raising awareness of the problem and launching a successful enforcement action against the landfill, the Pearland coalition did meet with success. As of 2023, TCEQ inspectors indicate there are no significant odor problems associated with the landfill (TCEQ, "Fact Sheet"). Again, olfactory rhetoric is not a perfect tool, though it can be used to good effect in iterative efforts. I speculate that its impact would be improved through residents' use of personal environmental-monitoring wearables combined with qualitative nosewitnessing since air-as-chemical-entity is privileged in the court system. The associated data could also assist policymakers in adjusting permitting processes to include anticipatory nuisance language, as in the Sriracha sauce case. Mediated visceral publics would then have greater leverage when deploying injury claims, as they would have a valuable combination of sense data and quantitative evidence.

One takeaway to consider hearkens back to the Sriracha sauce case in this book. Readers may recall that one of the reasons the residents of Irwindale were successful in court was because their building permit process for new construction included language about nuisance. Based upon the city of Irwindale's prior experiences with other industries that involved odor nuisance issues (i.e., the pet food plant and the brewery), local government leaders made sure to incorporate nuisance issues into the permitting process and lodged a legal complaint against Huy Fong Foods as soon as a nuisance issue emerged. Legal scholar Serena W. Williams names this an "anticipatory nuisance doctrine" informed by the failure of the legal system to address environmental racism in US courts (223). Pearland city leaders could revise their permitting language to include anticipatory nuisance doctrines. Fresno residents would have to persuade Fort Bend County board members to do this as well, which seems less likely given the intersectional dynamics in the unincorporated community. However, Fresno residents could also use inexpensive wearables and an associated app to record and compile their experiences and use that information to sway policymakers in negotiation sessions or for other, more direct-action initiatives.

Another takeaway for people who may find themselves in similar post-nuisance situations is to consider how the tripartite Pearland coalitional public came together to attempt to address the odor problem, developed and implemented an assessment protocol, deployed citizen science, and coordinated a collective effort that worked in some ways as a public relations campaign, which besmirched the local landfill operators' reputations among the community. Occasionally someone from the landfill who used the initials "FL" would respond to people who negatively reviewed the landfill site on Google Maps, which suggests that the operators understood the concerns. For example, in response to a resident who posted a one-star rating of the landfill two years ago (in 2020, after the lawsuit), FL wrote:

> Hi [local resident], Please accept our apologies for your frustration. Please provide your address and contact information via email at CCRM@Republicservices.com along with a copy of your post if you're still in need of any assistance. We hope to hear from you soon.

The resident's original comment is no longer posted; only FL's "response" remains. The resident either left a one-star review without comment or deleted their comment later to protect their privacy. Other commenters shamed Pearland residents who complained about the stench, pointing out that purchasing an expensive home right next to a landfill was unwise and suggesting that the residents received just desserts for their lack of due diligence about the landfill's proximity to the property they purchased. Victim blaming is another sort of injury claim in that it reframes an environmental issue as something that one should have known to avoid rather than addressing the perpetrators' negligence. This discloses a "site of exception that cultivates the exceptional subject" who ignores or facilitates continuing environmental harms (Rice 81). A "buyer beware" mentality, however, does not apply to many residents in the neighboring community of Fresno, as much of it predated the landfill.

Conclusion: Mixing Nosesay and Wearables to Enhance Results

The Pearland/Fresno case illustrates a blend of "expertise mixed with experience" across publics that align with the suggestions of Collins and Evans (9). Nosewitnessing efforts by residents in Pearland and Fresno positively contributed to the mix in this case study; however, I speculate that coalitional efforts could go a step further with targeted incorporation of wearable environmental-health technologies like those Donnie Sackey discusses in "One-Size-Fits-None: A Heuristic for Proactive Value Sensitive Environmental Design." Although this rests on an air-as-chemical-entity model, it also can address an air-as-lifeblood model in that residents would have more tools in their arsenal to combat corporate malfeasance and environmental injustices. The same holds true for the Sriracha sauce and Salton Sea case studies. Irwindale residents have had the most successful outcome because collaborative efforts resulted in pollution mitigation at the Sriracha sauce factory, which fully resolved the odor issue. Coalitional efforts in both Irwindale and Pearland illustrate how local municipalities can support residents' efforts to address environmental health concerns. Respectively, Irwindale and Pearland city leaders incorporated e-nose technologies that required technical expertise to better assess air pollution and point-source problems, yet Pearland made more effective use of citizen science in efforts to address the landfill than Irwindale did regarding odor issues at the Sriracha sauce factory. However, Irwindale still has a reeking pet food factory and brewery, so inexpensive wearables could support residents' efforts to address grandpersoned nuisance issues because recorded health data could provide quantifiable information that enhances ethos in policy reform requests, in legal cases, and in direct protest efforts. The wearables could also assist residents to understand and address personal and community risk exposure beyond legal ramifications. This isn't to suggest that people's personal testimony does not matter; it simply provides an additional layer of information residents can use to offset hegemonic Western constructs that devalue sensory experiences. In addition, because air-as-chemical-entity is coin of the court realm, residents may improve community health outcomes by including the data as evidence. At the Salton Sea, the use of wearables would be particularly useful as air quality monitoring stations are sparse and do not capture localized conditions as effectively as residents might need to make informed decisions about their safety when outdoors.

The role that a mediated visceral public can play in amplifying environmental issues through sensory rhetoric is a key takeaway of this case study. Another key takeaway is how coalitional efforts between residents, scientists, and localized governments can work effectively to address environmental problems despite attenuators' efforts to downplay risks. Moreover, attenuators can become unwitting amplifiers when they must account for negative environmental consequences in the public sphere. Using the RISE approach highlights environmental hazards that inequitably impact Fresno residents and the intersecting aspects of race, class, and access to representation that make the situation worse for the community. Finally, the Pearland Odor Task Force initiative offers an example from which other communities might draw inspiration or that scholars might consider when analyzing how such initiatives come to fruition or fail to do so in other places and spaces. For instance, Kalamazoo, Michigan, has an odor task force consisting of "members from local industry, community committees, local and state agencies, elected officials, and City staff," and it is designed to reduce the odor impact from Kalamazoo's wastewater and sewage treatment plant (City of Kalamazoo par. 3).

Environmental hazards like landfills, sewage, factories, and toxic dust are all over the place and interspersed among residential, commercial, and rural landscapes, which means that many communities must contend with health risks these hazards pose. All three case studies illustrate that communities contend with these hazards in a variety of ways, and RISE and the applied SCENT heuristic inform that those most at risk often face more difficulties in their efforts to redress environmental problems due to structural and intersecting axes of oppression. The more complicated the patchwork, the more difficult it is to make sense of the situation and figure out how to best address it to improve environmental health outcomes for all involved. When we zoom out to the broader planet, it is more difficult still.

CHAPTER 5

Launching a Call to Sense

Think globally, act locally.

—David Brower; Giovanna Di Chiro; René Dubos; Patrick Geddes

In 1968, people saw US astronauts' photographs of Earth as a fragile blue disk spinning against the imposing maw of outer space. Legal scholar Lawrence Tribe described the gravitational shift the images evoked as the "fourth discontinuity," preceded by Copernicus's, Darwin's, and Freud's insights, respectively (Edwards 1). The broadcast images created a profound perceptual shift in how many sensed Earth's—and by extension our—place in the universe. The pictures provide an "allegory of the inevitable unity that encompasses all human division and [multispecies] diversity and binds us to the natural world" (1). Back on terra firma, "inevitable unity" seems patchy at best. Nevertheless, there are moments of networked unity where people come together to address global environmental problems, as the Montreal Protocol and healing ozone patches illustrate.[1] As the case studies in this book disclose, we are not passive objects of material forces, though we are porous bodies and subject to their osmocosmic effects. We have and make choices. Choices have consequences that "glocally" collect in low places like the Salton Sea, at the top of heaps like the Blue Ridge Landfill, and in the middle of things like the Sriracha sauce factory (E. Frost 51).

---

1. The Montreal Protocol phased out global production of chemicals responsible for ozone depletion. It was agreed upon in 1987 and was the first universally ratified treaty in United Nations history.

David Brower, founder of Friends of the Earth, distilled the phrase "think globally, act locally"[2] in response to the images of Earth in space.[3] Environmental activists have since taken up the phrase and modified it: We ought to *act* globally and locally, meaning that people must extend beyond thinking about patchy local outcomes and instead act in a way that anticipates the global implications of our actions (Di Chiro 205–7; Gerlach 301). "Glocal" action, as a portmanteau of *global* and *local,* is the current phrase some deploy to express this braided effort (E. Frost 51; Gupta et al.). Macro and micro are thus connected and simultaneously patchworked, which is foundational to my argument throughout this book and a point that Indigenous peoples have made since time immemorial regarding our enmeshment in intergenerational webs of relation that extend across and beyond the Earth's surface (Cajete, *Look* and *Native*; Itchuaqiyaq, "Iñupiat"; Kimmerer; L. King et al.; LaDuke; Wildcat). That is, local socioenvironmental conditions are osmocosmically enmeshed within global effects and vice versa.

We are an interdependent species and necessarily abide by interdependent gravitational pulls at work in the larger universe. Our vestibular sense communicates this inherently. When out of balance, we cannot manage everyday tasks. This also speaks to the Earth's vestibular sense. Earth has a greater ability to contend with imbalance than we do as a species, which we can clearly sense when we face large-scale environmental changes. The consequences of global weirding that stem from our fossil fuel use are patchy: a record-setting wildfire here, a 1,000-year flood there, a Category 5 hurricane thither, a record heat wave hither. Many humans sense this on an embodied level as glocal impacts become increasingly clear, and the impact is felt most keenly in marginalized communities already at higher risk for contending with the felt effects of global heating (e.g., island nations, low-lying coastal areas, and semi-arid regions). Nosing around in the waste products of capitalist dysfunction is disturbing. While this book's case studies focus on local examples of environmental pollution and industrial waste production and the sensational efforts deployed to address them, the lack of care for landscape and sensescape patchworks everywhere capitalism exacts a toll informs the broader environmental harms we now face as we spin on our fragile blue planet. Patchy approaches to environmental harms are easier to cope with and address, though we still need to foster a shared sense of how to undertake global issues. Moreover, we

---

2. Several sources attribute the phrase to Brower and specifically the US environmental movement (Scheuering 86; A. Todd 113).

3. Scottish city planner Patrick Geddes first deployed the phrase in 1915 in *Cities in Evolution* (A. Todd 2).

must recognize and work to redress how inequitably distributed environmental damage is across the globe.

Socioenvironmental inequalities present in many contemporary societies could be otherwise, and they are shaped by choices and sensations that circulate in the mediated sensorium (Bower; Graeber and Wengrow). Of unity and sensation, Winderman and Mejia write, "Mapping the tentative unity that constitutes . . . a sensorium requires outlining the intersecting political, economic, social, cultural, environmental, and biological practices that connect present and absent . . . symptoms of dis-ease" (23). Informed by an intersectional ecofeminist sensory rhetorical approach (RISE), dis-ease in this book pertains to reckoning with environmental problems that affect majority-minoritized communities using a SCENT heuristic to evaluate how mediated visceral publics use olfactory (and other sensory) rhetoric to work toward environmental justice. Winderman and Mejia go on to say that "politics of the sensorium are perhaps most visceral during crisis" (27). It is the "heightening or failing of the senses to detect the source of [a] threat," which moves the sensorium "from the taken for granted to that which could be otherwise" in mediated visceral publics (27). The results can either lead to "a shoring up of the political structures which gave rise to the existing sensorium itself: the structures of power that mark some [senses,] sights, sounds, smells, tastes, and touches legible and legitimate and others illegible and illegitimate," or reconfigure once illegible senses and seemingly illegitimate perceptions like olfaction, nosewitnessing, and nosesay into suasive modes and models for invention that can reorient activist efforts and policymaking (27). Case in point, I trust readers will now have a deeper appreciation of the role olfaction (and by extension other senses) can play in deliberative, epideictic, and forensic rhetoric surrounding environmental injustice and how people work to redress it. Regardless of the sense perception being deployed, I also hope readers will be encouraged to evaluate how and where sensory persuasion occurs in other communities to address environmental concerns and whether the intervening results meet with success or failure in terms of direct action, policy decisions, and environmental health outcomes.

In this book, I have argued that people in Western cultures tend to give more attention to masculinized senses like vision and hearing than we do feminized senses like smell, taste, and touch. I have also argued that our sense of smell warrants more attention in rhetorical scholarship because olfaction persuades people to act on emergent environmental "threat vectors" (Winderman and Mejia 27). Winderman and Mejia's explication of how some senses and sensations are rendered legible and legitimate and others illegible and illegitimate maps on to language used in legal and technical domains that dismiss nosewitnessing, though I have argued that nosesay makes direct contributions to direct action and policymaking when efforts meet with iterative success in glocal patchworks.

Zooming out to global environmental concerns, a RISE approach coupled with the applied SCENT heuristic can also support readers to evaluate how nondiscursive sensation shapes language and action, including that surrounding global climate change. For example, divers who visit the Great Barrier Reef off the coast of Australia see and photograph mass coral bleaching, and some use the images to support coral restoration projects, raise awareness of global weirding's impacts, and inform decisions surrounding fossil fuel use (National Oceanic and Atmospheric Association). Researchers have also been mapping soundscape changes to evaluate how human activity and climate change impact "acoustic footprints" over time in places like the Amazon rainforest (Rappaport et al. 1). Multitudes have smelled the impact of record-setting wildfires. People physically feel weeks-long effects of triple-digit heat and bathtub-like coastal waters, which also prompt anxiety.

Climate psychologist and therapist Leslie Davenport explains that "climate anxiety" can lead to direct action, for anxiety informs awareness that can inspire people to subsequently address their own and others' behaviors (Yang). San Francisco resident Alfrid Artis recalls, "The first time I realized that the climate change crisis was causing anxiety in my life was the day when the sky in the San Francisco Bay Area was orange; that is not the color of the sky. And that had a profound and deep effect on me because it so clearly showed that the danger was real" (qtd. in Yang). Imagination was directly activated. Artis sensed the uncanny change in real time. Davenport characterizes "healthy climate anxiety" as something that is "built into us as people" because when we sense and "feel risks, threats, [and] experience losses," this causes "upset" that we can "acknowledge," and this "really means that you're paying attention, you care, you're empathetic to what's happening to our world" and can act to address it (qtd. in Yang). While some may have more intense anxiety than others, as a therapist, Davenport indicates that the psychosomatic sensations inform how people make decisions about "where they want to live, what they want to do," and "what their future may entail" (qtd. in Yang). To address the anxiety, Davenport empowers people by helping them identify ways to become part of the solution and not feel victimized. One way to do this is to sense your surround and talk with other people about it, which, as this book illustrates, is how composite sensations lead to mediated visceral publics that shape healthier environments.

The RISE approach is designed to foster and support coalitional actions that serve socioenvironmental justice projects, as it disrupts ableist notions of what it means to make sense, be sensible, and become sensitive to life on Earth. This final chapter (1) assembles transdisciplinary ecorhetorical alliances, (2) synthesizes a few takeaways and goals of the RISE approach, (3) creates additional links among risk communication, environmental, and sensory rhetorics, and (4) describes some limitations of the project and suggests how and why readers might want to launch related projects, including ways to bridge to academic activism. I use a RISE approach to interrogate environmental problems in a way that could have "rhetorical velocity" within several fields of inquiry, like environmental rhetoric studies, intersectional feminist science studies, technical and risk communication circles, and cultural rhetorics (Ridolfo and DeVoss). A RISE approach to analysis launches alliance-building as part of the book's overarching exigence. To develop and realize solutions for wicked environmental problems requires people to work toward full unity across networked patches like the Montreal Protocol illustrates, and as the Cahuilla and their Indigenous neighbors make plain in efforts to address Salton Sea conditions.

The book's case studies show how a RISE approach and olfactory rhetorical analysis are applied to evaluate how people work to intervene in environmental injustices in the mediated public sphere. Understanding how embodiment and relationality are tied to systemic environmental emplacement and "thing-power" is crucial when evaluating mediated visceral publics and their impact on direct action and policymaking designed to address both short- and long-term environmental risks (Bennett xvi). I argue that the two risks are entangled and that a RISE approach pays attention to both while attending to marginalized populations who routinely receive short shrift in risky situations regardless of duration. RISE is flexible enough to consider and help us intervene in both because it heightens our awareness of what moves us, goes through us, transforms our perceptions, and influences direct action and policymaking. For example, the Sriracha sauce case focuses on a successfully mitigated short-term injustice (capsaicin-based air pollution) perpetrated on a Latine community, but it also demonstrates the complex sociopolitical history of the region that is ingrained in the community's long-term public memory and nosewitnessing. The community's institutional memory prevailed, and the community's Latine leadership created change collaboratively. The Salton Sea study focuses primarily on short-term scent events arising from long-term environmental impacts within a desert environment to show how nose-witnessing moves people to act on accumulating environmental damage. Regarding the Salton Sea case, it remains unclear whether (and precisely how) residents and coalitional actors will prevail in keeping the sea as an oasis, but the stakes for the greater good are clear: No Salton Sea means poorer air quality, increased health risk, and less hospitable conditions for migrating birds and other life-forms. The Torres Martinez tribe is addressing their networked patches by tapping oral and petroglyphic memories and mapping those onto future osmocosmic imaginaries. In the Torres Martinez future past imaginary, time is restoried and retells radical adaptation techniques, providing a narrative of "sustainable times" built from a typology of "long-term thinking," "critique of growth," "slowing down," "cyclical temporality," and "increased discretionary time" (Bastian, "Retelling" 37–40, 42, 46, 45). The typology counters the accelerant of fast capitalism fueling global weirding. The Pearland/Fresno case illustrates how people actively use their perception of changing landfill conditions to inform public policy using citizen science to support mitigation efforts. Though the case is short-term in terms of dealing with the Blue Ridge Landfill's stench, it speaks to a larger concern about excessive Western (and global) consumption habits with eons-long implications.

Assembling Ecorhetorical Alliances and Transdisciplinary Webs of Relation in the Anthropocene

Scientists, academics, and some lay audiences name our contemporary epoch the "Anthropocene" to signpost the dramatic effect human presence is having toward life on Earth and its surface. Currently, the Anthropocene is a politically defined era of geological time during which human activity exerts a dominant influence on the environment, climate, and ecology of the Earth. The Holocene names the contemporary geologic time, and it began about 10,000 years ago. The Holocene differentiates from other epochs because its beginning signifies the end of the last major glaciation (ice age) and coincides with extinctions among a wide variety of large mammal species (larger than 100 pounds, or 45 kilograms) across multiple continents (e.g., wooly mammoths, saber-toothed cats, and paleohumans known as Cro-Magnon) (see Illinois State Museum).[4] Though not inaccurate, the idea representative of the Anthropocene projects an arrogant perspective, as our species' existence is but

---

4. This mass extinction event has been attributed to a complex combination of three essential things: rapid climate change, human overhunting of keystone species like the mammoth and mastodon, and hyperdisease (highly infectious diseases that jump species). Scientists suggest that increased human mobility into once-isolated areas facilitated hyperdisease among indigenous mammalian species 14,000 years ago. Sound familiar? It happened more recently as well when Europeans introduced and spread disease in the Americas (e.g., smallpox, syphilis). Currently, diseases like Ebola, HIV/AIDS, the Zika virus, avian and swine influenzas, and COVID-19 correlate with a sixth wave of mass extinction that some scientists say corroborates the Anthropocene (Crutzen).

a blip in Earth's geologic time span, although that points to the name-change impetus among disparate scientific circles. To explain, the Geological Society of America has been debating the name change from Holocene to Anthropocene and the latter's origin point for several years. The Anthropocene Working Group within the International Commission on Stratigraphy (ICS) must establish vigorous scientific evidence for the proposed name change to be formally accepted. For the official name change to be approved by ICS, the International Union of Geological Sciences must approve name ratification for the Anthropocene's formal addition to the geologic time scale—a chronological, scientific measurement that relates events in Earth's layers to duration to describe what has happened throughout our planet's history. Simply put, a name change of this order is a big deal.[5] Several scientific disciplines (climate scientists, stratigraphers, biologists, atmospheric chemists, geologists, etc.) cite evidence of human impact on biodiversity, geomorphology, sedimentary deposition, lithospheric change, and fossil and ice records as reasons that justify the new name (Finney and Edwards). Concerned scientists have created a new ecorhetorical term that has gained traction in other arenas. An emergent, rupturing concept like that of the Anthropocene acts as a fire object to underscore both the fragility of our very temporary stability as a species and the seriousness of the impact we are having on life on Earth—something Daniel Wildcat names a "global burning" (1). Ecopoetics scholar Lynn Keller suggests we lean into a "self-conscious Anthropocene," for this recognizes how human actions have elided sustainable time and the term "signals a powerful cultural phenomenon tied to reflexive, critical, and often anxious awareness" of the scalar impact of human effects on Earth (2–3). Such recognition holds dear sustainable time for our species and others we destroy with fossil fuel accelerants.

In the final chapter of this book, I want to hold out hope to readers that catastrophic climate change can be fully abated, yet in good faith I cannot—to do so would be folly and irresponsible. As of March 1, 2016, our planet's climate system breached the 2°C (3.6°F) mark—a mark that climate scientists have warned for decades is irreversibly catastrophic to Arctic and Antarctic ice sheets (Broecker and van Donk; Hansen et al.; Wendel). Corresponding

---

5. Stratigraphy is a branch of geology that studies and describes the order and relative position of strata (layers) and their relationship to the geologic time scale. Interpretation of stratigraphy is a recursive process that can change with the introduction of new information. While the geological time scale is often simplified in infographics that depict a linear process of deposition, the reality of interpretation is a messy, folded business due to the dynamic nature of plate tectonics. The ICS has not yet adopted the term *Anthropocene*, as the commission appears to think the term is a political, not scientific, term. See Finney and Edwards's discussion of the topic for a more nuanced understanding of the debate.

with the largest coral bleaching (coral death) episode scientists had ever witnessed, the 2°C threshold marked the warmest year in human civilization and recordkeeping.[6] Carbonic gas at the level we nosewitness today is at Pliocene levels that existed three to five million years ago, when Australopithecines like "Lucy" walked the earth (Witze). Put simply, the Arctic "winter" season in 2016 (and to date) is June-like. Ice typically melts in June in the Northern Hemisphere. Coral cannot handle the resulting heat or the change in ocean acidity. The breach point appears permanent, and it does not bode well for the goal of keeping or returning the Earth's overall temperature at or to pre-industrial levels. Every year since the 2016 breach reveals increases in global heating trends. Climate scientists note the 1850–1900 time span as the point at which global temperature rise began to be documented (Holthaus, par. 6). We have crossed a tipping point from which there is likely no return, and the US National Aeronautics and Space Administration (NASA) reports that 2024 is currently the hottest year ever recorded in brief human history (Hansen et al.; Zeebe et al.; NASA). Hailing from the book's introduction, Indigenous thinkers like Daniel Wildcat situate my thinking here and provide a timely reminder of the ecocritical, ecofeminist, and Indigenous works that align with the approach I offer readers (e.g., Adamson et al.; Cajete, *Look* and *Native*; Carson; Gaard, *Ecological*, "Misunderstanding," and "Toward"; Itchuaqiyaq, "Iñupiat"; Kimmerer; LaDuke; Rìos, "Cultivating"). Wildcat writes,

> The most difficult changes required [to address global heating] are not those of a physical, material, or technological character, but changes in worldviews and the taken-for-granted values and beliefs that are embedded in modern, Western-influenced societies. . . . What humankind actually requires is a climate change—a cultural climate change, a change in our thinking and actions—if we are to have any reasonable expectation that we might mitigate . . . dramatic plant and animal extinction. . . . We must [understand] our human selves in what environmental scientists and ecologists, without the least hint of romanticism, call the web of life. (5)

Wildcat's rhetorical approach to climate change is cultural in nature, but it also notices our disciplinary and environmentally embodied interdependencies. This is important in a RISE approach to scientific research and how it is characterized across contexts. The scientific method enjoys academic privilege because it can present empirical evidence to an audience, but it often fails in

---

6. A small part of the coral bleaching (massive coral death) is attributable to a 2015–16 El Niño event, but the cumulative impact is clear in scientific circles.

the popular public sphere because uncertainty is embedded within its discursive strategies. A RISE approach to interrogating masculinized science questions the formation of hypotheses, how and why evidence is gathered, and the underlying assumptions inherent in a research question because bodies are on the line. That said, I value transdisciplinary approaches to wicked environmental problems like climate change—cultural and geophysical—because the exigency of extinction ought to make us sensitive to multiple perspectives and the rhetorical and bloody ruptures that rapid change facilitates.

Scientists can also question their own research and communication practices and revise their ideas. Recent studies indicate that climate scientists have been too *conservative* in their estimations of how fast Earth's ice sheets are melting (Brysse et al.; T. Slater et al.). Laboratory-based feedback models have underestimated the speed of global ice melt at greater than 2°C (3.6°F). Modeling a linear process, scientists predicted a global sea rise of ten-plus feet (more than three meters) over a couple hundred years. In March 2016, a group of eighteen world-renowned climate scientists published a peer-reviewed paper in *Atmospheric Chemistry and Physics* that predicts a ten-plus-feet (more than three-meter) sea level rise in approximately fifty years (Hansen et al. 3765, 3799). The article points out that past laboratory models omitted the complexity of nonlinear feedback loops that can lead to extremely rapid change. It may help to think of this as punctuated equilibrium. Punctuated equilibrium is characterized by short bursts of rapid change followed by relative periods of stability. Punctuated equilibrium is a king cobra: slow to rise but quick to strike, and if the strike meets flesh, suffering is sure to ensue. One must back away to avoid a painful encounter. To accent, the ten-foot sea-level rise noted above is expected within our predicted lifetimes and will certainly affect the next generation's lifetime. Coastal regions and island nations will be inundated—some are already being swamped (e.g., Fiji, Louisiana's Isle de Jean Charles [the Biloxi-Chitimacha-Choctaw tribal home], Kiribati, the Marshall Islands, Tuvalu, and Vanuatu) (Abadi; Breslin). Assuming the oceans' rising trajectory, wide-scale displacement of human populations is likely to lead to massive destabilization of existing governments. Global heating constitutes a "threat multiplier" that increases the likelihood of war (Goodman). Think of the ongoing Syrian and Ukrainian crises on a global scale.[7] Earth's system has been thrown out of order (into disequilibrium) because we have put too much carbon dioxide into the atmosphere through excessive use of fossil fuels,

---

7. Though some disagree (e.g., De Châtel; Pearce), many environmental law, social, and political scientists have already linked the Syrian crisis and other crises to global climate change and population pressure due to increased desertification of already arid regions (e.g., Fetzek and Mazos 145; Toscano; Wendel).

overconsumption of finite resources, lousy agricultural practices, and deforestation without replacement (Hansen et al.; Zeebe et al.).

It seems prudent, in fact crucial, that we turn toward radical adaptation tactics and collaborative problem-solving to slow the bleeding of life on Earth in our precarious era. As Wildcat indicates, hope, however dim, is enmeshed in cultural climate change. With hope, equilibrium could be reassembled, but it takes a while and a great deal of coordinated, concerted effort to salvage. Climate systems expert James Hansen explains:

> We understand that in a system that is out of equilibrium, a system in which the equilibrium is difficult to restore rapidly, a system in which major components such as the ocean and ice sheets have great inertia but are beginning to change, the existence of such amplifying feedbacks presents a situation of great concern. There is a possibility, a *real* danger, that we will hand young people and future generations a climate system that is practically out of their control.... [The] message our climate science delivers to society, policymakers, and the public alike is this: we have a global emergency. Fossil fuel CO_2 emissions should be reduced as rapidly as practical. (Hansen et al. 3801; my emphasis)

That formidable news delivered, rhetoric is about choosing the best means of persuasion available and acting on it, which includes reorienting traditional models of persuasion to include different inventional and suasive resources. The transdisciplinary web of relations I bring together in this book is designed to support us as we find the courage and glimmers of hope needed to sustain our collaborative efforts in time.[8]

Our persistence in living through an era of precarity is stressful and often unjust, yet "sensational" precarity can compel just action and bravery. Sensational precarity is when we sense something off in our environs that makes us notice our and others' vulnerabilities, which can result in discerning ways to analyze and rectify problems. Sensational precarity could also lead to and expose unjust action and cowardly acts by those in power (Chirindo 430–31). Precarity described in other circles illustrates lack of job security; unjust labor practices tied to gender, sexuality, race, age, and ability; environmental and political volatility; and compromised psychological and material welfare of human and nonhuman creatures. It also defines a new type of social class

---

[8]. The hope I share here is more than theoretical pie in the sky. My collaborative, transdisciplinary efforts to create an open-source instructional module for teachers is practical and has been funded by the National Science Foundation. The module was published in August 2016. See Phillips et al., "Mapping."

termed the "precariat" (Casid; Cassegard; Chirindo; Hovary; Molé; Ogawa). Precarity draws our attention to injustice through public and private forums and highlights changes in environmental and other conditions (Hesford et al.). Intersectional ecofeminists pay attention to both (Vij). Rhetoric scholar Kundai Chirindo's discussion of precarity includes how biological change is "precipitated in part by the need to adapt to changing environs. Just as adaptation among the species is catalyzed by shifting surroundings, so it goes with mutations in language" and, I would argue, in approaches to rhetorical inquiry that include the extradiscursive (432).

Once scholars interested in intersectional ecofeminism and rhetorics of sensation converse in (or about) selected precarious environments, we must appraise and interrupt ongoing injustices. And, while these certainly pertain to the human realm, we cannot ignore our enmeshed relations. An intersectional ecofeminist rhetor faces adversity head-on (hope or no) because that is the only viable option that makes sense given the circumstances catastrophic climate change and other wicked environmental problems suggest. When I attend the movies and watch some (usually white man's) bootstraps phantasmagoria that champions hope, the human spirit, and perseverance in the face of overwhelming odds, I cringe a little at the false hope the scene generates among US movie-goers, as that is the audience with whom I ordinarily sit (e.g., *The Martian, Interstellar, Star Wars, The Hunger Games*). On the one hand, I think, "What escapist baloney these fictions perpetuate!" On another, I say, "Yes. We can overcome," and I feel frustration at the paradox's seam. So, what, dear reader, ought we do next? I have provided a few ideas in this book for how we might redirect people's sensitivities toward each other and our shared environments by understanding, evaluating, and procedurally applying a SCENT heuristic, but we have ample room to expand collaboratively on this theme and to understand, acknowledge, work through, and limit our own and others' sufferings and extinctions. Redirecting sensitivities starts with coming to terms with how historically excluded and marginalized peoples and nonhumans deserve environmental justice across glocal contexts. This redirection extends to deploying olfactory persuasion in coalitional osmocosmic efforts to address different types of air pollution and their effects on bodies, as the case studies in this book illustrate. We can also deploy visual rhetorics to expose and redress environmental harms, as illustrated by the Cuyahoga River example. We can use sonic rhetorics to highlight changes in soundscapes when human activity has negative impacts on a vulnerable "acoustic niche" in the Amazon rainforest or elsewhere (Rappaport et al. 1). We can use tactile and haptic rhetorics to discuss the politics of touch at intersection with disability and beyond (Walters). I know you can also deploy your sensational imaginations to conjure other ways to not only become more sensitive to others but to bring environmental justice to the fore.

Recapping Goals and Questions Fostered by a RISE Approach

The conceptual and practical processes of writing, thinking, and analyzing through a RISE approach and developing a SCENT heuristic resulted in insights that may not have emerged had I trod differently. For example, because a RISE approach invests in the idea of nonhierarchical sensory entanglement tied to environmental settings, one must question ideological assumptions and revise them as one identifies rhetorical ruptures in one's thinking, writing, and revision strategies. One example of this is the role of embodied simulation and iterative reprocessing when thinking about the ephemeral yet visceral experiences people have in environmental injustice zones. Deploying archival activism amplifies visceral publics' concerns about air-as-lifeblood and attenuates the dismissal of their concerns by scientific policymaking in juxtaposition with prudent interpretation. Of course, RISE emerged through collaborative effort and my interdependent enmeshments and discussions with others. I know that a Black feminist or a disability studies scholar could take the basic recipe I have built and create their own method, approach, or analysis, expanding the affordances RISE and olfactory persuasion or other sensory rhetorics could offer in the pursuit of social and environmental justice.

Some Limitations and Research Openings

Although a RISE approach and SCENT heuristic are designed to address a variety of sense perceptions, I opted to focus on one: olfaction. Because olfaction and olfactory rhetoric are uncommon topics in rhetoric studies and a book must be limited in scope, this is a limitation of the book that offers research openings for other rhetoricians interested in an emergent area of sensory rhetorical scholarship beyond olfaction. That I chose an archival approach to mediated publics rather than an in situ approach meant that beyond embodied simulation and iterative reprocessing, I had little embodied engagement with the communities and physical sites of inquiry I examined. Environmental rhetoricians interested in mixed-methods approaches to sensory rhetorics could put the RISE approach and heuristic in conversation with field-based research or participatory action research to understand

and support environmental justice initiatives and to triangulate additional data. It was also difficult to succinctly point to or gauge "success" as people advocated for themselves and their communities in these messy, ongoing examples of environmental injustice. Success was often iterative and incremental. This, too, affords research openings for multisensory analyses. Using a RISE approach could reveal more evidence of success or failure across the sensorium in a landscape patch. For example, what does the water taste like in Fresno close to the landfill? Does the soil around the landfill show visible evidence of leachate? Does the sound or vibration of garbage trucks rolling into the facility create a nuisance? Are carrion birds or rodents visible? Is off-gassed methane burned off in exposed pipes, and does that create more light pollution at night or add more air pollution? If it is trapped and repurposed for energy, do the pumps create additional noise pollution? How might analyzing the combined sensorial effects prove more useful when gauging successful activist, policymaking, or mitigation efforts than olfactory rhetorical analysis alone could reveal in environmental injustice settings? While adding complexity to the writing and research processes, contending with wicked socioenvironmental injustices encourages a compound approach, and environmental rhetoricians could examine one site from several sensory rhetorical angles.

Articulating Affordances

To recap a few affordances, RISE and applying the SCENT heuristic are useful for unearthing environmental and social injustices because the combination enables us to describe and evaluate relationships between sensation, perception, intellection, and community; analyze (re)actions and agency; and unearth rupture or emergence in conceptual viewpoints, waypoints, and endpoints. That is, the approach I offer readers supports invention as it expands our notions of what rhetoric is and can do to foster cultural climate change and environmental justice. The approach makes explicit the emergent connections between nondiscursive sensation and understanding of environmental problems that place some bodies at more risk than others. Concurrently, it works to reconfigure an ableist Western sensory hierarchy. In its stead, RISE supports us to work toward a less ableist, more inclusive sensorium that incorporates a variety of perceptions (an aggregate system) to evaluate (and redress) environmental and social injustices across a variety of networked patches and time. The case study chapters demonstrate how RISE and the heuristic can be put to good use. As to how we can collaboratively expand RISE, it makes sense to form alliances with other social and environmental justice initiatives and other cultural and disciplinary perspectives.

RISE begs additional questions about what future sensory rhetorical research looks like, can do, and may facilitate. Broadly, questions posed may include the following:

- How effective are rhetorics of sensation in the public sphere?
- What can we identify in public outcry tied to sensation that has moved (or can move) political leaders and others to act in favor of public good rather than along purely partisan lines?
- Might transdisciplinary collaboration tied to study of sensation forge useful alliances between academics and other social partners seeking to change a political climate hostile toward academe and environmentally responsible legislation?
- How might rhetorics of sensation converse with aspects of technical communication, specifically risk communication studies, to consider how risk is inequitably distributed?

Environmental Rhetoric, Risk, and Rhetorics of Sensation

Risk and how to contend with its perceivable impacts has emerged repeatedly in this book. Applying the SCENT heuristic illuminates how people contend with aspects of risk in the mediated public sphere once composite sensations merge and result in visceral publics. In this section, I argue that sensory rhetorical inquiry offers rhetoricians interested in environmental risk communication scholarship more ways to notice how and when an environmental crisis creates a rhetorical rupture that results in direct and political action, debate, and change. Launching a call to sense, I take up the question of inequitable distribution of risk to imagine with you what the question can inspire in future scholarship.

Carolyn Rude notes that the kinds of research questions we ask shape the trajectory of a given field. Rude posits that research pivots on this "central question: *How do texts (print, digital, multimedia; visual, verbal) and related communication practices mediate knowledge, values, and action in a variety of social and professional contexts?*" (176). As subsets of this central question, Rude suggests that "social change" and "knowledge making" are strands of inquiry researchers address alongside "disciplinary identity, pedagogy, and professional practice" (176). A RISE approach raises questions regarding Rude's explication of a field's investment in knowledge-making and social change and what that involves beyond discursive texts. Rude's example inspires me to ask the following questions: Beyond what I have considered in this book, how do extra- or nondiscursive "texts" mediate knowledge, values, and action in a variety of social and professional contexts? In what other capacity might RISE support social change in rhetoric studies and related fields? Finally, regarding embodiment, what else might a RISE approach do to support rhetoricians to evaluate what is reasonable, noticeable, or risky if the "text" is an effect of stimulus on bodily relationality in an environment altered by human activity (e.g., air pollution's relationship to childhood asthma, injury to tree foliage, or bioindicators to dragonfly coloration)?[9] That is, what happens if we move RISE from "mediated" publics to solely in situ material experiences? What are the potential affordances and limitations of the approach to narrative lines of inquiry?

Rhetoric scholars have worked diligently to situate the embodiment of the person(s) doing the communicating and the person(s) receiving the action, and I would add to this other living and nonliving things precious to life, like water and the ozone layer (e.g., D. Davis, *Breaking*; S. Frost; Grabill and Simmons; Haas; Longo; Ríos, "Cultivating"; D. Ross; S. Ross; Rude; Sauer, "Embodied"). Said another way, contemporary rhetoric scholars might address how the sensations of embodied experiences inform risk interpretation in a given setting, as some already have (e.g., Pezzullo; Sackey). Beverly Sauer informs:

> To manage risk, both scientific experts and individual workers must observe, evaluate, and interpret rapidly changing sensory information. . . . The problem of risk thus challenges conventional rhetorical notions of instructions and procedures as generalized sets of practices that can be formulated prior to an understanding of material conditions in local environments and raises questions about [how] texts represent knowledge that is embodied, sensory, and uncertain. ("Embodied" 132)

Sauer's work supports my assertions throughout this book that nondiscursive sensation and embodied simulation is embedded in how people respond to risk in their environments whether at home, at work, or in some other place. She asks us to consider the kinds of information ("tacit knowledge") decision-makers use to evaluate risk and hazard, and she wants us to understand how risk and hazard are sensed ("Embodied" 142).

---

9. Increasing numbers of red dragonflies are bioindicators of ozone deterioration, and they are shapeshifting to adapt, or perhaps colorshifting. The red coloration filters out more harmful ultraviolet rays than the green dragonfly coloration (Cooper).

In this book, I have suggested how people use sensory rhetoric, specifically olfactory persuasion, to inform policymakers about catastrophic environmental changes and to take a proactive stance regarding environmental injustice that places some bodies at greater risk than others. Throughout the case studies, I also suggested how risk and hazard can be sensed and articulated. Olfactory persuasion is a concept I deployed to explain and evaluate how risk and hazard are sensed. I connect this to Sauer's line of reasoning that "tacit knowledge represents what cannot be expressed in words," yet acts as "hindsight" that directs future action in circumstances of "dynamic uncertainty" ("Embodied" 144, 146). Analyzing how sensory information is represented and categorized in written and other multimodal forms is part of Sauer's project that connects with mine. Although Sauer focuses specifically on "instructions and procedures," my book has taken a larger view to build a sensus communis that intervenes in environmental injustices for human and nonhuman life across networked patchworks (132). Thus, I take up and expand questions that Sauer raises regarding a "knower's embodied understanding of the material world," but there is a lot of work to be done to understand how sensory rhetorics affect humans and nonhumans in dangerous settings, and to determine how risks and hazards are exacerbated by racism, classism, sexism, ableism, speciesism, and so forth (132).

Finally, Sauer's point that workers and others may "violate written practices and procedures because the information represented in texts does not provide them with a specific kind of sensory information that they need to assess risk" speaks directly to my argument that a Western sensory hierarchy must be interrogated and that embodied simulation and iterative reprocessing inform how people use their experiences when in risky situations ("Embodied" 134). For example, if a road construction worker is told to listen for vehicle engines, but there are all-electric vehicles that make very little noise or the worker is hard of hearing, deaf, or wearing hearing protection, then the worker's safety instructions are inadequate. Likewise, if the same worker is told to watch for oncoming vehicles but is working in heavy construction dust or steam, then they may not be able to see approaching traffic clearly. Roadkill includes human and nonhuman casualties. Paying attention to sensory rhetorics and employing a RISE approach can limit risk and injury, resulting in safer practices and procedures. For example, if a project manager attuned to risk communication identified vernacular discourse circulating in the workplace related to workers not being able to see or hear oncoming traffic, then the manager would be able to identify and successfully address the issue before it resulted in harm to workers. Otherwise, families could end up becoming a visceral public because their loved ones were injured or killed on the job. RISE sensitivity could thus address concerns and lead directly to action that prevents damage before it occurs.

As I touched on briefly in the introductory chapter, my experiences working as a US EPA subcontractor to support teams to document hazardous waste sites inform my understanding of the environmental industry and environmental risk assessment. A RISE angle that linked sensory rhetorics to risk communication would have given me a better understanding of how my work pertained to race, gender, age, class, and ethnicity in hazardous waste removal and remediation efforts since these statistics did *not* routinely appear in EPA reports or in my work with the on-site field assistance teams. The embodied experiences of impacted community members affected by the waste were usually left out of reports or not recorded at all. For example, if a community member noticed an unusual odor or strange color in their drinking water, they may have reported it to the EPA, which would draw attention to a potential hazard. However, EPA subcontractors had billable hours that seldom included time for casual conversations with residents, and subcontractors followed the regulatory demand for empirical data in the form of soil, water, and air samples that were analyzed in a laboratory for specific chemical contaminants (e.g., air/water-as-chemical-entity). Yet successful efforts *do* incorporate residents' perceptions, as the Brunswick, Georgia, example and the three case study chapters show.

A RISE approach also considers the political and temporal implications of risk in environmental rhetoric and policymaking. For example, many studies of risk in technical communication and professional writing circles focus on environmental rhetorics that affect human populations, and contemporary studies can account for cultural differences and disparate worldviews that add complexity and ambiguity to how people examine and sense their environmental emplacements (e.g., Blythe et al.; E. Frost; D. Ross; S. Ross; Sandman; Sauer, "Communicating"). Rhetoric scholars Donnie Sackey and Dànielle Nicole DeVoss write that "one of the key promises of environmental rhetoric [is] not erasing ambiguity, but . . . equipping people with tools to recognize and navigate the ambiguity. . . . Ambiguity reigns, and the ability to traverse ambiguities rather than struggle against them is a key rhetorical skill" (199). Considering sensation under this rubric enables us to navigate the ambiguities of environmental risk communication while also considering how Brian Massumi's privileging of the concept of "vagueness" enables the "indeterminacy of emergence" to appear in our writing practices, thinking, and sensate processes around environmental issues. Hence, we might recognize the notion that a "vague" sensation or "ambiguous" feeling involves questioning what risks we are willing to accept in a given context and evaluating the underlying issues. The result allows rhetors to grow the ability to pay more attention to life on Earth and communicate accordingly. RISE also navigates the ambiguities between the human and beyond-the-human realm in environmental rhetorics and risk communication. That is, in a posthuman sense, since we are complexly entangled with nonhuman populations and elements, it is reasonable to ask how we might expand rhetorics of sensation to include these aspects in our assessment of risk and risk communication. One way to do this is to think through different sensory ecologies and how these are or could be tactically deployed to intervene in socioenvironmental problems. For example, in chapter 1, I provided an example of how Australian cockatoos tactilely, visually, sonically, and socially adapt to precarious circumstances in Sydney and how humans respond to them to limit the risk of garbage being strewn about, which is linked to habitat destruction that people can address.

Launching a Call to Sense

I titled this chapter "Launching a Call to Sense" to invite readers in rather than pretend a conclusion would braid all loose ends together and tie up the results with an unimaginative bow. Instead, RISE, olfactory persuasion, mediated olfactory rhetoric, and my application of the concepts make room for readers' own sensemaking activities when applying the SCENT heuristic. Socioenvironmental injustices are ongoing and tend not to have neat conclusions. Rather, research openings exist within this project that others might wish to take up. Finally, I transition to affordances RISE could pose for civic osmocosmic engagement for readers interested in bridging academic-to-activist purposes, which ends the book at the nondiscursive place from which I launched it: in my own stinking backyard.

As to how other academics could launch a sensational project from where I depart, the RISE approach and SCENT heuristic I offer converse well with scholarship in critical race theories, transnational feminism, disability studies, environmental rhetorics, cultural rhetorics, and Indigenous and decolonial theories and methodologies, to name a few. Transdisciplinary collaboration with climate scientists, geoscientists, and renewable energy scholars can also be fruitful in our shared effort to communicate how to restore (and the urgency of restoring) "energy balance" in our use of Earth's finite resources and the environmental injustice impacts of not working toward that goal (Hansen et al. 3799–801; Hayhoe; Oreskes). For example, I collaborated with a geoscientist and an environmental scientist to develop a transdisciplinary approach to mapping the environment with sensory perception. We developed a series of open-access pedagogy modules for use across disciplinary contexts to illustrate how contaminants move in an environment and to show how that risk is communicated (Darby et al.). Other rhetoricians interested in RISE as an approach could consider pedagogical applications for the SCENT heuristic to evaluate how students apply the method to other environmental justice issues. Environmental justice coalitions could develop a repository of case studies that apply the heuristic across international contexts to see how other cultural contexts shape outcomes. For example, if one were to apply the heuristic to a Japanese context, or in South Africa, or in New Zealand, what would a successful or unsuccessful outcome look like for a community? Does the litigious nature of the US impede environmental justice work or keep it in motion? How quickly does a visceral public form and circulate mediated artifacts in the public sphere in different places, and what tools do people use to circulate said messages? Is prudent interpretation prevalent outside of the US or in sovereign nations within it? What else might a RISE approach allow us to do to become more sensitive to our environmental entanglements and marshal the capacity and capability to act and address injustices?

Bridging to Academic Activism in Civic Service

I have deployed olfactory persuasion (and rhetorics of sensation more broadly) to support my community's efforts to first resist, and now contend with, a massive hog-confinement facility that was constructed a stone's throw from Sandy Creek, a small central Illinois tributary to the Illinois River. Sharing this more personal story is a work in progress that draws upon Blythe et al.'s explication of what "critical action research" is supposed to do: assist communities. Their epigraph informs:

> Personal stories and social histories of resistance and change, the failures no less than the successes, need to be widely shared. Otherwise, we are left with the impression that community issues and struggles are born out of nothing—or that only extraordinary heroic people can get involved and make a difference. (Marino qtd. in Blythe et al. 272)

I am an ordinary person who believes in making a difference. Most days, I feel fortunate to live and work in the places I do, to have a sense of community, to be able to teach and learn, to write what I am passionate about, and to know love, health, and relative (if temporary) ease. During the years I have been writing this book, I have fought against the hog facility alongside my neighbors, and watched my father, mother, and mother- and father-in-law die horrible, drawn-out deaths. Three of the four were caused or exacerbated by environmental hazards and information suppression, as I touch upon in the preface. I also witnessed my daughter and son grow to become feminists, and I feel absolutely supported and cared for by my life partner. Life is good, and as an intersectional ecofeminist, I am fully aware that I have a heap of unearned privilege. I work to pay it forward to those who have less and deserve more and encourage readers who can to do so as well.

As an illustration of academic activism that bridges to civic service, my community and I collaborated with environmental law students at Washington University in St. Louis throughout the proposed hog facility case. Residents lost, and now we endure the stench. The law students who engaged in civic service to our community have moved on, but two young women from my immediate community have now finished law school, inspired, in part, by the monumental disruption to our lives and our relative powerlessness. My community's web of relations now includes many families from Iowa whose lives have been ruptured by our shared misery and resistance to the corporate overlord known as VMC Management that built the facilities and reshaped our smellscape and watershed health. All this is to say that academic life and community activism have collided in ways that I could not have anticipated when I began this project. Unpacking how olfactory suasion might exert force existed mostly as a theoretical construct in my head when my neighbors and I read the request for the hog facility building permit and the Illinois Department of Agriculture's lax rules about siting and regulating such operations. Faced with the possibility of having to live with air pollution of a "natural" sort (think Salton Sea) combined with the knowledge of nonhuman animal suffering associated with these facilities tempered the steel of my resolve to be an ally to more communities than I imagined was possible when I began the project. Rhetoric of sensation encompasses all the feelings—the embodiments—of joy, frustration, and resistance we experience when we are trying to advocate for something, someone, or someplace that we love. Surely, there are other scholars reading this book that want to and do bridge their academic-activist work in support of a civic osmocosm. Below, I outline a few suggestions for how and what environmental rhetoricians can do using a RISE approach to build toward academic-activist work:

- When a sensory event occurs in your community, talk about it with your neighbors and use your rhetorical skills to identify and amplify legitimate concerns.

- Contribute your expertise when asked or volunteer, but do so in coalition with community needs and values in mind.
- Address injury claims in public meetings about environmental hazard placement.
- Persist in resisting attenuators' attempts to dismiss a community's sensible concerns at circulation in their sensory rhetorical ecology.
- Help shape ethical and equitable public policy designed to address environmental injustices.
- Listen to nearby communities and contribute to public memory to keep as-yet-unresolved environmental injustices in the spotlight until they are appropriately redressed.
- Pay attention to extradiscursive arguments and amplify how they shape environmental policies.
- If you cannot be physically proximal to a community's environmental justice concerns, use embodied simulation, iterative reprocessing, and archival activism to amplify their actions anyway.

Someone facing or researching a (dis)similar situation could draw strength and resolve from a RISE approach, or apply olfactory- or sensory-rhetorical analysis and make use of the SCENT heuristic to do some good for life on Earth.

ACKNOWLEDGMENTS

Writing is relational and a book only comes to fruition as one shares ideas in conversation with others on the page and in person. Thanks to so many who gave knowledge, time, funds, and other sense-making resources that contributed to the book's development, including Texas Tech University's Humanities Center and Director Mike Borshuk, Offices of the Provost and President, Office of Research and Innovation, Department of English, Technical Communication and Rhetoric Program, and Women Faculty Writing Program.

Illinois State University feminist mentors in rhetoric and professional writing, thank you: Julie Jung, Angela M. Haas, Julie Cheville, Amy Robillard, and Jerry Savage. I owe a few Redbird friends a special debt of gratitude. Julie Collins Bates, I value your friendship, expertise, principles, and editorial finesse. Irina Nersessova, I appreciate our talks and continued camaraderie. Gretchen Frank, thanks for sending me all the olfaction stories!

Thank you, current and former Texas Tech colleagues for verbal or written feedback at different stages and on different chapters of the book: Michael Faris, Kendall Gerdes, Steve Holmes, Jennifer Nish, Jason Tham, and Scott Weedon. Thanks to Kellie Gray, Amy Koerber, Callie Kostelich, Beau Pihlaja, Becky Rickly, and David Roach for your words of encouragement as my colleagues throughout this process. Thank you to the growing sensory rhetorics community: Steph Ceraso, Debra Hawhee, Jon Stone, and Jennifer LeMesurier. I appreciate your work and sensational spaces of collaboration. Anita

Fitzgerald, thank you for your invaluable feedback on the book. I'm so grateful. Kimberly Radek Hall, such stalwart friendship across time and place is so rare. Thank you.

Thanks to Tara Cyphers and the New Directions in Rhetoric and Materiality series editors Allison Rowland, Christa Teston, Shui-Yin Sharon Yam, and Wendy S. Hesford. I am especially grateful for the thorough and thoughtful anonymous reviews of the book. I appreciate the reviewers' work and their ethic of care.

To my children, Morgan and Ethan, you are the soul of this book, and it is dedicated to your breathable futures. Mike, you are my heart. Writing a book during a lockdown in a global pandemic would have been much worse without you by my side.

WORKS CITED

Abadi, Mark. "These Island Nations Could Be Underwater in as Little as 50 Years." *Business Insider Science,* 30 Dec. 2015.

Abram, David. *The Spell of the Sensuous: Perception and Language in a More-than-Human World.* Pantheon Books, 1996.

Adamson, Joni, et al., editors. *The Environmental Justice Reader: Politics, Poetics, and Pedagogy.* U of Arizona, 2002.

Ahmed, Jalelah. "Odor Task Force Says It Knows Origin of Neighborhood Stink." *Houston Fox 26,* 4 Oct. 2016, https://www.fox26houston.com/news/odor-task-force-says-it-knows-origin-of-neighborhood-stink.

Ahmed, Sara. *The Cultural Politics of Emotion.* 2nd ed., Routledge, 2014.

Alaimo, Stacy. *Bodily Natures: Science, Environment, and the Material Self.* Indiana UP, 2010.

Albrecht, Leslie. "Barclays Center's 'Signature Scent' Tickles Noses, Curiosity." *DNAInfo,* 20 May 2013, https://www.dnainfo.com/new-york/20130520/prospect-heights/barclays-centers-signature-scent-tickles-noses-curiosity.

Anderson, Erik. "Project Takes Aim at Controlling Salton Sea Dust." *KPBS, BBC Newshour,* 12 Mar. 2019, https://www.kpbs.org/news/midday-edition/2019/03/12/controlling-dust-californias-salton-sea.

Appadurai, Arjun. "Gastro-Politics in Hindu South Asia." *American Ethnologist,* vol. 8, no. 3, 1981, pp. 494–511, https://doi.org/10.1525/ae.1981.8.3.02a00050.

Arendt, Hannah. "Origins of Totalitarianism." *On Violence: A Reader,* edited by Bruce B. Lawrence and Aisha Karim, Duke UP, 2007, pp. 417–33.

Aristotle. *De Anima.* Translated by Hugh Lawson-Tancred, Penguin, 1987.

Armstrong, Susan J., and Richard G. Botzler, editors. *Animal Ethics Reader.* Routledge, 2003.

Arola, Kristin. "A Land-Based Digital Design Rhetoric." *The Routledge Handbook of Digital Writing and Rhetoric,* edited by Johnathan Alexander and Jacqueline Rhodes, Routledge, 2018, pp. 199–214.

Associated Press. "Southern California Stench Linked to Salton Sea." *The Oregonian,* 11 Sept. 2012, https://www.oregonlive.com/today/2012/09/southern_california_stench_lin.html.

Avila, Ernie. Twitter (X) post, 10 Sept. 2012, 9:23 a.m., https://twitter.com/BigErn909/status/245195821975478272?ref_src=twsrc%5Etfw.

Banes, Sally. "Olfactory Performances." *The Drama Review,* vol. 45, no. 1, 2001, pp. 68–76.

Banks, Sedina. "The Erin Brockovich Effect: How Media Shapes Toxics Policy." *Environs: Environmental Law and Policy Journal,* vol. 26, no. 2, 2003, pp. 219–52. *HeinOnline,* https://heinonline.org/HOL/P?h=hein.journals/environs26&i=225.

Banzhaf, Spencer, et al. "Environmental Justice: The Economics of Race, Place, and Pollution." *Journal of Economic Perspectives,* vol. 33, no. 1, 2019, pp. 185–208.

Barad, Karen. *Meeting the Universe Halfway: Quantum Physics and the Entanglement of Matter and Meaning.* Duke UP, 2007.

Barajas, Julia. "Years of Putrid Odors, Scores of Complaints. The Fight over a Facility That Recycles Dead Animals in Southeast LA." *LAist, Southern California Public Broadcasting Service,* 5 Oct. 2023, https://laist.com/news/climate-environment/rendering-plants-odors-southeast-los-angeles-vernon-aqmd-complaints#interviews-with-local-residents.

Bardach, Eugene S., and Eric M. Patashnik. *A Practical Guide for Policy Analysis: The Eightfold Path to More Effective Problem Solving.* 6th ed., Sage Publishing, 2019.

Bardsley, Douglas K., et al. "Seeking Knowledge of Traditional Indigenous Burning Practices to Inform Regional Bushfire Management." *Local Environment,* vol. 24, no. 8, 2019, pp. 727–45.

Barth, Friedrich G., et al., editors. *Sensory Perception: Mind and Matter.* Springer-Verlag/Wien, 2012.

Barthes, Roland. *Writing Degree Zero.* Translated by Annette Lavers and Colin Smith, Hill and Wang, 2012.

Barthlott, Wilhelm, et al. "Plant Surfaces: Structures and Functions for Biomimetic Innovations." *Nano-Micro Letters,* vol. 9, no. 23, 2017, pp. 1–40, https://doi.org/10.1007/s40820-016-0125-1.

Barwich, Ann-Sophie. *Smellosophy.* Harvard UP, 2020.

Bastian, Michelle. "Liberating Clocks: Developing a Critical Horology to Rethink the Potential of Clock Time." *New Formations: A Journal of Culture/Theory/Politics,* vol. 92, pp. 41–55.

Bastian, Michelle. "Retelling Time in Grassroots Sustainable Economy Movements." *GeoHumanities,* vol. 5, no. 1, 2019, 36–53.

Bataille, George. *The Accursed Share: An Essay on the General Economy, Volumes II and III.* Zone Books, 1991.

Bates, Julie Collins. "Activist Archival Research, Environmental Intervention, and the Flint Water Crisis." *Reflections,* vol. 19, no. 2, 2020, pp. 208–39.

Bates, Julie Collins. *Toward an Interventionary Rhetoric for Technical Communication Studies.* 2017. Illinois State U, PhD dissertation.

Baumann, Hans. "Seeking Better Ways for the Art Community to Collaborate with Indigenous Communities." *AWorkstation,* 7 Apr. 2022, https://aworkstation.com/seeking-better-ways-for-the-art-community-to-collaborate-with-indigenous-communities/.

Becerra, Hector, and Frank Shyong. "Sriracha Spat: 11 Complaints Prompt AQMD 'Odor Surveillance.'" *Los Angeles Times,* 29 Oct. 2013.

Benjamin, Walter. "The Work of Art in the Age of Mechanical Reproduction." *Illuminations*, edited by Hannah Arendt, translated by Harry Zohn, Schocken Books, 1969, pp. 1–26.

Bennett, Jane. *Vibrant Matter: A Political Ecology of Things*. Duke UP, 2010.

Bergen, Benjamin K. *Louder Than Words: The New Science of How the Mind Makes Meaning*. Basic Books, 2012.

Berger, Martin A. *Sight Unseen: Whiteness and American Visual Culture*. U of California P, 2005.

Berlant, Lauren. "Structures of Unfeeling: *Mysterious Skin*." *International Journal of Politics, Culture and Society*, vol. 28, no. 3, pp. 191–213.

Berman, Tzeporhah. "The Rape of Mother Nature? Women in the Language of Environmental Discourse." *The Ecolinguistics Reader: Language, Ecology, and Environment*, edited by Alwin Fill and Peter Mülhäusler, Bloomsbury, 2001, pp. 258–69.

Besley, John C., and Matthew Nisbet. "How Scientists View the Media, the Public, and the Political Process." *Public Understanding of Science*, vol. 22, 2013, pp. 644–59.

Biden, Joe. "How to Rebuild the US Environmental Protection Agency." *Nature (London)*, vol. 588, no. 7838, 16 Dec. 2020, pp. 369–70, https://ttu-primo.hosted.exlibrisgroup.com/permalink/f/1j33bpi/TN_cdi_webofscience_primary_000624454300001.

Billets, Stephen, and Amy Dindal. "History and Accomplishments of the U.S. Environmental Protection Agency's Superfund Innovative Technology Evaluation (SITE) Monitoring and Measurement Technology (MMT) Program." *Journal of Testing and Evaluation*, vol. 35, no. 5, 2007, pp. 486–95.

Blair, Carole. "Contemporary U.S. Memorial Sites as Exemplars of Rhetoric's Materiality." *Rhetorical Bodies*, edited by Jack Selzer and Sharon Crowley, U of Wisconsin P, 1999, pp. 16–57.

Blair, Carole. "Reflections on Criticism and Bodies: Parables from Public Places." *Western Journal of Communication*, vol. 65, no. 3, 2001, pp. 271–94, https://doi.org/10.1080/10570310109374706.

Blair, Carole, et al. "Introduction: Rhetoric/Memory/Place." *Places of Public Memory: The Rhetoric of Museums and Memorials*, edited by Greg Dickinson et al., U of Alabama P, 2010, pp. 1–54.

Blodgett, Bonnie. *Remembering Smell: A Memoir of Losing and Discovering the Primal Sense*. Houghton Mifflin Harcourt, 2010.

Blue Ridge Landfill and Republic Services. "Odor Control Plan." 5 Apr. 2018, https://www.pearlandtx.gov/home/showpublisheddocument/20800/636592340193730000.

Blythe, Stuart, et al. "Action Research and Wicked Environmental Problems: Exploring Appropriate Roles for Researchers in Professional Communication." *Journal of Business and Technical Communication*, vol. 22, no. 3, 2008, pp. 272–98.

Böhme, Gernot. *Critique of Aesthetic Capitalism*. Translated by Edmund Jephcott, Mimesis International, 2017. Atmospheric Spaces 1.

Böhme, Jakob. *The Supersensual Life*. 1624. Translated by William Law, 1995, http://www.gnosis.org/library/super.htm.

Boissoneault, Lorraine. "The Cuyahoga River Caught Fire at Least a Dozen Times, but No One Cared until 1969." *Smithsonian Magazine*, 19 June 2019, www.smithsonianmag.com/history/cuyahoga-river-caught-fire-least-dozen-times-no-one-cared-until-1969-180972444/.

Booher, Amanda K., and Julie Jung. "Introduction: Situating Feminist Rhetorical Science Studies." *Feminist Rhetorical Science Studies: Human Bodies, Posthumanist Worlds*, edited by Booher and Jung, Southern Illinois UP, 2018, pp. 1–49.

Bourdieu, Pierre. *Distinction*. 1984. Translated by Paul Kegan, Routledge, 2010.

Bourne, Joel, Jr. "Salton Sea." *National Geographic,* Feb. 2005.

Bower, Bruce. "Ancient 'Mega-Cities' Reshape the History of the First Cities." *Science News,* 19 Feb. 2020, https://www.sciencenews.org/article/ancient-urban-megasites-may-reshape-history-first-cities.

Bradford, Alina, and Daisy Dobrijevic. "Corpse Flower: Facts about the Smelly Plant." *Live Science,* 27 Oct. 2021, https://www.livescience.com/51947-corpse-flower-facts-about-the-smelly-plant.html.

Brennan, Teresa. *The Transmission of Affect.* Cornell UP, 2004.

Breslin, Sean. "Louisiana Tribe Officially Becomes America's First Climate Refugees." *The Weather Channel,* 22 Feb. 2016.

Brocardo, Patrícia S, et al. "Zinc Attenuates Malathion-Induced Depressant-Like Behavior and Confers Neuroprotection in the Rat Brain." *Toxicological Sciences,* vol 97, no. 1, 2007, pp. 140–48, https://doi.org/10.1093/toxsci/kfm024.

Broecker, Walter S., and J. van Donk. "Insolation Changes, Ice Volumes, and the O^{18} Record in Deep-Sea Cores." *Reviews of Geophysics and Space Physics,* vol. 8., 1970, pp. 169–97.

Brothers, Daniel, et al. "Loading of the San Andreas Fault by Flood-Induced Rupture of Faults beneath the Salton Sea." *Nature Geoscience,* vol. 4, no. 7, June 2011, pp. 486–92.

Brower, David R. "A Call to Action." *Earthcare: Global Protection of Natural Areas,* edited by Edmund A. Schofield, Routledge, 1979, pp. 61–74.

Brummett, Barry. "Some Implications of 'Process' or 'Intersubjectivity': Postmodern Rhetoric." *Philosophy and Rhetoric,* vol. 9., no. 1, 1976, pp. 21–51.

Brysse, Keynyn, et al. "Climate Change Prediction: Erring on the Side of Least Drama?" *Global Environmental Change,* vol. 23, no. 1, 2013, pp. 327–37, https://doi.org/10.1016/j.gloenvcha.2012.10.008.

Bugnyar, Thomas, et al. "Ravens Attribute Visual Access to Unseen Competitors." *Nature Communications,* vol. 7, no. 10506, Feb. 2016, pp. 1–6. *JSTOR,* https://doi.org/10.1038/ncomms10506.

Bullard, Robert D., editor. *The Quest for Environmental Justice: Human Rights and the Politics of Pollution.* Sierra Club Books, 2005.

Bullard, Robert D., and Beverly Wright. *The Wrong Complexion for Protection: How the Government Response to Disaster Endangers African American Communities.* New York UP, 2012.

Bullard, Robert D., et al. "Toxic Wastes and Race at Twenty: Why Race Still Matters after All of These Years." *Environmental Law,* vol. 38, no. 2, 2008, pp. 371–411. *Gale in Context: Science,* https://go.gale.com/ps/i.do?p=SCIC&u=txshracd2579&id=GALE%7CA179977592&v=2.1&it=r&sid=bookmark-SCIC&asid=a8db163a.

Burr, Abigail C., et al. "Salton Sea Dust Extract Exposure Promotes Lung Inflammation in Mice." *American Journal of Respiratory and Critical Care Medicine,* American Thoracic Society International Conference Abstracts, May 2019, https://doi.org/10.1164/ajrccm-conference.2019.199.1_MeetingAbstracts.A1833.

Bushdid, C., et al. "Humans Can Discriminate More Than 1 Trillion Olfactory Stimuli." *Science (American Association for the Advancement of Science),* vol. 343, no. 6177, 2014, pp. 1370–72, https://doi.org/10.1126/science.1249168.

Butler, Judith. *Bodies That Matter: On the Discursive Limits of Sex.* Routledge, 2011. https://doi.org/10.4324/9780203828274.

Cajete, Gregory. *Look to the Mountain: An Ecology of Indigenous Education.* Kivaki, 1994.

Cajete, Gregory. *Native Science: Natural Laws of Interdependence.* Clear Light, 2016.

Calderón-Garcidueñas, Lilian, et al. "Urban Air Pollution: Influences on Olfactory Function and Pathology on Exposed Children and Young Adults." *Experimental Toxicology Pathology,* vol. 62, no. 1, 2010, pp. 91–102.

California Department of Water Resources. "Salton Sea Species Conservation Habitat Monitoring and Adaptive Management Plan." California Natural Resources Agency, 2015.

California Institute of Contemporary Art. "TMCDI [sic] Tribal Community in Partnership with Hans Baumann." Summer 2021, https://icasandiego.org/art/tmcdi-tribal-community-in-partnership-with-hans-baumann/.

Cantor, Alida. "Hydrosocial Hinterlands: An Urban Political Ecology of Southern California's Hydrosocial Territory." *Environment and Planning E: Nature and Space,* vol. 4, no. 2, 2021, pp. 451–74, https://doi.org/10.1177/2514848620909384.

Cantor, Alida. "The Public Trust Doctrine and Critical Legal Geographies of Water in California." *Geoforum,* vol. 72, 2016, pp. 49–57.

Cantor, Aviva. "The Club, the Yoke, and the Leash: What We Can Learn from the Way a Culture Treats Animals." *Ms. Magazine,* 1983, pp. 27–29.

Carson, Rachel L. *Silent Spring.* 1962. Mariner, 2002.

Casid, Jill H. "Handle with Care." *TDR: The Drama Review,* vol. 56, no. 4, 2012, pp. 121–35.

Cassegard, Carl. "Let Us Live! Empowerment and the Rhetoric of Life in the Japanese Precarity Movement." *Positions,* vol. 22, no. 1, 2014, pp. 41–69.

Cedillo, Christina. "Q&A: Christina Cedillo, Assistant Professor of Writing and Rhetoric." Interviewed by Brandon Ruiz-Peña, *The Signal,* 12 Nov. 2019, https://www.uhclthesignal.com/wordpress/2019/11/12/qa-christina-cedillo-assistant-professor-of-writing-and-rhetoric/.

Center for Disaster Philanthropy. "2019–2029 Australian Bushfires." Mar. 2020, https://disasterphilanthropy.org/disasters/2019-australian-wildfires/.

Ceraso, Steph, and Jon Stone. "(Re)Making Sense: Composition and Rhetoric at the End of Rationality, J.16, Chicago, Illinois, 18 Feb. 2023." Conference on College Composition and Communication. Public address.

Cerulo, Karen A. "Scents and Sensibility: Olfaction, Sense-Making, and Meaning Attribution." *American Sociological Review,* vol, 83, no. 2, 2018, pp. 361–89, https://doi.org/10.1177/0003122418759679.

Cha, Eun S., et al. "Paraquat Application and Respiratory Health Effects among South Korean Farmers." *Occupational and Environmental Medicine,* vol. 69, no. 6, 2012, pp. 398–403.

Chakraborty, Jayajit, et al. "Comparing Disproportionate Exposure to Acute and Chronic Pollution Risks: A Case Study in Houston, Texas." *Risk Analysis,* vol. 34, no. 11, 2014, pp. 2005–20, http://dx.doi.org/10.1111/risa.12224.

Chamovitz, Daniel. *What a Plant Knows: A Field Guide to the Senses.* Farrar, Straus, and Giroux, 2020.

Chavis, Benjamin J., Jr., and Charles Lee. "Toxic Wastes and Race in the United States: A National Report on the Racial and Socio-Economic Characteristics of Communities with Hazardous Waste Sites." Commission for Racial Justice, United Church of Christ, 1987, pp. 1–79, http://uccfiles.com/pdf/ToxicWastes&Race.pdf.

Chen, Angela. "Changes Happening at the Salton Sea on a State and Federal Level." *KESQ News,* 7 July 2021, https://kesq.com/news/2021/07/07/changes-happening-at-the-salton-sea-on-a-state-federal-level/.

Chen, Denise, and Jeannett Haviland-Jones. "Human Olfactory Communication of Emotion." *Perceptual and Motor Skills,* vol. 91, no. 3, 2000, pp. 771–81, https://doi.org/10.2466/pms.2000.91.3.771.

Chen, Nancy N. "'Speaking Nearby': A Conversation with Trinh T. Minh-Ha." *Visual Anthropology Review,* vol. 8, no. 1, 1992, pp. 82–91.

Chirindo, Kundai. "Precarious Publics." *Quarterly Journal of Speech,* vol. 107, no. 4, 2021, pp. 430–34, https://doi.org/10.1080/00335630.2021.1983192.

Choi-Schagrin, Winston. "Sometimes, Life Stinks. So, He Invented the Nasal Ranger." *New York Times,* 31 Jan. 2022.

Christofides, Christiana. Conversation with the author. 17 Mar. 2022.

Christofides, Christiana. Email to the author. 31 Mar. 2022.

City of Irwindale. "2008 General Plan." June 2008. Updated 2020, https://www.irwindaleca.gov/DocumentCenter/View/38/General-Plan?bidId=.

City of Kalamazoo. "Air Quality and Odor Reduction." https://www.kalamazoocity.org/Residents/Water-Sewer-Service/More-About-Kalamazoos-Utility-Systems/Air-Quality-Odor-Reduction. Accessed 29 Jan. 2025.

Clark, Andy. *Supersizing the Mind: Embodiment, Action, and Cognitive Extension.* Oxford UP, 2010.

Clary-Lemon, Jennifer. "Gifts, Ancestors, and Relations: Notes toward an Indigenous New Materialism." *Enculturation: A Journal of Writing and Culture,* vol. 30, no. 1, 12 Nov. 2019.

Clary-Lemon, Jennifer. *Planting the Anthropocene: Rhetorics of Natureculture.* Utah State UP, 2019.

Classen, Constance. *The Color of Angels: Cosmology, Gender, and the Aesthetic Imagination.* Routledge, 1998.

Classen, Constance. *The Deepest Sense: A Cultural History of Touch.* U of Illinois P, 2012.

Classen, Constance. "The Witch's Senses: Sensory Ideologies and Transgressive Femininities from the Renaissance to Modernity." *Empire of the Senses,* edited by David Howes, Berg, 2005, pp. 70–84.

Classen, Constance. *Worlds of Sense: Exploring the Senses in History and across Cultures.* Routledge, 2023.

Classen, Constance, et al. *Aroma: The Cultural History of Smell.* Routledge, 1994.

Cohen, Alex. "Irwindale Ends Fight with Sriracha Factory." Southern California Public Radio. 89.3 KPCC, 29 May 2014.

Cohen, Michael J. "Hazard's Toll: The Costs of Inaction at the Salton Sea." *The Pacific Institute,* 2014, https://pacinst.org/publication/hazards-toll/.

Cohen, Michael J., et al. *Haven or Hazard: The Ecology and Future of the Salton Sea.* The Pacific Institute, 1999, https://pacinst.org/wp-content/uploads/1999/02/haven_or_hazard3.pdf.

Collins, Harry, and Robert Evans. *Rethinking Expertise.* U of Chicago P, 2007.

Coole, Diana, and Samantha Frost, editors. *New Materialisms: Ontology, Agency, and Politics.* Duke UP, 2010.

Cooper, Idelle. "An Examination of the Role of the Creative Process in Biological Research." Illinois State University Research Symposium, 29 Sept. 2010, Stevenson Hall, Normal, Illinois. Address.

Copping, Leonard G. "California Confirms 'Roundup' Will Be Labeled 'Cancer Causing.'" *Outlooks on Pest Management,* vol. 26, no. 5, Oct. 2015, p. 191.

"Coral Bleaching." *Great Barrier Reef Foundation,* https://www.barrierreef.org/the-reef/threats/coral-bleaching. Accessed 4 Aug. 2023.

Corbin, Alain. *The Foul and the Fragrant: Odor and the French Social Imagination.* Translated by Miriam Kochan, Harvard UP / Berg, 1986.

Cory, Therese Scarpelli. "Is Anything in the Intellect That Was Not First in Sense?: Empiricism and Knowledge of the Incorporeal in Aquinas." *Oxford Studies in Medieval Philosophy,* vol. 6, no. 1, 2018, pp. 100–144.

Crenshaw, Kimberlé. "Demarginalizing the Intersection of Race and Sex: A Black Feminist Critique of Antidiscrimination Doctrine, Feminist Theory and Antiracist Politics." *University of Chicago Legal Forum,* vol. 1, 1989, pp. 139–67.

Crenshaw, Kimberlé. "Mapping the Margins: Intersectionality, Identity Politics, and Violence against Women of Color," *Stanford Law Review,* vol. 43, no. 6, 1990, pp. 1241–99.

Croy, Ilona, and Thomas Hummel. "Olfaction as a Marker for Depression." *Journal of Neurology,* vol. 264, 2017, pp. 631–38, https://doi.org/10.1007/s00415-016-8227-8.

Crutzen, Paul J. "The 'Anthropocene.'" *Journal de Physique IV,* vol. 12, no. 10, 2002, pp. 1–5.

Damasio, Antonio. *Descartes' Error: Emotion, Reason, and the Human Brain.* Penguin, 2005.

Damasio, Antonio. *"The Feeling of What Happens": Body and Emotion in the Making of Consciousness.* Mariner, 2000.

Darby, Kate, et al. "Mapping the Environment with Sensory Perception." *InTeGrate,* Science Education Resource Center, 25 Sept. 2023, https://serc.carleton.edu/152677.

Davis, Diane. *Breaking Up (at) Totality: A Rhetoric of Laughter.* Southern Illinois UP, 2000.

Davis, Diane. "Rhetoricity at the End of the World." *Philosophy and Rhetoric,* vol. 50, no. 4, 2017, pp. 431–51.

Davis, Joseph E., editor. *Identity and Social Change.* Transaction, 2011.

d'Eaubonne, Françoise. *Le Feminise ou la Mort.* Pierre Horay, 1974.

DeBuys, William, and Joan Myers. *Salt Dreams: Land and Water in Low-Down California.* U of New Mexico P, 2001.

de Certeau, Michel. *The Practice of Everyday Life.* 1984. Translated by Steven Rendall, 3rd ed., U of California P, 2011.

De Châtel, Francesca. "The Role of Drought and Climate Change in the Syrian Uprising: Untangling the Triggers of the Revolution." *Middle Eastern Studies,* vol. 50, no. 4, 2014, pp. 521–35.

Delbert, Caroline. "The Nasal Ranger: A Hobbyist Weed Farm's Worst Enemy." *Popular Mechanics,* 15 Jan. 2020, https://www.popularmechanics.com/science/a30535438/nasal-ranger/.

Del Carmen, Rolando V. *Criminal Procedure: Law and Practice.* Wadsworth-Cengage, 2014.

Deleuze, Gilles, and Felix Guattari. *A Thousand Plateaus: Capitalism and Schizophrenia.* Translated by Brian Massumi, U of Minnesota P, 1987.

Deloria, Vine, Jr. *Spirit and Reason.* Fulcrum, 1999.

de Onís, Catalina M. *Energy Islands: Metaphors of Power, Extractivism, and Justice in Puerto Rico.* U of California P, 2021.

"Desert Cahuilla Wetland." *Torres Martinez Desert Cahuilla Indians Programs,* https://torresmartinez.org/wetlands/. Accessed 28 July 2023.

DeVasto, Danielle, et al. "Stasis and Matters of Concern: The Conviction of the L'Aquila Seven." *Journal of Business and Technical Communication,* vol. 30, no. 2, 2016, pp. 131–64.

DiCaglio, Sara. "Towards an Olfactory Rhetoric: Scent, Affect, Material, Embodiment." *Bodies of Knowledge: Embodied Rhetorics in Theory and Practice,* edited by A. Abby Knoblauch and Marie E. Moeller, Utah State UP, 2022, pp. 57–73.

Di Chiro, Giovanna. "Local Actions, Global Visions: Remaking Environmental Expertise." *Frontiers: A Journal of Women's Studies*, vol. 18, no. 2, 1997, pp. 203–31.

Dolmage, Jay, and Cynthia Lewiecki-Wilson. "Refiguring Rhetorica: Linking Feminist Rhetoric and Disability Studies." *Rhetorica in Motion: Researching Feminist Rhetorical Methods and Methodologies*, edited by Eileen Schell and K. J. Rawson, U of Pittsburgh P, 2010, pp. 23–38.

Douglas, Mary. *Purity and Danger: An Analysis of Concepts of Pollution and Taboo*. Routledge, 2002.

Driskill, Qwo-Li. *Asegi Stories: Cherokee Queer and Two-Spirit Memory*. U of Arizona P, 2016.

Drobnick, Jim, editor. *The Smell Culture Reader*. Berg, 2006.

Druschke, Caroline Gottschalk. "A Trophic Future for Rhetorical Ecologies." *Enculturation*, vol. 28, no. 1, 20 Feb. 2019, https://enculturation.net/a-trophic-future.

Druschke, Caroline Gottschalk, et al. "Centering Fishing Agency in Coastal Dam Removal and River Restoration." *Water Alternatives*, vol. 10, no. 3, 2017, pp. 724–43.

Dubos, René. "Think Globally, Act Locally." *Celebrations of Life*, by Dubos, McGraw-Hill, 1981, pp. 83–130.

Dulin, Matt. "Pearland Ranked Nation's 7th Most Prosperous City in Analysis of Census Data." *Community Impact*, 24 May 2018.

Dulin, Matt. "Travis County Court Dismisses Pearland's Lawsuit against Blue Ridge Landfill." *Community Impact*, 13 Feb. 2019, https://communityimpact.com/houston/pearland-friendswood/city-county/2019/02/13/travis-county-court-dismisses-pearlands-lawsuit-against-blue-ridge-landfill/.

Dumit, Joseph. "Neuroexistentialism." *Sensorium: Embodied Experience, Technology, and Contemporary Art*, edited by Caroline A. Jones, Massachusetts Institute of Technology P, 2006, pp. 182–89.

Edbauer, Jenny. "Unframing Models of Public Distribution: From Rhetorical Situation to Rhetorical Ecologies." *Rhetoric Society Quarterly*, vol. 35, no. 4, pp. 5–24, http://dx.doi.org/10.1080/02773940509391320.

Edwards, Paul N. *A Vast Machine: Computer Models, Climate Data, and the Politics of Global Warming*. Massachusetts Institute of Technology P, 2010.

"Elephant Facts." Georgia Department of Natural Resources, 2022. https://elephantaidinternational.org/elephant-facts/?gclid=CjwKCAiAjs2bBhACEiwALTBWZUW0gmT8uuwdOaHjiM558_vXkdtyoW9sovXIBuioHccVhfBilVHIfRoCZV0QAvD_BwE.

Ellms, J. W., and W. C. Lawrence. "The Causes of Obnoxious Tastes and Odors Sometimes Occurring in the Cleveland Water Supply." *American Water Works Association*, vol. 9, no. 3, May 1922, pp. 463–73. *JSTOR*, www.jstor.org/stable/41224884?seq=9#metadata_info_tab_contents.

Endevelt-Shapria, Yaara, et al. "Altered Responses to Social Chemosignals in Autism Spectrum Disorder." *Nature Neuroscience*, vol. 21, 2018, pp. 111–19, https://doi.org/10.1038/s41593-017-0024-x.

Endres, Danielle. "The Rhetoric of Nuclear Colonialism: Rhetorical Exclusion of American Indian Arguments in the Yucca Mountain Nuclear Waste Siting Decision." *Communication and Critical/Cultural Studies*, vol. 6, no. 1, 2009, pp. 39–60, https://doi.org./10/1080/14791420802632103.

Enríquez-Loya, Aydé, and Kendall Léon. "Transdisciplinary Rhetorical Work in Technical Writing and Composition: Environmental Justice Issues in California." *College English*, vol. 82, no. 5, 2020, pp. 449–59.

"Environmental Justice and Environmental Racism." *Greenaction for Health and Environmental Justice*, https://greenaction.org/what-is-environmental-justice/. Accessed 3 Apr. 2022.

Epstein, Kate. "How to Strive toward Bias-Free Writing." Texas Tech Humanities Center Workshop, 3 Feb. 2022, Texas Tech University, Lubbock. Address.

Evans, Thayer. "Pearland Reaches Settlement with Blue Ridge Landfill." *Pearland Chronicle*, 25 May 2009, https://www.chron.com/neighborhood/pearland-news/article/Pearland-reaches-settlement-with-Blue-Ridge-1582840.php.

"Eyewitness." *Oxford English Dictionary*, Oxford UP, 2024, https://www.oed.com/dictionary/eyewitness_n?tab=meaning_and_use#4910883.

Farrell, Thomas. "The Weight of Rhetoric: Studies in Cultural Delirium." *Philosophy and Rhetoric*, vol. 41, no. 4, 2008, pp. 467–87.

Farzan, Shohreh, and Jill Johnson. "USC AIRE Children's Study." *USC Environmental Health Centers*, https://envhealthcenters.usc.edu/usc-aire-childrens-study. Accessed 10 June 2021.

Favot, Sarah. "Congressman Invites Sriracha Hot Sauce Factory to Move." *Los Angeles Daily News*, 27 Apr. 2014.

Feldman Barrett, Lisa. *Seven and a Half Lessons about the Brain*. Houghton Mifflin Harcourt, 2020.

Feldman, Claudia, and Eric Hanson. "Fire Highlights Need in Unincorporated Fresno." *Houston Chronicle*, 25 Feb. 2007, https://www.chron.com/news/houston-texas/article/Fire-highlights-need-in-unincorporated-Fresno-1800639.php.

Ferdman, Roberto A. "The Highly Unusual Company behind Sriracha, the World's Coolest Hot Sauce." *Quartz*, 21 Oct. 2013, https://qz.com/132738/the-highly-unusual-company-behind-sriracha-the-worlds-coolest-hot-sauce/.

Fetzek, Shiloh, and Jeffrey Mazos. "Climate, Scarcity and Conflict." *Survival*, vol. 56, no. 5, 2014, pp. 143–70.

Finney, Stanley C., and Lucy E. Edwards. "The 'Anthropocene' Epoch: Scientific Decision or Political Statement?" *Geological Society of America Today*, vol. 26, no. 3, 2016, pp. 4–10.

FL. Comment on "Republic Services Blue Ridge." *Google Maps*, 2020, https://www.google.com/maps/contrib/113893494549787208917/place/ChIJzxGWxFHsQIYRKj6vGlIZa48/@29.1072384,-90.6822358,6z/data=!4m4!1m3!8m2!1e1!2s113893494549787208917?hl=en-US.

Flaccus, Gillian. "Weird News: Southern California Engulfed by Rotten-Egg Smell." *Salon*, 11 Sept. 2012, 9:53 p.m., https://www.salon.com/2012/09/11/weird_news_southern_california_engulfed_by_rotten_egg_smell/.

Forsman, Timothy N. "What the QSA Means for the Salton Sea: California's Big Blank Check." *Arizona State Law Journal*, vol. 46, no. 1, 2014, pp. 365–88.

Foundation for Community Research. "Statistical Review: Summary of Key Association Data and Information 2020." https://foundation.caionline.org/publications/factbook/statistical-review/.

Franks, Raymond. "BFI Blue Ridge Community Statement." 16 Jan. 2006. Letter to Judge Hebert of Fort Bend County, Texas.

Friesen, Amanda, et al. "Political Attitudes Vary with Detection of Androstenone." *Politics and the Life Sciences*, vol. 29, no. 1, 2020, pp. 26–37, https://doi.org/10.1017/pls.2019.18.

Frost, Erin A. "Transcultural Risk Communication on Dauphine Island." *Technical Communication Quarterly*, vol. 22, no. 1, 2013, pp. 50–66, https://doi.org/10.1080/10572252.2013.726483.

Frost, Samantha. "Fear and the Illusion of Autonomy." Coole and Frost, pp. 158–77.

Gaard, Greta. *Ecological Politics: Ecofeminists and the Greens*. Temple UP, 1998.

Gaard, Greta. "Misunderstanding Ecofeminism." *Z Magazine*, vol. 3, no. 1, 1998, pp. 20–24.

Gaard, Greta. "Toward a Queer Ecofeminism." *New Perspectives on Environmental Justice: Gender, Sexuality, and Activism*, edited by Rachel Stein, Rutgers UP, 2004, pp. 21–44.

Geddes, Patrick. *Cities in Evolution: An Introduction to the Town Planning Movement and to the Study of Civics*. Williams and Norgate, 1915.

"Gen. 3:6." *Bible Gateway*. New International Version, Biblica, 2011.

Gerlach, Luther P. "The Structure of Social Movements." *Networks and Netwars: The Future of Terror, Crime, and Militancy*, edited by John Arquilla and David Ronfeldt, Rand, 2001, pp. 289–310.

Ghosh, Amitav. *The Great Derangement: Climate Change and the Unthinkable*. U of Chicago P, 2016.

Gilbert, Avery. *What the Nose Knows: The Science of Scent in Everyday Life*. Crown, 2008.

Gilio-Whitaker, Dina. *As Long as Grass Grows: The Indigenous Fight for Environmental Justice, from Colonization to Standing Rock*. Beacon, 2020.

Glynn Environmental Coalition. "Who We Are." https://www.glynnenvironmental.org/about. Accessed 4 Apr. 2023.

Goodman, Sherri. Interview by William Kakenmaster. *E-International Relations*, 24 Jan. 2019, www.e-ir.info/2019/01/24/interview-sherri-goodman/.

Goolsby, Denise. "Salton Sea Key to Atomic Bombs Dropped 70 Years Ago." *Desert Sun*, 5 Aug. 2015, https://www.desertsun.com/story/news/veterans/2015/08/05/storyteller-hiroshima-th-anniversary/31193807/.

Grabill, Jeffrey T., and Michele Simmons. "Toward a Critical Rhetoric of Risk Communication: Producing Citizens and the Role of Technical Communicators." *Technical Communication Quarterly*, vol. 7, no. 4, 1998, pp. 415–41.

Graeber, David, and David Wengrow. *The Dawn of Everything: A New History of Humanity*. Farrar, Straus and Giroux, 2021.

Graham, S. Scott. *Where's the Rhetoric: Imagining a Unified Field*. The Ohio State UP, 2020.

Graham, S. Scott, et al. "Statistical Genre Analysis: Toward Big Data Methodologies in Technical Communication." *Technical Communication Quarterly*, vol. 24, no. 1, 2015, pp. 70–104.

Grandin, Temple. "Handling Methods and Facilities to Reduce Stress on Cattle." *Veterinary Clinics of North America: Food Animal Practices*, vol 14, no. 2, 1998, pp. 3250–341.

Grant, Richard. "Do Trees Talk to Each Other?" *Smithsonian*, Mar. 2018, https://www.smithsonianmag.com/science-nature/the-whispering-trees-180968084/.

Grineski, Sara E., et al. "Hazardous Air Pollutants and Flooding: A Comparative Interurban Study of Environmental Injustice." *GeoJournal*, vol. 80, 2014, pp. 145–58, http://dx.doi.org/10.1007/s10708-014-9542-1.

Grosz, Elizabeth. "Feminism, Materialism, and Freedom." *New Materialisms: Ontology, Agency, and Politics*, edited by Diana Coole and Samantha Frost, Duke UP, 2010, pp. 139–57.

Gunn, Joshua. "ShitText: Toward a New Coprophilic Style." *Text and Performance Quarterly*, vol. 26, no. 1, 2006, pp. 79–97.

Gupta, Joyeeta, et al. "Climate Change: A 'Glocal' Problem Requiring 'Glocal' Action." *Environmental Sciences*, vol. 4, no. 3, 2007, pp. 139–48, https://doi.org/10.1080/15693430701742677.

Haas, Angela M. "Race, Rhetoric, and Technology: A Case Study of Decolonial Technical Communication Theory, Methodology, and Pedagogy." *Journal of Business and Technical Communication*, vol. 26, no. 3, 2012, pp. 277–310.

Haas, Angela M., and Erin A. Frost. "Toward an Apparent Decolonial Feminist Rhetoric of Risk." *Topic-Driven Environmental Rhetoric*, edited by Derek Ross, Routledge, 2017, pp. 168–86.

Haberly, Lewis B. "Parallel-Distributed Processing in Olfactory Cortex: New Insights from Morphological and Physiological Analysis of Neuronal Circuitry." *Chemical Senses*, vol. 26, no. 5, 2001, pp. 551–76.

Han, Pengfei, et al. "Olfactory Loss Is Associated with Reduced Hippocampal Activation in Response to Emotional Pictures." *NeuroImage*, vol. 188, 2019, pp. 84–91.

Hansen, James, et al. "Ice Melt, Sea Level Rise and Superstorms: Evidence from Paleoclimate Data, Climate Modeling, and Modern Observations That 2°C Global Warming Could Be Dangerous." *Journal of Atmospheric Chemistry and Physics*, vol. 16, 2016, pp. 3781–812.

Harvey, Susan Ashbrook. *Scenting Salvation: Ancient Christianity and the Olfactory Imagination*. U of California P, 2006.

Hauser, Gerard A. *Vernacular Voices: The Rhetoric of Publics and Public Spheres*. U of South Carolina P, 2008.

Hawhee, Debra. *Rhetoric in Tooth and Claw: Animals, Language, Sensation*. U of Chicago P, 2016.

Hawhee, Debra. "Rhetoric's Sensorium." *Quarterly Journal of Speech*, vol. 101, no. 1, 2014, pp. 2–17. EBSCO, https://doi.org/10.1080/00335630.2015.995925.

Hawhee, Debra. *A Sense of Urgency: How the Climate Crisis Is Changing Rhetoric*. U of Chicago, 2023.

Hawhee, Debra. "Toward a Bestial Rhetoric." *Philosophy and Rhetoric*, vol. 44, no. 1, 2011, pp. 81–87.

Hawhee, Debra, and Vanessa Beasley. "Rhetoric and Sensation: Seminar Description." *Rhetoric Society of America Summer Institute*, 2015, https://www.rhetoricsociety.org/aws/RSA/pt/sd/news_article/89384/_blank/layout_details/false.

Hayhoe, Katharine. *Saving Us: A Climate Scientist's Case for Hope and Healing in a Divided World*. Atria One Signal Publishers, 2021.

Hayles, N. Katherine. *How We Became Posthuman: Virtual Bodies in Cybernetics, Literature, and Informatics*. U of Chicago P, 1999.

Hayles, N. Katherine. "Traumas of Code." *Critical Inquiry*, vol. 33, 2006, pp. 136–57.

Hayles, N. Katherine. "Virtual Bodies and Flickering Signifiers." *October*, vol. 66, 1993, pp. 69–91.

"Hearsay." *Oxford English Dictionary*, Oxford UP, 2024, https://www.oed.com/dictionary/hearsay_n?tab=meaning_and_use#1886161.

Henshaw, Victoria, et al., editors. *Designing with Smell: Practices, Techniques, and Challenges*. Routledge, 2018.

Herder, Johann G. "Essay on the Origin of Language." Translated by Alexander Gode. *On the Origin of Language: Two Essays by Jean-Jacques Rousseau and Johann Gottfried Herder (Milestones of Thought)*, edited by John H. Moran. Frederick Ungar, 1966, pp. 87–176.

Hernandez, Maricarmen, et al. "Immigration, Mobility, and Environmental Injustice: A Comparative Study of Hispanic People's Residential Decision-Making and Exposure to Hazardous Air Pollutants in Greater Houston, Texas." *Geoforum*, vol. 60, 2015, pp. 83–94.

Hernández-López, Ernesto. "Sriracha Shutdown: Hot Sauce Lessons on Local Privilege and Race." *Seton Hall Law Review*, vol. 46, no. 1, 2015, pp. 189–242.

Herz, Rachel S. *The Scent of Desire: Discovering Our Enigmatic Sense of Smell*. Harper Collins, 2007.

Hesford, Wendy S. *Violent Exceptions: Children's Human Rights and Humanitarian Rhetorics*. The Ohio State UP, 2021.

Hesford, Wendy S., et al., editors. *Precarious Rhetorics*. The Ohio State UP, 2018.

Hessburg, Paul F., et al. "Wildfire and Climate Change Adaptation of Western North American Forests: A Case for Intentional Management." *Ecological Applications*, vol. 31, no. 8, 2021, pp. 1–17.

Highmore, Ben. *Cultural Feelings: Mood, Mediation, and Cultural Politics*. Routledge, 2017.

Hill Collins, Patricia. *Intersectionality as Critical Social Theory*. Duke UP, 2019.

Hillel, Daniel. "Salinity Management." *Encyclopedia of Soils in the Environment*, Elsevier, 2005, pp. 435–42.

Hinton, Devon, et al. "Olfactory-Triggered Panic Attacks among the Khmer Refugees: A Contextual Approach." *Transcultural Psychiatry*, vol. 41, no. 2, 2004, pp. 155–99, https://doi.org/10.1177/1363461504043564.

Holthaus, Eric. "When Will the World Really Be 2 Degrees Hotter Than It Used to Be?" *FiveThirtyEight*, 23 Mar. 2016, https://fivethirtyeight.com/features/when-will-the-world-really-be-2-degrees-hotter-than-it-used-to-be/.

"Holy Mole: Mexico City." *Mexico One Plate at a Time*, created by Rick Bayless, season 1, episode 22, Frontera Media Productions / American Public Television, 6 June 2003.

Houdek, Matthew, and Ersula J. Ore. "Cultivating Otherwise Worlds and Breathable Futures." *Rhetoric, Politics and Culture*, vol. 1, no. 1, 2021, pp. 85–95.

Hovary, Claire L. A. "The Informal Economy and the ILO: A Legal Perspective." *International Journal of Comparative Labour Law and Industrial Relations*, vol. 30, no. 4, 2014, pp. 391–411.

"How a Man Left to Die Made Sriracha." *YouTube*, uploaded by Hook, 19 Jan. 2021, https://www.youtube.com/watch?v=kNXvuCEC2S8.

Howes, David. "Olfactory Art: Introduction." *Designing with Smell*, edited by Victoria Henshaw et al., Routledge, 2018, pp. 5–9.

Howes, David. "On the Odour of the Soul: Spatial Representation and Olfactory Classification in Eastern Indonesia and Western Melanesia." *Bijdragen tot de Taal-, Land-en Volkenkunde*, vol. 144, no. 1, 1988, pp. 84–113.

Howes, David. *Sensual Relations: Engaging the Senses in Culture and Social Theory*. U of Michigan P, 2003.

Howes, David, and Constance Classen. *Ways of Sensing: Understanding the Senses in Society*. 2014, Routledge.

Hunt, Kathleen, et al. "The Radical Potential of Public Hearings: A Rhetorical Assessment of Resistance and Indecorous Voice in Public Participation Processes." *Confronting the Challenges of Public Participation: Issues in Environmental Planning and Health Decision-Making*, edited by Jean Goodwin, 2016, pp. 65–79, Iowa State University Digital Repository, https://dr.lib.iastate.edu/handle/20.500.12876/2809.

Hustak, Carla, and Natasha Myers. "Involutionary Momentum: Affective Ecologies and the Sciences of Plant/Insect Encounters." *Differences: A Journal of Feminist Cultural Studies*, vol. 25, no. 3, 2012, pp. 75–118, https://doi.org/10.1215/10407391-1892907.

Hutchins, Edwin. *Cognition in the Wild*. Massachusetts Institute of Technology P, 1995.

Illinois State Museum. "The Late Pleistocene Extinctions." 7 Apr. 2016, https://exhibits.museum.state.il.us/exhibits/larson/lp_extinction.html.

Ingold, Tim. *The Perception of the Environment: Essays on Livelihood, Dwelling and Skill*. Routledge, 2000.

IQAir. "Salton Sea Park Air Monitoring." https://www.iqair.com/us/air-quality-map?lat=33.50896&lng=-115.91954&placeId=59a5191c3e70006e2ca167do. Accessed 28 Oct. 2021.

Irigaray, Luce. *This Sex Which Is Not One.* Translated by Catherine Porter, Cornell UP, 1985.

Itchuaqiyaq, Cana U. "Iñupiat Ilitqusiat: An Indigenous Ethics Approach for Working with Marginalized Knowledges in Technical Communication." *Equipping Technical Communicators for Social Justice Work: Theories, Methodologies, and Pedagogies,* edited by Rebecca Walton and Godwin Agboka, Utah State UP, 2021, pp. 33–48.

Itchuaqiyaq, Cana U. "When the Sound Is Frozen: Extracting Climate Data from Inuit Narratives." *Technical Communication for Environmental Action,* edited by Sean D. Williams, State U of New York P, 2023, pp. 19–38.

Jack, Jordynn. "Chronotopic Expertise: Enacting Water Ontologies in a Wind-Energy Debate in Ontario, Canada." *Rhetoric Society Quarterly,* vol. 52, no. 4, 2022, pp. 325–40.

Jarvis, Jacob. "Fact Check: Did Donald Trump Suggest People Inject Poison to Cure COVID?" *Newsweek,* 16 Aug. 2021, https://www.newsweek.com/fact-check-did-donald-trump-suggest-people-inject-poison-cure-covid-1619105.

Jay, Martin. "In the Realm of the Senses: An Introduction." *American Historical Review Forum: The Senses in History,* vol. 116, no. 2, 2011, pp. 307–15.

Jenner, Mark S. R. "Follow Your Nose? Smell, Smelling, and Their Histories." *American Historical Review,* vol. 116, no. 2, 2011, pp. 335–51.

Johnson, Jenell. "'A Man's Mouth Is His Castle': The Midcentury Fluoridation Controversy and the Visceral Public." *Quarterly Journal of Speech,* vol. 102, no. 1, 2016, pp. 1–20, https://doi.org/10.1080/00335630.1135506.

Johnson, Jill, et al. "The Disappearing Salton Sea: A Critical Reflection on the Emerging Environment Threat of Disappearing Saline Lakes and Potential Impact on Children's Health," *Science of the Total Environment,* vol. 663, May 2019, pp. 804–17, https://doi.org/10.1016/j.scitotenv.2019.01.365.

Jones, Jaimy. "Pearland, Katy Politicians Face Off over Landfill Lawsuit." *Houston Chronicle,* 1 Aug. 2018, https://www.chron.com/neighborhood/pearland/news/article/Pearland-Katy-politicians-face-off-over-landfill-13122894.php.

Jütte, Robert. "The Sense of Smell in Historical Perspective." *Sensory Perception: Mind and Matter,* edited by Friedrich G. Barth et al., Springer-Verlag/Wien, 2012, pp. 313–32.

Kadifa, Margaret. "West Pearland Residents Frustrated about Timeline to Stop 'Putrid Garbage Stink.'" *Houston Chronicle,* 10 Feb. 2017, https://www.chron.com/neighborhood/pearland/news/article/West-Pearland-residents-frustrated-about-timeline-10923824.php.

Kagan, Elena J. Dissenting opinion. *West Virginia v. EPA,* US Supreme Court Document US 20-1530, no. 597, 30 June 2022. *Cornell Legal Information Institute,* https://www.law.cornell.edu/supremecourt/text/20-1530.

Kamara, Doxey. "Latinx vs. Latine." *The Tulane Hullabaloo,* 29 Sept. 2021, https://tulanehullabaloo.com/57213/intersections/opinion-latinx-vs-latine/.

Kamczyc, Alex. "Republic Services Reports 15 Percent Growth in Total Revenue for 2021." *Recycling Today,* 15 Feb. 2022, https://www.recyclingtoday.com/article/republic-services-reports-growth-in-total-revenue/.

Keller, Lynn. *Recomposing Ecopoetics: North American Poetry of the Self-Conscious Anthropocene.* U of Virginia P, 2017.

Kellogg, Kristi, and Kerry Acker. "What Is Chorizo? 10 Things You Need to Know about the Spicy Sausage." *Epicurious,* 12 July 2018, https://www.epicurious.com/ingredients/what-is-chorizo-and-how-to-use-the-spiccy-sauage-article.

Kempisty, David M., and LeeAnn Racz, editors. *Forever Chemicals: Environmental, Economic, and Social Equity Concerns with PFAS in the Environment.* CRC Press, 2021.

Kennan, George. *The Salton Sea: An Account of Harriman's Fight with the Colorado River.* Macmillan, 1917.

Kennedy, George A., "A Hoot in the Dark: The Evolution of General Rhetoric." *Philosophy and Rhetoric,* vol. 25, no. 1, 1992, pp. 1–21.

Kerr, Thomas, et al. "The One-Eyed King: Positioning Universal Design within Learning and Teaching at a Tertiary Institution." *Rhetoric and Reality: Critical Perspectives on Educational Technology,* edited by B. Hegarty et al., Ascilite Dunedin, 2014, pp. 698–702.

Kerschbaum, Stephanie L. *Signs of Disability.* New York UP, 2022.

KESQ News. "Sen. Boxer Praises Support for Salton Sea Restoration in President's Budget." 11 Apr. 2013, https://kesq.com/news/2013/04/11/sen-boxer-praises-support-for-salton-sea-restoration-in-presidents-budget/.

Kimmerer, Robin Wall. *Braiding Sweetgrass.* Milkweed, 2013.

King, Denae W., et al. "An Initial Assessment of a Forgotten Minority Community: Key Informant's Perceptions of Environmental Health in Fresno, Texas." *Californian Journal of Health Promotion,* vol. 4, no. 1, 2006, pp. 22–31, https://www.ncbi.nlm.nih.gov/pmc/articles/PMC4196245/.

King, Denae W., et al. "Residential Perceptions of Environmental Exposures and Associated Health Effects in the Fresno, Texas Community." *Californian Journal of Health Promotion,* special issue on health disparities and social justice, vol. 5, 2007, pp. 48–57, https://cjhp.scholasticahq.com/article/93489.

King, Lisa, et al., editors. *Survivance, Sovereignty, and Story: Teaching American Indian Rhetorics.* Utah State UP, 2015.

Kinney, Thomas J. "The Political Unconscious of Rhetoric: The Case of the Master-Planned Community." *Rhetorical Agendas, Political, Ethical, Spiritual,* edited by Patricia Bizzell, Lawrence Erlbaum Associates, 2006, pp. 251–60.

Kirksey, Eben, et al. "Feeding the Flock: Wild Cockatoos and Their Facebook Friends." *Environment and Planning E: Nature and Space,* vol. 1, no. 4, 2018, pp. 602–20.

Klump, Barbara C., et al. "Is Bin-Opening in Cockatoos Leading to an Innovation Arms Race with Humans?" *Current Biology,* vol. 32, no. 17, 2022, pp. 910–11, https://doi.org/10.1016/j.cub.2022.08.008.

Knoblauch, Abby. "Bodies of Knowledge: Definitions, Delineations, and Implications of Embodied Writing in the Academy." *Composition Studies,* vol. 40, no. 2, 2012, pp. 50–65.

Koehler, Kirsten A., et al. "Potential Impact of Owens (Dry) Lake Dust on Warm and Cold Cloud Formation." *Journal of Geophysical Research Atmospheres,* vol. 112, no. D12210, 2007, pp. 1–12.

Koerber, Amy. "The Rhetorical Infrastructure of Sexual Misconduct in Michigan State University's Abuse Scandal." *Rhetoric of Health and Medicine,* vol. 5, no. 3, 2022, pp. 250–79.

Kohn, Eduardo. *How Forests Think.* U of California P, 2013.

Kovács, Tibor, et al. "Olfactory Centres in Alzheimer's Disease: Olfactory Bulb Is Involved in Early Braak's Stages." *Neuroreport,* vol. 12, no. 2, 2001, pp. 285–88.

Kumar, Ashok, et al. "An Application of EJSCREEN for the Examination of Environmental Justice in Metropolitan Areas of Ohio, USA." *Sustainability Studies: Environmental and Energy Management,* edited by G. Venkatesan et al., Bentham Books, 2022, pp. 112–26.

LaDuke, Winona. *All Our Relations: Native Struggles for Land and Life.* South End, 1999.

Lake, Frank K., and Amy Cardinal Christianson. "Indigenous Fire Stewardship." *Encyclopedia of Wildfires and Wildland-Urban Interface Fires,* 2020, pp. 714–22, https://doi.org/10.1007/978-3-319-51727-8_225-1.

Lakoff, George, and Mark Johnson. *Philosophy in the Flesh.* Basic, 1999.

Langer, Susan K. *Philosophy in a New Key: A Study in the Symbolism of Reason, Rite, and Art.* 1942. 3rd ed., Harvard UP, 1957.

Law, John, and Annemarie Mol. "Situating Technoscience: An Inquiry into Spatialities." *Environment and Planning D: Society and Space*, vol. 19, no. 5, 2001, pp. 505–630.

Law, John, and Vicky Singleton. "Object Lessons." *Organization*, vol. 12, no. 3, 2005, pp. 331–55.

Laylander, Don. "The Regional Consequences of Lake Cahuilla." *The San Diego State University Occasional Archaeological Papers*, vol. 1, 2006, https://soap.sdsu.edu/Volume1/LakeCahuilla/cahuilla.htm.

Leiss, William, and Douglas Powell. *Mad Cows and Mother's Milk: The Perils of Poor Risk Communication.* 2nd ed., McGill-Queen's UP, 2004.

Lemke, Thomas. "An Alternative Model of Politics? Prospects and Problems of Jane Bennett's Vital Materialism." *Theory, Culture, and Society*, vol. 35, no. 6, 2018, pp. 31–54.

Leopold, Aldo. *A Sand County Almanac: And Sketches Here and There.* Oxford UP, 1949.

Le Rouge, Mary. "Rhetorical Practices in East Palestine: Following Environmental Disaster." Conference on College Composition and Communication, H.21, 5 Apr. 2024, Spokane Convention Center, Spokane.

Liévanos, Raoul S. "Race, Deprivation, and Immigration Isolation: The Spatial Demography of Air-Toxic Clusters in the Continental United States." *Social Science Research*, vol. 54, 2015, 50–67.

Lindberg, Eric. "As Salton Sea Shrinks, Experts Fear Far-Reaching Health Consequences." *USC News*, 28 Aug. 2019, https://news.usc.edu/159380/salton-sea-shrinking-asthma-respiratory-health-air-quality/.

Linder, S. H., et al. "Cumulative Cancer Risk of Air Pollution in Houston: Disparities in Risk Burden and Social Disadvantage." *Environmental Science Technology*, vol. 42, no. 12, 2008, pp. 4312–22.

Long, Elenore. *Community Literacy and the Rhetoric of Local Publics.* Parlor Press, 2008.

Longo, Bernadette. "An Approach for Applying Cultural Study Theory to Technical Writing Research." *Technical Communication Quarterly*, vol. 7, no. 1, 1998, pp. 53–74.

Low, Kelvin E. Y. *Scents and Scents-Sibilities: Smell and Everyday Life Experiences.* Cambridge, 2009.

Lübke, Katrin T., and Bettina M. Pause. "Always Follow Your Nose: The Functional Significance of Social Chemosignals in Human Reproduction and Survival." *Hormones and Behavior*, vol. 68, 2015, pp. 134–44, https://doi.org/10.1016/j.yhbeh.2014.10.001.

Luhmann, Niklas. *Social Systems.* 1984 Gr. Translated by John Bednarz Jr. with Dirk Baeker, Stanford UP, 1995.

Mackendrick, Norah. "Foodscape." *Contexts*, vol. 13, no. 3, 2014, pp. 16–18.

Manning, Erin. *The Politics of Touch: Sense, Movement, Sovereignty.* U of Minnesota P, 2007.

Maroukis, Thomas C. *We Are Not a Vanishing People: The Society of American Indians, 1911–1923.* U of Arizona P, 2021.

Martinez, Aja Y. *Counterstory: The Rhetoric and Writing of Critical Race Theory.* National Council of Teachers of English, 2020.

Marquez, Vanesa. Twitter (X) post, 10 Sept. 2012, 11:21 a.m., https://twitter.com/vanessathought/status/245225544990474240?ref_src=twsrc%5Etfw.

Mason, Jennifer, and Katherine Davies. "Coming to Our Senses? A Critical Approach to Sensory Methodology." *Qualitative Research*, vol. 9, no. 5, 2009, pp. 587–603.

Massumi, Brian. *Parables for the Virtual: Movement, Affect, and Sensation.* Duke UP, 2002.

Mazis, Glen A. *Merleau-Ponty and the Face of the World: Silence, Ethics, Imagination, and Poetic Ontology.* State U of New York P, 2017.

Mbembe, Achille. "Necropolitics." Translated by Libby Meintjes. *Public Culture,* vol. 15, no. 1, pp. 11–40.

McClanahan, Bill, and Nigel South. "All Knowledge Begins with the Senses: Towards a Sensory Criminology." *British Journal of Criminology,* vol. 60, no. 1, 2020, pp. 3–23. JSTOR, https://doi.org/10.1093/bjc/azz052.

McDavid Schmidt, Kimberly, and Rebecca Beucher. "Affective Intensities: Emotion, Race, Gender and the Push and Pull of Bodies." *English Teaching: Critique and Practice,* vol. 19, no. 4, pp. 403–16, https://doi.org/10.1108/ETPC-11-2019-0147.

McDonnell, Patrick J. "Cause of Bird Deaths at Salton Sea Eludes Experts." *Los Angeles Times,* 16 Mar. 1992, https://www.latimes.com/archives/la-xpm-1992-03-16-mn-2824-story.html.

McEvilley, Thomas. *The Shape of Ancient Thought: Comparative Studies in Greek and Indian Philosophies.* Allworth, 2002.

McGee, Harold. *Nose Dive: A Field Guide to the World's Smells.* Penguin, 2020.

McKerrow, Raymie E. "Corporeality and Cultural Rhetoric: A Site for Rhetoric's Future." *Southern Communication Journal,* vol. 63, no. 4, 1998, pp. 315–28, https://doi.org/10.1080/10417949809373105.

McNeley, James K. *Holy Wind in Navajo Philosophy.* U of Arizona P, 1981.

McSorley, Kevin. "Sensate Regimes of War: Smell, Tracing, and Violence." *Security Dialogue,* vol. 51, nos. 2–3, 2020, pp. 155–73, https://doi.org/10.1177/0967010619893231.

Medway, Dominic, and Gary Warnaby. "Designing Smell into the Consumer Experience." *Designing with Smell,* edited by Victoria Henshaw et al., Routledge, 2018 pp. 123–30.

Merleau-Ponty, Maurice, and Claude Lefort. *The Visible and the Invisible, Followed by Working Notes.* 1964 Fr. Translated by Alphonso Lingis, Northwestern UP, 1968.

Metzler, Chris, and Jeff Springer, directors. *Plagues and Pleasures on the Salton Sea.* Tilapia Films, 2007.

Middleton, Michael, et al. *Participatory Critical Rhetoric: Theoretical and Methodological Foundations for Studying Rhetoric in Situ.* Lexington Books, 2015.

Mies, Maria, and Vandana Shiva. *Ecofeminism.* Zed, 2014.

Minorsky, Peter V. "The Functions of Foliar Nyctinasty: A Review and Hypothesis." *Biological Reviews,* vol. 84, no. 1, 2019, pp. 216–29.

Minsky, Laurence, et al. "Inside the Invisible but Influential World of Scent Branding." *Harvard Business Review,* 11 Apr. 2018, https://hbr.org/2018/04/inside-the-invisible-but-influential-world-of-scent-branding.

Mirzoeff, Nicholas, editor. *The Visual Culture Reader.* 3rd ed., Routledge, 2012.

Molé, Noelle J. "Existential Damages: The Injury of Precarity Goes to Court." *Cultural Anthropology,* vol. 28, no. 1, 2013, pp. 22–43.

Molyneux, Maxine, and Deborah Lynn Steinberg. "Mies and Shiva's Ecofeminism: A New Testament?" *Feminist Review,* vol. 49, spring 1995, pp. 86–107.

Moore, David J., et al. "Exploring the Role of Individual Differences in Affect Intensity on the Consumer's Response to Advertising Appeals." *Advances in Consumer Research North American Advances,* vol. 21, 1994, pp. 181–87.

Morgan, Tara. "From Choricero to Chorizo: The Rare Pepper That Makes Traditional Basque Sausage Sing." *Edible Idaho Magazine*, 15 June 2015, https://edibleidaho.ediblecommunities.com/recipes/choricero-chorizo-rare-pepper-makes-traditional-basque-sausate-sing.

Mostafa, Taymour, et al. "Pheromones in Sex and Reproduction: Do They Have a Role in Humans?" *Journal of Advanced Research*, vol. 3, no. 1, 2012, pp. 1–9, https://doi.org/10.1016/j.jare.2011.03.003.

Moteki, Hideaki. "Anosmia, Trigeminal Nerve Dysfunction, and COVID-19: A Personal Account." *Acta Oto-Laryngologica Case Reports*, vol. 6, no. 1, 2021, pp. 88–90, https://doi.org/10.1080/2 3772484.2021.2002696.

Muchembled, Robert. *Smells: A Cultural History of Odours in Early Modern Times*. 2017 Fr. Translated by Susan Pickford, Polity Press, 2020.

Muir, John. *Nature Writings*. Literary Classics, 1997.

Müller, Caroline, et al. "The Power of Infochemicals in Mediating Individualized Niches." *Trends in Ecology and Evolution*, vol. 35, no. 11, 2020, pp. 981–89, https://doi.org/10.1016/j.tree.2020.07.001.

Murray, Joddy. *Non-Discursive Rhetoric: Image and Affect in Multimodal Composition*. State U of New York P, 2009.

Nadaraja, Dinish, et al. "The Sustainability Assessment of Plantation Agriculture: A Systematic Review of Sustainability Indicators." *Sustainable Production and Consumption*, vol. 26, 2021, pp. 892–910, https://doi.org/10.1016/j.spc.2020.12.042.

National Aeronautics and Space Administration. "Global Temperature Anomalies from 1880 to 2024." 10 Jan. 2025, https://svs.gsfc.nasa/5450.

National Oceanic and Atmospheric Association. "National Environmental Satellite, Data, and Information Service Coral Reef Watch." 7 Mar. 2016.

Nevitt, Gabrielle A. "Sensory Ecology on the High Seas: The Odor World of the Procellariiform Seabirds." *The Journal of Experimental Biology*, vol. 211, no. 11, 2008, pp. 1706–13, https://doi.org/10.1242/jeb/.015412.

Newburger, Emma. "Ghost Towns and Toxic Fumes: How an Idyllic California Lake Became a Disaster." *CNBC*, 6 Nov. 2021, https://www.cnbc.com/2021/11/06/californias-salton-sea-spewing-toxic-fumes-creating-ghost-towns-.html.

Nguyen, Tien. "Tour the Sriracha Factory Again and See What Started the Whole Pepper Crisis." *LA Weekly*, 12 Sept. 2014.

Nijhuis, Michelle. "Accidental Refuge: Should We Save the Salton Sea?" *High Country News*, 19 June 2000.

Nishimi, Kristen, et al., "Master-Planned Communities in the United States as Novel Contexts for Individual and Population-Level Research." *Preventative Medicine*, vol. 154, 3 Nov. 2021, pp. 1–7, https://doi.org/10.1016/j.ypmed.2021.106864.

Nixon, Rob. *Slow Violence and the Environmentalism of the Poor*. Harvard UP, 2011.

Odor Task Force Minutes. April 27, 2016. City of Pearland, Texas, https://www.pearlandtx.gov/home/showpublisheddocument/13129/636059026333317000.

Odor Task Force Minutes. May 25, 2016. City of Pearland, Texas, https://www.pearlandtx.gov/home/showpublisheddocument/13135/636059027814777000.

Odor Task Force Minutes. August 17, 2016. City of Pearland, Texas, https://www.pearlandtx.gov/home/showpublisheddocument/14627/636105684858630000.

Ogawa, Akihiro. "Young Precariat at the Forefront: Anti-Nuclear Rallies in Post-Fukushima Japan." *Inter-Asia Cultural Studies*, vol. 14, no. 2, 2013, pp. 317–26.

Olalde, Mark. "Will California Finally Fulfill Its Promise to Fix the Salton Sea?" *High Country News*, 21 Dec. 2020, hcn.org/issues/53.1/south-water-will-california-finally-fulfill-its-promise-to-fix-the-salton-sea.

Oreskes, Naomi. *Why Trust Science?* Princeton UP, 2021.

Overweg, Cynthia. "Hildegard of Bingen: The Nun Who Loved the Earth." *Quest*, vol. 105, no. 3, 2017, pp. 21–25.

Panagia, Davide. *The Political Life of Sensation*. Duke UP, 2009.

Parr, Joy. "Smells Like?: Sources of Uncertainty in the History of the Great Lakes Environment." *Environmental History*, vol. 11, no. 2, Apr. 2006, pp. 269–99.

Parrish, Alex C. *Adaptive Rhetoric: Evolution, Culture, and the Art of Persuasion*. Routledge, 2015.

Parrish, Sabine. "Competitive Coffee Making and the Crafting of the Ideal Barista." *Gastronomica*, vol. 20, no. 2, 2020, pp. 79–90, https://doi.org/10.1525/gfc.2020.20.2.79.

Parsons, Talcott, et al. "Some Fundamental Categories of the Theory of Action." *Toward a General Theory of Action*, edited by Talcott Parsons and Edward A. Shils, Harvard UP, 1951, pp. 3–29.

Pasadena Star-News. "Sriracha Hot Sauce Controversy: Timeline of Events." *Pasadena Star-News Air Quality*, 12 Mar. 2014.

Patel, Zara M. "The Evidence for Olfactory Training in Treating Patients with Olfactory Loss." *Otolaryngology and Head and Neck Surgery*, vol. 25, no. 1, 2017, pp. 43–46, https://doi.org/10.1097/MOO.0000000000000328.

Patencio, Francisco, and Margaret Boynton. *Stories and Legends of the Palm Spring Indians*, Burtyrki Books, 2020.

Pearce, Fred. "Climate's Conflict Zone." *New Scientist*, vol. 228, no. 3050, 2015, pp. 26–30.

Pearce, Fred. *When the Rivers Run Dry: Water—the Defining Problem of the Twenty-First Century*. 2nd ed., Beacon, 2018.

People ex rel. City of Irwindale, a Municipal Corporation, and Fred Galante, City Attorney for the City of Irwindale v. Huy Fong Foods, Inc., a California Corporation, and Does 1 through 20. Case No. BC525856. 2013. 1–10. Superior Court of the State of California County of Los Angeles–Central District. 28 Oct. 2013.

Pew Research Center. "The Rise of Asian Americans." 4 Apr. 2013, https://www.pewresearch.org/social-trends/2012/06/19/the-rise-of-asian-americans/.

Pezzullo, Phaedra C. *Toxic Tourism: Rhetorics of Pollution, Travel, and Environmental Justice*. U of Alabama P, 2007.

Phillips, Lisa L. "Sensing Publics: Environmental Rhetoric in East Palestine." *Conference on College Composition and Communication*, H.21, 5 Apr. 2024, Spokane Convention Center, Spokane.

Phillips, Lisa L., et al. "Mapping the Environment with Sensory Perception." *Science Education Resource Center*, 10 May 2016, https://serc.carleton.edu/integrate/teaching_materials/map_sense/index.html.

Pink, Sarah. *Doing Sensory Ethnography*. Sage, 2009.

Pitzer, Gary. "Long Troubled Salton Sea May Finally Be Getting What It Most Needs: Action—and Money." *Water Education Foundation*, 28 July 2021, https://www.watereducation.org/western-water/long-troubled-salton-sea-may-finally-be-getting-what-it-most-needs-action-and-money.

Plato. *Six Great Dialogues: Apology, Crito, Phaedo, Phaedrus, Symposium, The Republic*. Translated by Benjamin Jowett, edited by Mary Waldrep and Tom Crawford, Dover, 2007.

Polakovic, Gary. "Farm Runoff: It's an Ongoing Challenge." *The Press-Enterprise*, http://www.sci.sdsu.edu/salton/FarmRunoff.html. Accessed 14 June 2021.

Pollard, Justin. "The Eccentric Engineer." *Engineering and Technology*, vol. 8, no. 10., 2013, p. 92, http://dx.doi.org/10.1049/et.2013.1033.

Poudyal, Bibhushana, and Mala Rai. "The Smell of the Other and Self-Alienation: A Mani(fold)festo of Race, Ethnicity, and Rhetorical (In)Accessibility to Food." *Food Justice Activism and Pedagogies: Literacies and Rhetorics for Transforming Food Systems in Local and Transnational Contexts*, edited by Eileen E. Schell et al., Lexington Books, 2023, pp. 71–83.

Propen, Amy D. *Locating Visual-Material Rhetorics: The Map, the Mill, and the GPS*. Parlor Press, 2012.

Rai, Candice, and Caroline Druschke Gottschalk, editors. *Field Rhetoric: Ethnography, Ecology, and Engagement in the Places of Persuasion*. U of Alabama P, 2018.

Rappaport, Danielle I., et al. "Animal Soundscapes Reveal Key Markers of Amazon Forest Degradation from Fire and Logging." *Proceedings from the National Academy of Sciences*, vol. 119, no. 18, 2022, pp. 1–11, https://doi.org/10.1073/pnas.2102878119.

Rathje, William, and Cullen Murphy. *Rubbish! The Archaeology of Garbage*. 1992. U of Arizona P, 2001.

Ravenscroft, Alison. "Strange Weather: Indigenous Materialisms, New Materialism, and Colonialism." *Cambridge Journal of Postcolonial Literary Theory*, vol. 5, no. 3, Sept. 2018, pp. 355–70.

Reaves, Elissa. "Atrazine." United States Environmental Protection Agency, Docket Number EPA-HQ-OPP-2013-0266, 14 Sept. 2020, https://www.epa.gov/sites/default/files/2020-09/documents/atrazine-id-signed-final.pdf.

Reheis, Marith C. "Dust Deposition Downwind of Owens (Dry) Lake, 1991–1994: Preliminary Findings." *Journal of Geophysical Research Atmospheres*, vol. 102, no. D22, 1997, pp. 25999–6008.

Reid, Alex. "Composing with Deliberate Speed: Writing Humanity's Future Sensorium." *Rhetorical Speculations: The Future of Writing, Rhetoric, and Technology*, edited by Scott Sundvall, Utah State UP, 2019, pp. 69–87.

Reinarz, Johnathon. *Past Scents: Historical Perspectives on Smell*. U of Illinois P, 2014.

Remeikis, Amy. "Scott Morrison's Hawaiian Horror Show: How a PR Disaster Unfolded." *The Guardian*, 20 Dec. 2019, https://www.theguardian.com/australia-news/2019/dec/21/scott-morrison-hawaii-horror-show-pr-disaster-unfolded.

"Republic Services Net Worth 2010–2021." *Macrotrends*, https://www.macrotrends.net/stocks/charts/RSG/republic-services/net-worth. Accessed 24 Mar. 2022.

Rice, Jenny. *Distant Publics: Development Rhetoric and the Subject of Crisis*. U Pittsburgh P, 2012.

Ridolfo, Jim, and Dànielle N. DeVoss. "Composing for Recomposition: Rhetorical Velocity and Delivery." *Kairos: A Journal of Rhetoric, Technology, and Pedagogy*, vol. 3, no. 2, http://www.technorhetoric.net/13.2/topoi/ridolfo_devoss/index.html.

Ríos, Gabriela Raquel. "Cultivating Land-Based Literacies and Rhetorics." *LiCS: Literacy in Composition Studies*, vol. 3, no. 1, 2015, pp. 60–70.

Ríos, Gabriela Raquel. "Performing Nahua Rhetorics for Civic Engagement." *Survivance, Sovereignty, and Story: Teaching American Indian Rhetorics*, edited by Lisa King et al., Utah State UP, 2015, pp. 79–95.

Rittel, Horst, and Melvin Webber. "Dilemmas in a General Theory of Planning." *Policy Sciences*, vol. 4, no. 2, 1973, pp. 155–69.

Robinson, Cedric J., et al. "Racial Capitalism: The Nonobjective Character of Capitalist Development." *Black Marxism, Revised and Updated Third Edition: The Making of the Black Radical Tradition.* 3rd ed., U of North Carolina P, 2021, pp. 9–28. *JSTOR*, http://www.jstor.org/stable/10.5149/9781469663746_robinson.

Rodriguez, Katheryn, et al. *Exposing the Desert III: Policy and Programs at the Salton Sea*, Center for Health Disparities, University of California, Riverside, 12 July 2021, https://storymaps.arcgis.com/stories/618867f8c870414d8cc0962776e73f63.

Ross, Derek G., editor. *Topic-Driven Environmental Rhetoric.* Routledge, 2017.

Ross, Susan M. "A Feminist Perspective on Technical Communication Action: Exploring How Alternative Worldviews Affect Environmental Remediation Efforts." *Technical Communication Quarterly*, vol. 3, no. 3, 1994, pp. 325–42.

Rowland, Allison L. *Zoetropes and the Politics of Humanhood.* The Ohio State UP, 2020.

Rubin, Gretchen. *Life in Five Senses: How Exploring the Senses Got Me out of My Head and into the World.* Crown, 2023.

Rude, Carolyn D. "Mapping the Research Questions in Technical Communication." *Journal of Business and Technical Communication*, vol. 23, no. 2, 2009, pp. 174–215.

Rudy, A. P. "Imperial Contradictions: Is the Valley a Watershed, Region, or Cyborg?" *Journal of Rural Studies*, vol. 21, no. 1, 2005, pp. 19–38.

Sackey, Donnie J. "One-Size-Fits None: A Heuristic for Proactive Value Sensitive Environmental Design." *Technical Communication Quarterly*, vol. 29, no. 1, 2020, pp. 33–48, https://doi.org/10.1080/10572252.2019.1634767.

Sackey, Donnie J., and Dànielle N. DeVoss. "Ecology, Ecologies, and Institutions Eco and Composition." *Ecology, Writing Theory, and New Media: Writing Ecology*, edited by Sidney I. Dobrin, Routledge, 2012, pp. 195–212.

Salleh, Ariel. Foreword. *Ecofeminism*, by Maria Mies and Vandana Shiva, Zed, 2014, pp. ix–xii.

Salton Sea Air Quality Mitigation Program. "Emissions Estimate." 31 Dec. 2020, https://saltonseaprogram.com/aqm/data-portal/data-portal.php#.

Salton Sea Authority. "Timeline of Salton Sea History." 2017, https://saltonsea.com/get-informed/history/.

"Salton Sea Fingered as Culprit in California Stink." *The Weather Channel*, 13 Sept. 2012, https://www.oregonlive.com/today/2012/09/southern_california_stench_lin.html.

Sanburn, Josh. "The Poisoning of an American City." *Time*, vol. 187, no. 3, 1 Feb. 2016, https://time.com/magazine/us/4188304/february-1st-2016-vol-187-no-3-u-s/.

Sandman, Peter M. "Getting to Maybe: Some Communications Aspects of Siting Hazardous Waste Facilities." *Seton Hall Legislative Journal*, 1986, pp. 437–65.

Sansom, Garett, et al. "Vulnerable Populations Exposed to Lead-Contaminated Drinking Water within Houston Ship Channel Communities." *Environmental Research and Public Health*, vol. 16, no. 15, 2019, pp. 1–8, https://doi.org/10.3390/ijerph16152745.

Sauer, Beverly A. "Communicating Risk in a Cross-Cultural Comparison of Rhetorical and Social Understandings in U.S. and British Mine Safety Training Programs." *Journal of Business and Technical Communication*, vol. 10, no. 3, 1996, pp. 306–29.

Sauer, Beverly A. "Embodied Knowledge: The Textual Representation of Embodied Sensory Information in a Dynamic and Uncertain Material Environment." *Written Communication*, vol. 15, no. 2, 1998, pp. 131–69.

Scander, Henrik, and Bo Marcus Jackobsson. "Gastronomy Competition and Restaurant Practice: Sommeliers' Understanding of the Game of Social Craft." *International Journal of Gas-*

tronomy and Food Science, vol. 29, no. 100567, 2022, pp. 1–8, https://doi.org/10.1016/j.ijgfs.2022.100567.

Scheuering, Rachel W. *Shapers of the Great Debate on Conservation: A Biographical Dictionary.* Greenwood, 2004.

Schiffman, Susan S., and C. Mike Williams. "Science of Odor as a Potential Health Issue." *Journal of Environmental Quality*, vol. 34, no. 1, 2005, pp. 129–38.

Schmitt, Casey R., et al. "Rhetorical Approaches in Environmental Communication." *The Handbook of International Trends in Environmental Communication*, edited by Bruno Takahashi et al., Routledge, 2021, pp. 70–87.

Scott, J. Blake. *Risky Rhetorics: AIDS and the Cultural Practices of HIV Testing.* Southern Illinois UP, 2003.

Senda-Cook, Samantha. "Long Memories: Material Rhetoric as Evidence of Memory and a Potential Future." *Western Journal of Communication*, vol. 84, no. 4, 2020, pp. 419–38.

Senda-Cook, Samantha, et al. "Rhetorical Cartographies: (Counter)Mapping Urban Spaces." *Field Rhetoric: Ethnography, Ecology, and Engagement in the Places of Persuasion*, edited by Candice Rai and Caroline Gottschalk Druschke, 2018, U of Alabama P, pp. 95–119.

Serrano, Fermín, et al. "White Paper on Citizen Science." *European Commission*, 2015, pp. 1–36.

Sexton, K. et al. "Comparative Assessment of Air Pollution-Related Health Risks in Houston. *Environmental Health Perspectives*, vol. 115, no. 10, 2007, pp. 1388–93.

Sheehan, Matt. *The Transpacific Experiment: How China and California Collaborate and Compete for Our Future.* Counterpoint, 2020.

Shepherd, Gordon M. "Perception without a Thalamus: How Does Olfaction Do It?" *Neuron*, vol. 46, no. 2, 2005, pp. 166–68, https://doi.org/10.1016/j.neuron.2005.03.012.

Sherwin, Richard K. "Dialects and Dominance: A Study of Rhetorical Fields in the Law of Confessions." *University of Pennsylvania Law Review*, vol. 136, no. 3, 1988, pp. 730–848.

Shyong, Frank, et al. "Some Neighbors Say Sriracha Factory's Smell Is Creating Headaches." *Los Angeles Times*, 29 Oct. 2013, https://www.latimes.com/local/la-me-1030-sriracha-smell-20131030-story.html.

Silvestrini, Gabriella. "Rousseau, Pufendorf and the Eighteenth-Century Natural Law Tradition." *History of European Ideas*, vol. 36, no. 3, 2010, pp. 280–301.

Simard, Suzanne W., et al. "Net Transfer of Carbon between Ectomycorrhizal Tree Species in the Field." *Nature (London)*, vol. 388, no. 6642, 1997, pp. 579–82.

Simmons, W. Michele. *Participation and Power: Civic Discourse in Environmental Policy Decisions.* State U of New York P, 2007.

Simon, Matt. "The Salton Sea: Death and Politics in the Great American Water Wars." *Wired*, 14 Sept. 2012, https://www.wired.com/2012/09/salton-sea-saga/.

Singer, Norie R. "Toward Intersectional Ecofeminist Communication Studies." *Communication Theory*, vol. 30, no. 3, 2020, pp. 268–89, https://doi.org//10.1093/ct/qtz023.

Singh, Maanvi. "'The Air Is Toxic': How an Idyllic California Lake Became a Nightmare." *The Guardian*, 24 July 2021, https://www.theguardian.com/us-news/2021/jul/23/salton-sea-california-lake-dust-drought-climate.

Škof, Lenart, and Petri Berndtson. Introduction. *Atmospheres of Breathing.* State U of New York P, 2018, pp. i–xxvii.

Slater, Philip. *The Pursuit of Loneliness: American Culture at the Breaking Point.* 1970. 20th anniversary ed., Beacon, 1990.

Slater, Thomas, et al. "Review Article: Earth's Ice Imbalance." *The Cryosphere*, vol. 15, no. 1, 2021, pp. 233–46, https://doi.org/10.5194/tc-15-233-2021.

Smell Something, Tell Something! "Brunswick, Georgia, community group," *Facebook*, 5 Jan. 2019. https://www.facebook.com/groups/1852807574805035.

Smell Something, Tell Something! "I was awoken," *Facebook*, 10 Jan. 2023, https://www.facebook.com/groups/1852807574805035/posts/5721722004580220.

Smith, Mark A. *How Race Is Made: Slavery, Segregation, and the Senses*. U of North Carolina P, 2006.

Solar News Group. "California Sues Sriracha Factory for Fumes." *Reuters*, Solar News Online, 4 Nov. 2013.

Soler, Zachary M., et al. "A Primer on Viral-Associated Olfactory Loss in the Era of COVID-19." *International Forum of Allergy and Rhinology*, vol. 10, no. 7, pp. 814–20, https://doi.org/10.1002/alr.22578.

South Coast Air Quality Monitoring Data. "Current Hourly Air Quality Index Map." https://scaqmd-online.maps.arcgis.com/apps/webappviewer/index.html?id=3d51b5d2fc8d42d9af8c04f3c00f88d3. Accessed 20 Oct. 2021.

Spence, Charles. "Scenting Entertainment: Virtual Reality Storytelling, Theme Park Rides, Gambling, and Video-Gaming." *i-Perception*, vol. 12, no. 4, 2021, pp. 1–26, https://doi.org/10.1177/20416695211034538.

St. Croix Sensory. "Nasal Ranger—Field Olfactometer." https://www.fivesenses.com/equipment/nasalranger/nasalranger/. Accessed 14 Feb. 2022.

Stearney, Lynn M. "Feminism, Ecofeminism, and the Maternal Archetype: Motherhood as a Feminine Universal." *Communication Quarterly*, vol. 42, no. 2, 1994, pp. 145–59, https://doi.org/10.1080/01463379409369923.

Stephens, Sonia. H., and Daniel P. Richards. "Storymapping and Sea Level Rise: Listening to Global Risks at Street Level." *Communication Design Quarterly*, vol. 8, no. 1, 2020, pp. 5–18.

Stevens, Martin. *Sensory Ecology, Behaviour, and Evolution*. Oxford, 2013.

Stewart, Jude. *Revelations in Air: A Guidebook to Smell*. Penguin, 2021.

Stringfellow, Kim. *Greetings from the Salton Sea: Folly and Intervention in the Southern California Landscape, 1905–2005*. U of Chicago P, Center for American Places, 2011.

Sturken, Marita, and Lisa Cartwright. *Practices of Looking: An Introduction to Visual Culture*. 2nd ed., Oxford UP, 2009.

Sugiura, Lisa, et al. "Ethical Challenges in Online Research: Public/Private Perceptions." *Research Ethics*, vol. 13, nos. 3–4, 2017, pp. 184–99.

Sunseri, Charlotte. "Food Politics of Alliance in a California Frontier Chinatown." *International Journal of Historical Archaeology*, vol. 19, no. 2, 2015, pp. 416–31.

Synnott, Anthony. *The Body Social: Symbolism, Self, and Society*. Routledge, 1993.

Tanner, Caroline M., et al. "The Disease Intersection of Susceptibility and Exposure: Chemical Exposures and Neurodegenerative Disease Risk." *Alzheimer's and Dementia*, vol. 10, no. 3, 2014, pp. S213–S225.

Tanner, Caroline M., et al. "Rotenone, Paraquat, and Parkinson's Disease." *Environmental Health Perspectives*, vol. 119, no. 6, pp. 1–18, http://doi.org/10.1289/ehp.1002839.

Taylor, Paul S. "Plantation Agriculture in the United States: Seventeenth to Twentieth Centuries." *Land Economics*, vol. 30, no. 2, 1954, pp. 141–52.

Texas Commission on Environmental Quality. "Fact Sheet: Pearland Odor Complaints." https://www.tceq.texas.gov/agency/subjects-of-interest/air-quality/odors-in-pearland. Accessed 31 Aug. 2023.

Texas Commission on Environmental Quality. "In the Matter of an Enforcement Action Concerning Blue Ridge Landfill TX, LP, Docket No. 2016-1923-AIR-E." 10 July 2017, https://www.pearlandtx.gov/home/showpublisheddocument/17104/636359828012570000-433277.

Texas Commission on Environmental Quality. "Odor Complaint Investigation Procedures." https://www.pearlandtx.gov/home/showpublisheddocument/22227/636679585934600000. Accessed 7 Feb. 2022.

Thomas, Gordon, and Max M. Witts. *Ruin from the Air: The Atomic Mission to Hiroshima.* Hamish Hamilton, 1997.

Thompson, Claire S. "Scent and Brand Storytelling." *Designing with Smell*, edited by Victoria Henshaw et al., Routledge, 2018, pp. 140–47.

Thomson, Jess. "California Lake Flooded for First Time in 110 Years after Atmospheric River." *Newsweek*, 23 Apr. 2023, https://www.newsweek.com/california-lake-flooded-rainfall-nasa-drought-1792176.

Thoreau, Henry D. *Walden*. 1854. Edited by Jeffrey S. Cramer, Yale, 2004.

Timbrell, Jamie. "Mix It Up with Mole." *Culinary Trends*, spring 2009, pp. 14–15, https://moam.info/culinary-trends-early-spring-issue_5a3633d71723dd8c64bb696a.html.

Todd, Anne M. *Communicating Environmental Patriotism: A Rhetorical History of the American Environmental Movement.* Routledge, 2013.

Todd, Zoe. "An Indigenous Feminist's Take on the Ontological Turn: 'Ontology' Is Just Another Word for Colonialism." *Journal of Historical Sociology*, vol. 29, no. 1, 2016, pp. 4–22, https://doi.org/10.1111/johs.12124.

Toscano, Julia. "Climate Change Displacement and Forced Migration: An International Crisis." *Arizona Journal of Environmental Law and Policy*, vol. 6, 2015, pp. 457–90.

Trumbo, Craig W. "Risk, Rhetoric, and the Reactor Next Door." *Technical Communication, Deliberative Rhetoric, and Environmental Discourse*, edited by Nancy W. Coppola and Bill Karis, Ablex, 2000, pp. 191–223.

Tsing, Anna Lowenhaupt. *The Mushroom at the End of the World: On the Possibility of Life in Capitalist Ruins.* Princeton UP, 2015.

Tsing, Anna Lowenhaupt, et al., editors. *Arts of Living on a Damaged Planet: Ghost and Monsters of the Anthropocene.* U of Minnesota P, 2017.

Tuan, Yi-Fu. *Landscapes of Fear.* 1979. U of Minnesota P, 2013.

Tuan, Yi-Fu. *Passing Strange and Wonderful: Aesthetics, Nature, and Culture.* 1993. Kodansha America, 1995.

Ulrich, Amanda. "More than 17000 Native Trees Planted on Exposed Lakebed Next to Salton Sea." *The Desert Sun*, 20 Jan. 2022, https://www.desertsun.com/story/news/environment/2022/01/20/more-than-1-700-native-trees-planted-exposed-lakebed-next-salton-sea/6585559001/.

Ulrich, Amanda. "Torres Martinez Tribe Host Poster Contest to Honor 'Past, Present, and Future' Salton Sea." *The Desert Sun*, 27 Dec. 2020, https://www.desertsun.com/story/news/2020/12/27/torres-martinez-tribe-hosts-poster-contest-honor-culture-around-salton-sea/3932756001/.

United States Census Bureau. "Baldwin Park, California." 19 July 2019, https://www.census.gov/quickfacts/baldwinparkcitycalifornia?.

United States Census Bureau. "Fresno CDP, Texas." 1 July 2020, https://www.census.gov/quickfacts/fact/table/fresnocdptexas/AGE775222.

United States Census Bureau. "Income and Poverty in the United States: 2020." 14 Sept. 2021, https://www.census.gov/library/publications/2021/demo/p60-273.html.

United States Census Bureau. "Irwindale, California." 2010–2019, https://www.census.gov/search-results.html?q=Irwindale%2C+California&page=1&stateGeo=none&searchtype=web&cssp=SERP&_charset_=UTF-8.

United States Census Bureau. "Quick Facts Imperial County, California." https://www.census.gov/quickfacts/imperialcountycalifornia. Accessed 11 June 2022.

United States Census Bureau. "Quick Facts Katy, Texas." https://www.census.gov/quickfacts/fact/table/katycitytexas/PST045222. Accessed 31 Aug. 2023.

United States Census Bureau. "Quick Facts Pearland, Texas." https://www.census.gov/quickfacts/fact/table/pearlandcitytexas/INC110219. Accessed 31 Jan. 2022.

United States Census Bureau. "Supplemental Poverty Measure."10 Sept. 2024, https://www.census.gov/topics/income-poverty/supplemental-poverty-measure.html.

United States Court of Appeals for the Fifth Circuit. Case No. 19-40062, Summary Calendar, *Jing Gao et al. v. Blue Ridge Landfill*. 30 Oct. 2019. *Justia*, https://cases.justia.com/federal/appellate-courts/ca5/19-40062/19-40062-2019-10-30.pdf?ts=1572460258.

United States Department of Agriculture. "Plant Hardiness Zone Map." 2012, https://planthardiness.ars.usda.gov/.

United States Environmental Protection Agency. "Cuyahoga River AOC." 2022, https://www.epa.gov/great-lakes-aocs/cuyahoga-river-aoc.

United States Environmental Protection Agency. "National Overview: Facts and Figures on Materials, Wastes, and Recycling." 2018, https://www.epa.gov/facts-and-figures-about-materials-waste-and-recycling/national-overview-facts-and-figures-materials.

United States Environmental Protection Agency. "Pacific Southwest, Region 9: Superfund." *EPA.gov*, 6 Feb. 2014.

Valverde, Mariana. "The Law of Bad Smells: Making and Adjudicating Offensiveness Claims in Contemporary Local Law." *Canadian Journal of Law and Society*, vol. 34, no. 2, 2019, pp. 327–41, https://doi.org/10.1017/cls.2019.20.

Vannini, Phillip, et al. *The Senses in Self, Society, and Culture: A Sociology of the Senses*. Routledge, 2012.

Vij, Ritu. "Affective Fields of Precarity: Gendered Antinomies in Contemporary Japan." *Alternatives: Global, Local, Political*, vol. 38, no. 2, 2013, pp. 122–38.

Voyles, Traci B. *The Settler Sea: California's Salton Sea and the Consequences of Colonialism*. U of Nebraska P, 2021.

Wajcman, Judy. *Pressed for Time: The Acceleration of Time in Digital Capitalism*. U of Chicago P, 2014.

Walters, Shannon. *Rhetorical Touch: Disability, Identification, Haptics*. U of South Carolina P, 2014.

Walwema, Josephine. "Chapter 10: Participatory Policy Enacting Technical Communication for a Shared Water Future." *Technical Communication for Environmental Action*, edited by Sean D. Williams, State U of New York P, 2023, pp. 245–66.

Wander, Philip. "The Ideological Turn in Modern Criticism." *Communication Studies*, vol. 34, no. 1, pp. 1–18, https://doi.org/10.1080/10510978309368110.

Warner, Michael. *Publics and Counterpublics*. Zone Books, 2005.

Warren, Karen. "The Power and Promise of Ecological Feminism." *Environmental Ethics*, vol. 12, 1990, pp. 125–46.

Watts, Vanessa. "Indigenous Place-Thought and Agency amongst Humans and Non-Humans (First Woman and Sky Women Go on a European World Tour!)." *Decolonization: Indigeneity, Education and Society*, vol. 2, no. 1, 2013, pp. 20–34.

Weidner, Ned. "Rotting Fish in Paradise: Putrefaction, Ecophobia, and Olfactory Imaginations of Southern California." *Configurations*, vol. 25, no. 2, 2017, pp. 237–51, https://doi.org/10.1353/con.2017.0014.

Wendel, JoAnna. "Current Carbon Emissions Unprecedented in 66 Million Years." *Earth and Space Science News Eos*, vol. 97, no. 23, Mar. 2016.

Wildcat, Daniel R. *Red Alert! Saving the Planet with Indigenous Knowledge*. Fulcrum, 2009.

Williams, Casey M. *Analysis of Factors Related to Science Teachers' Perceptions about Climate Change: Implications for Educators*. 2019. Texas Tech U, PhD dissertation. ProQuest. https://hdl.handle.net/2346/85313.

Williams, Serena W. "The Anticipatory Nuisance Doctrine: One Common Law Theory for Use in Environmental Justice Cases." *William and Mary Environmental Law and Policy Review*, vol. 19, no. 2, 1995, pp. 223–51, https://scholarship.law.wm.edu/wmelpr/vol19/iss2/3.

Wilson, Donald A., and Richard J. Stevenson. *Learning to Smell: Olfactory Perception from Neurobiology to Behavior*. Johns Hopkins UP, 2006.

Wilson, Edward O. *Consilience: The Unity of Knowledge*. Vintage, 1999.

Winderman, Emily and Robert Mejia. "The COVID-19 Sensorium and Its Vectors, Victims, and Violators." *Communication and Critical/Cultural Studies*, vol. 19, no. 1, 2022, pp. 22–29, https://doi.org/10.1080/14791420.2021.2020861.

Winner, Langdon. *The Whale and the Reactor: A Search for Limits in an Age of High Technology*. U of Chicago P, 1989.

Witze, Alexandra. "What the Pliocene Epoch Can Teach Us about Future Warming on Earth." *Science News*, 28 Nov. 2017, https://www.sciencenews.org/article/what-pliocene-epoch-can-teach-us-about-future-warming-earth.

Wohlleben, Peter. *The Hidden Life of Trees: What They Feel, How They Communicate—Discoveries from a Secret World*. Translated by Jane Billinghurst, Greystone Books, 2016.

Wolfe, Benjamin. "Why Does the Sea Smell Like the Sea?" *Popular Science*, 19 Aug. 2014, https://www.popsci.com/seasmells/.

Womach, J. "Agriculture: A Glossary of Terms, Programs, and Laws." *Congressional Research Service*, 2005, https://ttu-primo.hosted.exlibrisgroup.com/permalink/f/1j33bpi/TN_cdi_proquest_congressional_congresearch_crs_2005_rsi_0052.

Wood, H. P. "The Colorado River." *Imperial Valley Press*, 20 Apr. 1901, https://cdnc.ucr.edu/?a=d&d=IVP19010420.2.27.

World Health Organization. "An Estimated 12.6 Million Deaths Each Year Are Attributable to Unhealthy Environments." 15 Mar. 2016, https://www.who.int/news/item/15-03-2016-an-estimated-12-6-million-deaths-each-year-are-attributable-to-unhealthy-environments.

Wu, Ellen. *The Color of Success: Asian Americans and the Origins of the Model Minority*. Princeton UP, 2013.

Yang, John. "Climate Change Causing a Sense of Despair? Here Are Some Ways to Combat It." *Public Broadcasting Service News*, 30 July 2023, https://www.pbs.org/newshour/show/climate-change-causing-a-sense-of-despair-here-are-some-ways-to-combat-it.

Yao, Fangfang, et al. "Satellites Reveal Widespread Decline in Global Lake Water Storage." *Science*, vol. 380, no. 6646, 2023, pp. 743–49, https://doi.org/10.1126/science.abo2812.

Yates, Julian S., et al. "Multiple Ontologies of Water: Politics, Conflict and Implications for Governance." *Environment and Planning D: Society and Space*, vol. 35, no. 5, 2017, pp. 797–815, https://doi.org/10.1177/0263775817700395.

Yates-Doerr, Emily, and Annemarie Mol. "Cuts of Meat: Disentangling Western Nature-Cultures." *Cambridge Anthropology*, vol. 30, no. 2, 2012, pp. 48–64, https://doi.org/10.3167/ca.2012.300204.

Yeshurun, Yaara, and Noam Sobel. "An Odor Is Not Worth a Thousand Words: From Multidimensional Odors to Unidimensional Odor Objects." *Annual Review of Psychology*, vol. 61, 2010, pp. 219–41, https://doi.org/10.1146/annurev.psych.60.110707.163639.

Yurk, Valerie. "Pacific Northwest Heat Wave Killed More than One Billion Sea Creatures." *Scientific American*, 15 July 2021, https://www.scientificamerican.com/article/pacific-northwest-heat-wave-killed-more-than-1-billion-sea-creatures/.

Zeebe, Richard E., et al. "Anthropogenic Carbon Release Rate Unprecedented during the Past 66 Million Years." *Nature Geoscience*, 21 Mar. 2016.

Zelenko, Michael. "Dust Rising." *Verge*, 6 June 2018, https://www.theverge.com/2018/6/6/17433294/salton-sea-crisis-drying-up-asthma-toxic-dust-pictures.

Zelizer, Barbie. *About to Die: How News Images Move the Public*. Oxford UP, 2010.

Zenou, Yves, and Nicolas Boccard. "Racial Discrimination and Redlining in Cities." *Journal of Urban Economics*, vol. 48, 2000, pp. 260–85, http://doi.10.1006/juec.1999.2166.

Zheng, Zen T. "Residents Oppose Landfill Expansion near Fresno." *Houston Chronicle*, 7 July 2006, https://www.chron.com/news/article/Residents-oppose-landfill-expansion-near-Fresno-1862348.php.

Zheng, Zen T. "State Accepting Comments on Landfill: Residents Resist Project; Owners Defend Operation." *Houston Chronicle*, 13 July 2006, https://www.chron.com/news/article/State-accepting-comments-on-landfill-1905869.php.

Zou, Yong-ming, et al. "Olfactory Dysfunction in Alzheimer's Disease." *Neuropsychiatric Disease Treatment*, vol. 12, 2016, pp. 869–75, https://doi.org/10.2147/NDT.S104886.

INDEX

activism, academic, 175–77
affective intensities, 42–43
agency: of alive-and-dead matter, 93n1; distributed, 49–50, 57; nonhuman, 12–13, 47, 93–94, 93n1, 100–101; thing-power, 124
agitation, 105–7
Ahmed, Sara, 27
air-toxic cluster tracts, xi
air/water-as-chemical-entities perspective: about, 71–72; Blue Ridge Landfill case and, 155; Salton Sea case and, 111; Sriracha case and, 75–77; toxic vapor analyzers and, 149–50
air/water-as-lifeblood perspective: about, 71–72; archival activism and, 168; Blue Ridge Landfill case and, 149–50, 155; Salton Sea case and, 103, 115–16; Sriracha case and, 75–77, 88. See also Indigenous knowledges
air/water-as-resource perspective: about, 71–72; Salton Sea case and, 102–3; Sriracha case and, 75–77
Albrecht, Leslie, 24
algal blooms, 116
Allied Waste, 137–38

Alzheimer's disease, ix
ambiguity, 173–74
amplifiers, 139–42
amygdala, 24
Andaman Islanders, 40
animacy, 12–13, 115, 121
anosmia, 25, 39, 70, 77
Anthropocene, 162–63
anticipatory nuisance doctrines, 153
ArcGIS StoryMaps, 62–63
Arola, Kristin, 6
Artis, Alfrid, 160
attenuators, 139–42
Australia: bushfires, 46, 54–55; cockatoo tactical communication, 65

Bailey, Lisa, 77
Barthes, Roland, 14
Bastian, Michelle, 126
Bataille, George, 94
Bates, Julie Collins, 130–31
Baumann, Hans, 122

Beasley, Vanessa, xi
Belardo, Mary, 117–18
Bennett, Jane, 101
Berlant, Lauren, 45
Berman, Tzeporhah, 38
Berndtson, Petri, 25
bioinformation exchange, 96–97
BIPOC communities: Blue Ridge Landfill case and, 127, 136–37, 142; circulation in, 64; critical horology and, 126; dominant power structures and, 4; entropy and, 133; intersectional ecofeminism and, 54, 58, 64; precautionary principle and, 68; RISE and, 60, 62; SCENT heuristic and, 60, 67; slow violence and, 103–4; toxic tours and, 16; voices of, 19. *See also* Indigenous knowledges; intersectionality; race and ethnicity
Blair, Carole, 15
Blue Ridge Landfill (Fresno/Pearland, TX): about, 125–30; amplifiers, attenuators, and coalitional publics, 139–42; citizen science and, 134–35; class action lawsuit and olfactory rhetoric, 151–54; digital sniffers, wearables, and human training, 146–50, 154–55; enforcement decree, 139; expansion plans, 133–34, 136, 138; Fresno context, 135–39; intersectional concerns and, 136–37; Nuisance Odor Protocol (TCEQ) and FIDO charts, 149; odor concerns and public commentary, 143–46; Odor Task Force, 127, 134, 146; Pearland context, 131–35; population demographics, 142–43; Sriracha case compared to, 135, 153
Böhme, Jakob, 38
Bono, Mary, 110
Bono, Sonny, 110
Booher, Amanda, 12
Boulder Dam, 108
Boxer, Barbara, 99
brain processing, 24, 100
Breceda, Mark, 75
Brennan, Teresa, 42, 43–44
Brockovich, Erin, 64
Brower, David, 158
Brummett, Barry, 3n1
Brunswick, GA, 63–67

Bullard, Robert, xii, 103
Butler, Judith, 58

Cahuilla peoples: in history of Salton Sea, 98–99; oral traditions, 102, 106, 114–16; Torres Martinez Cahuilla and Salton Sea, 102, 102n3, 104–5, 107, 121–23, 162. *See also* Indigenous knowledges
California Development Company, 106
Canadian wildfires, 66
capitalism, racial, 107
capsaicin, 75, 77, 82
Cerulo, Karen, 16–17
Chavez, Jose, 91
chemical entities, air/water as. *See* air/water-as-chemical-entities perspective
chemoreception, 34–35, 41–42
Chirindo, Kundai, 167
chronoception, 39–40, 40n3
chronotopic time, 125–26
circulation: affective intensity and, 43; chemoreception and, 34–35; extradiscursive sensations circulated in mediated publics, 5–9; nonhuman agency and, 101; of nosewitness accounts in Sriracha case, 71; scent events, bodies, and, 16; SCENT heuristic and, 64, 65; sensory ecology and, 97, 140–41
citizen science, 134–35, 147
civic osmocosms, 70
Clary-Lemon, Jennifer, 18
Classen, Constance, 3, 36–37, 125
Clean Water Act, 113
climate change: climate anxiety, 160; ecorhetorical alliances and transdisciplinary webs of relation in Anthropocene, 162–68; global heating as "global weirding," 123, 158; Montreal Protocol, 157, 161
coalitional publics, 139–40, 143, 147, 154–55
cockatoos, 65
Cohen, Michael, 116
Collins, Harry, 127–28, 154
Collins, Timothy, 136–37
Colorado River, 102, 106–7. *See also* Salton Sea
communal sensations, 43

composite sensations: about, 57; Cuyahoga River fire and, 68; future action and, 1; nosewitnessing and, 128–29, 134; SCENT heuristic and, 59–61, 64, 170; sensorium and, xi; visceral publics and, 45, 49, 57, 130, 160

context, in SCENT heuristic, 60, 63

contingency, double, 105–6

coral bleaching, 160

Corbin, Alain, 14

cosmologies, 18–19, 39–40

COVID-19, 51

Crenshaw, Kimberlé, 21, 58

critical action research, 175–77

critical horology, 126

Crowfoot, Wade, 118–20

cultural attunement, 66

Cuyahoga River fire, Cleveland, 7–9, 7 fig. 1, 68

cyanobacteria blooms, 116

databases, 62–63

Davenport, Leslie, 160

Davis, Diane, 50, 140–41

Dawson, Janis, 91

de Certeau, Michel, 61n9

DeBuys, William, 98

Del Carmen, Rolando V., 70

Deleuze, Gilles, 45

deliberative rhetoric, 1

Desana, 40

DeVoss, Dànielle Nicole, 173

DiCaglio, Sara, 12

digital sniffer technologies, 146–50

Disneyland, 24

distal senses, 36–40

Dolmage, Jay, 35–36

Druschke, Caroline Gottschalk, 24

Dulin, Matt, 151

Dumit, Joseph, 46

ecofeminism (about), 21–23. See also intersectional ecofeminism; RISE approach

ecophobia, 94

elephants, 57

embodiment: Blue Ridge Landfill case and, 128, 139, 144–45; extradiscursive conditions and, 5; legal rhetoric and disembodiment, 86–87; meaning of, 51–52; memory, embodied, 44, 56; nonhuman, 53; in our environments, 51–56; relationality, emplacement, and, 50, 55–56, 161; relationality and embodied rhetoric, 52–55; rhetoricity, embodied, 24; RISE and, 11, 58–59; Salton Sea case and, 112, 117; in SCENT heuristic, 60, 63–64; sensorium as sensing body, 45–46; sensory rhetorics and, 9, 176; simulation, embodied, 16–18, 168, 171–72; Sriracha case and, 76–81; topos of, 50; trauma, responses to, 27; vestibular sense and, 158

emotion: affective intensities, 42–43; disgust and, 20; feeling vs., 43; olfaction and, 12, 25–27

emplacement: defined, 50; embodiment, relationality, and, 161; embodiment of place, 55–56; relationality and, 50–51; in Salton Sea case, 98–102; Salton Sea case and, 98–99; in SCENT heuristic, 60, 63–64; Sriracha case and, 76–81, 86–87

Endres, Danielle, 85–86

enmeshments: agitation and, 105; foodscape, foodways, and, 78–79; Indigenous cosmologies and, 18; legal, 28; local-global, 158; nonhuman and human, 82, 101; political, 49; proximal senses and, 40; Salton Sea case and, 140; sensorium and, 46; Sriracha case and, 82, 89

e-nose wearables, 149–50, 154–55

entanglement: Blue Ridge Landfill case and, 141; embodied, 54–56; of embodiment and relationality as risks, 161; flickering signifiers and, 96; intersectional ecofeminism and, 101; Salton Sea case and, 99; sensory ecology and, 97; Tsing on, 40, 97

environment, viii n1, ix–x

environmental injustice: Blue Ridge Landfill case and, 136–37, 143; intersectional ecofeminism and, 58; olfactory persuasion and, 29; precarity and, 167; RISE and, 169, 174–75; Salton Sea case and, 103–5; in San Gabriel Valley, CA, 72–74; SCENT heuristic and analysis of, 59–64; sensus communis and, 172; Sriracha case and, 71–72, 89; Superfund and, 8. See also BIPOC communities; intersectionality; race and ethnicity

environmental justice and olfactory rhetoric, 27–29

Environmental Protection Agency (EPA), 8, 8n7, 173

epideictic rhetoric, 1–2

epistemological inquiry, 6

ethics: body as topos for counterethics, 50; of entanglements, 54; relationality and, 49–50; speaking "nearby," 19; virtue ethics, 129

eutrophic conditions, 116

Evans, Robert, 127–28, 154

exceptional public subjects, 55–56, 143

experiential positioning system, 56

expertise, 127–28, 134

extinction, sensory, 26–27

extradiscursive rhetoric: about, 68–69; embodied simulation and, 17; paying attention to, 177; precarity and, 167; Salton Sea case and, 93

extradiscursive sensation, 5–9, 58–59

Farrell, Thomas, x

feedback loops, 113, 165

feeling, 43, 55

feeling structure, 11

feminism. *See* intersectional ecofeminism; RISE approach

FIDO charts (frequency, intensity, duration and offensiveness), 149

fires: Australia, 46, 54–55; Canada, 66; Cuyahoga River, Cleveland, 7–9, 7 fig. 1, 68; Maui, 66; Pacific Northwest, 46; smoke, smell of, 51, 53; Texas, 66

fish kills. *See* Salton Sea

flickering signifiers, 96

Flint, MI, 7

Floyd, George, 57

foodscape, 78

foodways and foodway politics, 78–80, 82–83

forensic rhetoric, 1

Foss, Karen, 58

Foss, Sonja, 58

Fresno, TX. *See* Blue Ridge Landfill

Gaard, Gretta, 22

Galaz, Kathy, 79

garbage worker strikes, 14

García, Amor, 100

Garcia, Sergio, 77–78

gendered sensory hierarchy, 36–39

Ghosh, Amitav, 5

global heating as "global weirding," 123, 158. *See also* climate change

"glocal" action, 158

Glynn Environmental Coalition, 67

Graham, Scott, 13–14

Grandin, Temple, 47n5

Great Barrier Reef, 160

Grineski, Sara, 136–37

Grosz, Elizabeth, 96

Guattari, Felix, 45

Gunn, Joshua, 85

gustatory rhetorics, 10

Hansen, James, 166

haptic rhetorics, 10, 14, 167

Harriman, E. H., 107

Hauser, Gerard, 139–40

Hawhee, Debra, xi, 1, 2, 9–10, 25, 33, 35–37, 40–43, 47, 57–58

Hayhoe, Katherine, 123

Hayles, N. Katherine, 52n6, 96

Hernandez, Maricarmen, 136–37

Hernández-López, Ernesto, 83

heuristic. *See* SCENT heuristic

Highmore, Ben, 45

Hildegard of Bingen, 38

Hill, Lucian, 146–47

Hill Collins, Patricia, 21, 58

Hinkley, CA, 64

hippocampus, 24

hog facility, Illinois, vii–viii, 14–15, 175–76

Holocene, 162–63

hope, 15, 166, 167

Horvitz, Steve, 99
Houdek, Matthew, xi, 19
Howes, David, 125
Hunt, Kathleen, 85–86
Hustak, Carla, 4
Huy Fong Foods. *See* Sriracha factory

indecorous voice, 85–86
Indigenous knowledges: animacy, concepts of, 12–13, 115, 121; Cahuilla and Salton Sea, 102; "indigenuity," 120–22; ontological traditions, 19; RISE and, 18; Salton Sea case and, 104–5, 118–19; sensory cosmologies, 39–40; seventh-generation model, 48–49; Western cosmologies vs., 18–19. *See also* air/water-as-lifeblood perspective; Cahuilla peoples
Indigenous realism, 49
information technology, bio-based, 96
injury claims: about, 82, 112–13; Blue Ridge Landfill case and, 133, 136, 143–46; Salton Sea case and, 109–10, 112–13, 118; Sriracha case and, 82; victim blaming, 154
injustice. *See* environmental injustice
intelligibility, 40–41
International Commission on Stratigraphy (ICS), 163
interoception, 34
intersectional ecofeminism: embodiment and, 54; entanglements and, 101; precarity and, 167; senses and, 58–59. *See also* RISE approach
intersectionality: about, 21, 58; air-toxic cluster tracts and, xi; Blue Ridge Landfill case and, 136–37; ecofeminism and, 22–23; virtue ethics and, 129. *See also* environmental injustice; race and ethnicity
Irigaray, Luce, 2
Irwindale, CA. *See* Sriracha factory
"it" as neuter nominative rhetoric, 86
Itchuaqiyaq, Cana Uluak, 49
iterative processing, 16–18, 168, 172

Jack, Jordynn, 71–72, 102
Jerome J605 analyzer, 149
Johnson, Jenelle, 20

Johnson, Jill, 77
Johnson, Mark, 40n3
Juárez, Miriam, 100, 112
Jung, Julie, 12

Kagan, Elena, 8n7
kairotic time, 125–26
Kalamazoo, MI, 156
Keller, Lynn, 163
Kennan, George, 106
Kennedy, George, 141
Kimmerer, Robin Wall, 39, 115
kincentric model, 48–49. *See also* relationality
Knoblauch, Abby, 52
knowledge: embodied (*see* embodiment); folk wisdom, 128; Indigenous (*see* Indigenous knowledges); scientific, technical, and legal vs. public, sensory, and embodied, 127–28

Lakoff, George, 40n3
landfills. *See* Blue Ridge Landfill
Langer, Susanne, 11–12
language: anticipatory, 68; chronoception and, 40n3; embodied, 52; legal, 153; non-discursive sensation and, 160
Law, John, 8n6, 47
lawsuits: Blue Ridge Landfill class action suit, 131, 151–54; Hinkley, CA, 64; Sriracha case, 75–76, 81–82, 84–88
legal rhetoric, 86, 129–30, 146
legal standing, 151
Leiss, William, 6
Lewiecki-Wilson, Cynthia, 35–36
lifeblood, air/water as. *See* air/water-as-lifeblood perspective
living dead. *See* necropolitics
Long, Elenore, 140
Luhmann, Niklas, 105

Malathion, ix
Manning, Erin, 37
Māori chronoception, 39–40
Massumi, Brian, 173

masting, 41–42

Maui wildfires, 66

Mbembe, Achille, 72–73

McGinley, Chuck, 150

McSorley, Kevin, 11

mediated visceral publics. *See* visceral publics

Mejia, Robert, 45, 159–60

memory: embodied, 44, 56; public, 2, 36, 76, 144, 161, 177; subjects of nonmemory and narratives of memory, 9

memory claims, 110, 143–46

Menily (Moon Goddess/Maiden), 114–16

Merleau-Ponty, Maurice, 47

midden piles, 132

Minh-ha, Trinh T., 19

Montreal Protocol, 157, 161

more-than-humans, xi, 10–14, 58

Morrison, Scott, 54–55

Mother Earth, 38–39

mycorrhizal network, 41

Myers, Natasha, 4

narratives in SCENT heuristic, 60–61, 63–64

Nasal Ranger technology, 148, 148 fig. 6, 150

necropolitics, 72–73, 76, 93

Nixon, Rob, 64, 112

nondiscursive rhetoric: about, 68–69; embodied simulation and, 17, 171–72; extradiscursive vs., 4n2; RISE and, 56; Salton Sea case and, 93; sensory ecology and, 140

nondiscursive sensation: about, 2; embodied simulation and, 171; RISE and, 160, 169; Sauer on, 171; sensory rhetorics and, 58–59; Sriracha case and, 89

nonhumans: agency and, 12–13, 47, 93–94, 93n1, 100–101; care for, 10; composite sensations and, 57; embodied capacity of, 53; enmeshments, nonhuman and human, 82, 101; kincentric model and, 48–49; nosesay and, 62; odors, olfaction, and, 2–3; posthuman entanglement, 174; Salton Sea case and, 115–16; SCENT heuristic and, 65, 67; sensorium and, xi; sensory ecologies and, 45, 141; Sriracha case and, 82

nosesay, 62, 84–86, 130

nosewitnessing, 62, 128–29, 134, 154–55

nuisance: anticipatory nuisance doctrines, 153; anti-nuisance clauses, 67, 71; Blue Ridge Landfill case and, 127, 131, 134–35, 137, 145–54; composite sensations and, 68; odor nuisance modeling, 147; official inaction and, 65–66; "permanent nuisance" designation, 152; precautionary principle and, 68; Sriracha case and, 71, 75–83, 87–88

O'Brien, Robert H., 75–76, 87–88, 130

ocularcentric paradigm, 2, 4, 16, 35–36, 62

odor nuisance modeling, 147

olfaction: about, 23–27; as "Cinderella" sense, 1, 4; culture and, 3–4; olfactory sensibility, 112–14. *See also* olfactory rhetoric; *and specific cases*

olfactory bulb, 100

olfactory persuasion: about, 1, 3; Brunswick, GA, and, 64, 65–66; civic osmocosms and, 70, 71; hog facility and, 175, 176; importance of, 29; redirection of sensitivities and, 167; RISE and, 168; risk, hazard, and, 172; Salton Sea case and, 91; SCENT heuristic and, 174; Sriracha case and, 71, 87–89

olfactory rhetoric: about, 2–3, 27–29; in Blue Ridge Landfill case, 144–46, 149, 151, 153; emotional processing and, 25; environmental justice and, 29; extradiscursive conditions and, 5; feeling structure and, 10; RISE approach and, 20; in Salton Sea case, 93, 123; in Škof and Berndtson, 25; in Sriracha case, 70, 77–78, 87–89; Sriracha case and, 74

Olivo, Dora, 133

ontological frames, 71–72

ontological inquiry, 6

Ore, Ersula, xi, 19

Ortiz, H. Manuel, 76, 81

osmocosm: about, 25–26; civic, 70–71, 74–76, 176; glocal action and, 157–58; mapping onto osmocosmic imaginaries, 162; redirection of sensitivities and, 167

Paliewicz, Nicholas, 85–86

Panagia, David, 46

Paraquat, ix

Parkinson's disease, ix
Parr, Joy, 91, 100
Parrish, Alex, 5
Parsons, Talcott, 105
patch dynamics, 94–98
Patencio, Francisco, 115n5
Pearland, TX. *See* Blue Ridge Landfill
perception: bubble of, 47; cultural training and, 3–4; double contingency and, 105; embodied sensation and, 51; foodway politics and, 80; intersectional affluence and, 142–43; nosesay and, 85; of public nuisance, 77, 79; RISE and, 56–57, 161, 169; selective, 53–54, 53n7, 56, 88; sensations, intelligibility, and, 40–41; sensorium and, 12, 45–47
Pérez, Manuel, 99
"permanent nuisance" designation, 152
Pezzullo, Phaedra, 16, 17–18
phenomenology, 100
phronesis, 76, 129
plants, embodied response in, 53
point- and nonpoint-source pollution, 103, 117, 129
policymaking, scientific, 128–30, 152
posthumanist approaches, 12. *See also* more-than-humans; nonhumans
Poudyal, Bibhushana, 83–84
Powell, Douglas, 6
precarity, 94–95, 97, 166–67
privilege: academic, 164–65; to escape or avoid environmental crises, 54; posthumanist approaches and, 12; Sriracha case and, 83–84; white, 60
proprioception, 34
proximal senses, 36–40
prudent interpretation, 129, 152
public memory, 2, 36, 144, 161, 177
public talk, 109
publics: defined, 139; injury claims and, 82; local and coalitional, 139–41, 143, 154–55; mediated, x, 5–9, 51, 59; nonscientific, 128; Rice's exceptional public subject, 55, 143; sensorium and, 46; visceral (*see* visceral publics)
punctuated equilibrium, 165

Quiroz, Otoniel, 121–22

race and ethnicity: anticipatory nuisance doctrine and, 153; Blue Ridge Landfill case and, 133, 136–37; capitalism, racial, 107; entropy and, 133; environmental racism, defined, xi n4; foodway politics and, 78, 82–83; intersectional ecofeminism and, 21–22, 58; necropolitics and, 76; RISE and, 31; Salton Sea and environmental racism, 111–12; selective perception and, 53n7; self-alienation and, 83–84; Superfund and, 8. *See also* BIPOC communities; environmental injustice; intersectionality
Rai, Mala, 83–84
Reagan, Ronald, 74
realism, Indigenous, 49
reciprocity, relational: kincentric thinking and, 86; nonhumans as beings-of-the-world and, 55; patchy geographies and, 106; Salton Sea case and, 114–16, 123; in sensorium, 48; Skywoman and, 39; Sriracha case and, 88–89; water/air-as-lifeblood and, 72
relationality: about, 48; embodied rhetoric, RISE, and, 52–56; embodiment, environmental emplacement, and, 161; extradiscursive sensations and, 5–9; Indigenous models, 48–49; patchy, in Salton Sea, 95–96; within sensorium, 48–51; sensorium and, 45; Sriracha case and, 86–89. *See also* reciprocity, relational
report writing and wound sites, 118
Republic Services, Inc., 134, 137, 141–42, 151–53. *See also* Blue Ridge Landfill
resilience, 114–16
resource, air/water as. *See* air/water-as-resource perspective
rhetoric as a "what" or a "how," 13–14, 15
rhetorical labor, interdisciplinary, 13
rhetoricians, speech vs. English, 14
rhetorics: gustatory, 10; haptic, 10, 14, 167; sonic, 10, 14, 35–36, 167; tactile, 167; visual, 10, 14, 35–36, 105, 167. *See also* olfactory rhetoric; sensory rhetorical approach
Rice, Jenny: "crises of place," 99; on exceptional public subjects, 55–56, 143; on

injury claims and wound sites, 82, 109–10, 112–13, 118; "interventions into imperiled places," x; on memory claims, 8–9; on public feeling, 88; on public memory of spaces, 1–2, 144; on public talk, 109; on urban development, 133

RISE approach (intersectional ecofeminist sensory rhetorical approach): about, x, 19–20; affordances and audiences of, 9–18, 169–70; defining, 56–59; dis-ease and, 159; ideological assumptions, questioning and revising, 168; Indigenous knowledges and, 18; limitations and research openings, 168–69; public talk and, 109; relationality within, 49–51; Salton Sea case and, 101–2, 124; scientific research and, 164–65; sense, call to, 174–75; and "sensory rhetorical," 58–59. *See also* SCENT heuristic; *and specific cases*

risk assessment and communication, xi–xii, 170–74

risk characterization, 6

Rittel, Horst, 23n9, 95

Robinson, Cedric, 107

Ross, Mary, 133

Roundup, ix

Rousseau, Jean-Jacques, 50

Rude, Carolyn, 170–71

Ruiz, Frank, 111

ruptures: Salton Sea and, 95–97, 124; sensorium and, 46–47; Sriracha case and, 72–73, 87, 89; volcanic eruptions as, 50

Sackey, Donnie, 23, 117, 155, 173

Salleh, Ariel, 22

Salton Sea: agitation, double contingency, and, 105–6; Blue Ridge Landfill case compared to, 130; emplacement and context, 98–102; environmental and developmental history of, 106–12; fish kills, 91–94, 111; indigenuity and, 120–22; map, 92 fig. 3; Menily myth, resilience, and reciprocity, 114–16; monitoring, data collection, and research studies, 116–19; olfactory sensibility, the toilet assumption, and, 112–14; patch dynamics and precarity, 94–98; patchy mitigation successes, 119–21; Torres Martinez Cahuilla initiatives, 104, 121–23; unintentional design and salty patchworks, 102–5;

wearables and, 155; zones of indetermination and variegated materialism, 123–24

Salton Sea Naval Base, 108

Sauer, Beverly, 171–72

scent events: about, 15–16, 23; agitation and, 106; Blue Ridge Landfill case and, 127, 130, 135; in Brunswick, GA, 63–64; extradiscursive conditions and, 5; foodway politics and, 80; nosesay and, 85; public will triggered by, 120; Salton Sea case and, 91, 93, 95–97, 100–101, 105, 111, 113, 120, 122–23; SCENT heuristic and, 62–63; short-term, 18, 161; thick description and, 59

SCENT heuristic: affordances, 169–70; Blue Ridge Landfill case and, 127–28; context, 60, 63; emplacement and embodiment, 60, 63–64; four-stage procedure and application of, 61–68; generalization and, 90; limitations and research openings, 168–69; narratives, 60–61, 63–64; Salton Sea case and, 93, 95–96; sense, call to, 174–75; sensing and searching, 59, 61–63; Sriracha case and, 70–71; tactics, 61, 65–66; transformation, 61, 66–67

Schlange, Andrew, 92–93, 120

Schwabe, Kurt, 119

scientific policymaking, 128–30, 152

self-alienation from foodways, 83–84

sensation: affective experience and, 45; communal, 43; criticism or theory, toggling with, 9–10; embodiment and, 52–56; extradiscursive sensation, 5–9, 58–59; knowledge and, 11, 27; as meaningful, 3; Panagia on, 46; perception, intelligibility, and, 40–41; relationality and, 51; rhetorics of, 50, 57–58, 89–90, 167, 170–76; RISE and, 20; ruptures of, 105–12; somatosensation, 34; unity and, 159; Western categorization of, 34–40. *See also* composite sensations; embodiment; nondiscursive sensation; sensory rhetorical approach

sensing and searching, in SCENT heuristic, 59, 61–63

sensitivities, redirection of, 167

sensorium: composite sensations in, 1; as concept, xi; defining, xi, 44–48; expanding approaches to, 35–36; relationality and, 50; RISE and, 58–59, 169; unity, sensation, and, 159; unknown within, 12

sensory categorization, Western, 34–40

sensory ecologies: about, 10; affective intensities and, 40–44; amplifiers, attenuators, and, 139–42; bioinformation exchange and, 96–97; Blue Ridge Landfill case and, 140; nonhumans and, 45, 141; sensorium and, 45

sensory extinction, 26–27

sensory rhetorical approach: about, x–xi, 9–10; embodiment in environments, 51–56; relationality within sensorium, 48–51; RISE approach, defining, 56–59; risk communication and, 170–74; SCENT heuristic, 59–61; sensorium, defining, 44–48; sensory ecologies and affective intensities, 40–44; staged procedural approach for SCENT heuristic, 61–68; Western sensory categorization, 34–40. *See also* olfactory persuasion; olfactory rhetoric; RISE approach

Serrato, Thomas, 79

settler-colonial approaches: analyzing, 67; Colorado River and, 106; precarity and, 97; racial capitalism, 107; Salton Sea case and, 102–4; water/air-as-chemical-entities perspective and, 71–72

seventh-generation model, 48–49

Sherwin, Richard, 129, 152

Sila, 12–13

Simmons, Michele, 134

Simon, Matt, 94, 100

simulation, embodied, 16–18, 168, 171–72

Singer, Norie R., 12, 22

Singh, Maanvi, 100

Singleton, Vicky, 8n6, 47

Škof, Lenart, 25

Skywoman, 39

Slater, Philip, 113–14

slow violence, 64, 72–73, 77, 103–4, 112, 113

"Smell Something, Tell Something!" Facebook group, 64, 65–66

smelling salts, 25

sniffer technologies, 146–50

Soil, Water, Air Protection Enterprise (SWAPE), 74–75

somatosensation, 34

sonic rhetorics, 10, 14, 35–36, 167

Sriracha factory (Irwindale, CA): air/water as resource or chemical entity or lifeblood and, 71–72, 75–77; atmospheric elements and odor surveillance, 74–76; Blue Ridge Landfill case compared to, 130, 135, 153; emergent phenomena and sensational enmeshments, 89–90; emplaced and embodied events, phronesis, and foodways, 76–81; judicial response, 87–88; legal rhetoric and rhetorical disembodiment, 86–87; narrative and context, 71–72; plaintiff actions, nonhuman-human enmeshments, injury claims, and food politics, 81–86; reciprocal relationality and, 88–89; regional history of environmental injustice, 72–74; SCENT heuristic and, 70–71

standing, legal, 151

statutes of limitations, 152–53

Stewart, Jude, 116

StoryMaps (ArcGIS), 62–63

Sunseri, Charlotte, 78

Superfund (CERCLA): about, 8; in Brunswick, GA, 63; in Fresno, TX, 129, 136, 138; San Gabriel Valley groundwater contamination site, 73–74

Supreme Court, US, 8n7

tactics, sensory-rhetorical, 61, 61n9, 65–66

tactile rhetorics, 167

Tapia, Arthur, 81

Tapia, Sofia, 81

Tate, John R., 84, 86

temporal regimes. *See* time and temporal regimes

Texas Commission on Environmental Quality (TCEQ), 125, 127, 139–40, 146–53. *See also* Blue Ridge Landfill

Texas wildfires, 66

thick description, 59

thiols, 39

Thomas, Donna, 133, 138

time and temporal regimes: chronoception, 39–40, 40n3; kairotic and chronotopic time, 125–26; restoried time, 162; seventh-generation model, 48–49

Todd, Zoe, 12–13, 18

toilet assumption, 113–14

Torres Martinez Desert Cahuilla Indians (TMCDI), 102, 102n3, 104–5, 107, 121–23, 162. *See also* Cahuilla peoples; Indigenous knowledges

Tortez, Thomas, Jr., 104, 110

toxic tours, 16, 17–18

toxic vapor analyzers, 149

Tran, David, 70, 74–76, 83, 88–90

transformation in SCENT heuristic, 61, 66–67

trees, 41–42

Tribe, Lawrence, 157

Trumbo, Craig, 139

Tsing, Anna, 40, 94, 97, 114, 118

unintentional design, 94, 98

Vázquez, Noemí, 112–13

vibratory communication, 57

violence, slow, 64, 72–73, 77, 103–4, 112, 113

virtue ethics, 129–30

visceral publics: about, 20–23; archival activism and, 168; Blue Ridge Landfill case and, 127, 130, 136, 155–56; civic osmocosms and, 70; composite sensations and, 45, 57, 140; exceptional public subjects and, 143; folk wisdom and, 128, 139; Salton Sea case and, 91, 93, 101, 111–12; sensorium and, 159; sensory rhetoric and, 32, 42–43; Sriracha case and, 70–71, 85–86, 88; tactics and, 65; thing-power and, 161; transformation and, 66–67

visual rhetorics, 10, 14, 35–36, 105, 167

Voyles, Traci, 102, 120

Warner, Michael, 140

water as chemical entity, resource, or lifeblood. *See* air/water-as-chemical-entities perspective; air/water-as-lifeblood perspective; air/water-as-resource perspective

wearable technologies, 149–50, 154–55

Webber, Melvin, 23n9, 95

Wendover Airforce Base, 108

Western thinking: air/water as resource or chemical entity or lifeblood ontologies, 71–72; Indigenous vs. Western cosmologies, 18–19; sensory categorization, 34–40

Whang, Young Ja, 78–79

wicked environmental problems, 23, 94–95, 119–20, 124, 165

Wildcat, Daniel, 49, 56, 120, 163, 164, 166

Williams, Serena W., 153

Winderman, Emily, 45, 159–60

wound sites, 109–10, 112–13, 118, 132–33

Wright, Beverly, 103

Zepeda, Yolanda Priscilla, 81

zones of indetermination, 96, 123–24

NEW DIRECTIONS IN RHETORIC AND MATERIALITY
ALLISON L. ROWLAND, CHRISTA TESTON, AND SHUI-YIN SHARON YAM,
SERIES EDITORS

Current conversations about rhetoric signal ongoing attentiveness to and critical appraisal of material-discursive phenomena. New Directions in Rhetoric and Materiality provides a forum for responding to and extending such conversations, but also asks that books published in the series attend to social events of consequence unfolding around the world—such as violence based on misinformation, continued police brutality, immigration legislation and migration crises, and more. The series therefore seeks to amplify books that examine rhetoric's relationship to materiality while also confronting material-rhetorical forces of oppression, power imbalances, and differential vulnerabilities.

Olfactory Rhetoric: Sniffing Out Environmental Problems
    LISA L. PHILLIPS

Patient Sense: Rhetorical Body Work in the Age of Technology
    LILLIAN CAMPBELL

Trafficking Rhetoric: Race, Migration, and the Making of Modern-Day Slavery
    ANNIE HILL

Nuclear Decolonization: Indigenous Resistance to High-Level Nuclear Waste Siting
    DANIELLE ENDRES

Decolonial Conversations in Posthuman and New Material Rhetorics
    EDITED BY JENNIFER CLARY-LEMON AND DAVID M. GRANT

Untimely Women: Radically Recasting Feminist Rhetorical History
    JASON BARRETT-FOX

Violent Exceptions: Children's Human Rights and Humanitarian Rhetorics
    WENDY S. HESFORD

Zoetropes and the Politics of Humanhood
    ALLISON L. ROWLAND

Ecologies of Harm: Rhetorics of Violence in the United States
    MEGAN EATMAN

Raveling the Brain: Toward a Transdisciplinary Neurorhetoric
    JORDYNN JACK

Post-Digital Rhetoric and the New Aesthetic
    JUSTIN HODGSON

Not One More! Feminicidio on the Border
    NINA MARIA LOZANO

Visualizing Posthuman Conservation in the Age of the Anthropocene
    AMY D. PROPEN

Precarious Rhetorics
    EDITED BY WENDY S. HESFORD, ADELA C. LICONA, AND CHRISTA TESTON

www.ingramcontent.com/pod-product-compliance
Lightning Source LLC
Chambersburg PA
CBHW030136240426
43672CB00005B/151